Dinosaurs, Dragons, and the BIBLE

Bodie Hodge

First printing: May 2023
Second printing: September 2023

Copyright © 2023 by Bodie Hodge. All rights reserved. No part of this book may be reproduced, copied, broadcast, stored, or shared in any form whatsoever without written permission from the publisher, except in the case of brief quotations in articles and reviews. For information write:
Master Books, P.O. Box 726, Green Forest, AR 72638
Master Books® is a division of the New Leaf Publishing Group, LLC.

ISBN: 978-1-68344-344-5
ISBN: 978-1-61458-842-9 (digital)
Library of Congress Control Number: 2023934658
Cover by Diana Bogardus

Please consider requesting that a copy of this volume be purchased by your local library system.

Printed in the United States of America

Please visit our website for other great titles:
www.masterbooks.com

For information regarding promotional opportunities, please contact the publicity department at pr@nlpg.com

Master
Books®
A Division of New Leaf Publishing Group
www.masterbooks.com

Contents

Dedication

I would like to dedicate this book to my family who have persevered with me through this long endeavor — Renee, Kylie, Caleb, Lacey, and Lexiana.

Professional Dedication

To the families of the late Dr. David Menton, Dr. Kevin Anderson, and Dr. John Morris. Their work and dedication has been an inspiration and a precursor to so much that I have done. I feel like I'm standing on the shoulders of giants when I read and refer to their work. I am eternally grateful for their steadfast love of Christ and stance on the authority of Scripture that is reflected in their lives, teachings, and research.

Acknowledgments

Ken Ham, Rob Webb, Bryan Osborne, Dr. Georgia Purdom, Frost Smith, Dr. Andy McIntosh, Dr. David Menton, Buddy Davis, Dr. Gabriela Haynes, Dan Lietha, Cameron Suter, Maria Suter, Joel Leineweber, Harry Sanders, Roger Patterson, Neil Seeds, and the team at Master Books — who are excellent as always.

Notes

Scripture passages are from the New King James Version (NKJV) unless discussing older or comparative translations, where they are specifically denoted. Other versions used are the English Standard Version (ESV) and the King James Version (KJV). Some old and foreign translations are used and denoted directly in the text.

Words that are capitalized for consistency:
- Ark (of Noah)
- Flood (of Noah's day)
- Scripture, Word of God, and Bible, but not adjectives "biblical" or "scriptural"
- Ice Age when speaking of the event that was triggered by the Flood, not the secular multitudes of "ice ages."
- Day 1, Day 2, Day 3, Day 4, Day 5, Day 6, Day 7, and Creation Week
- The pronouns of God/Christ, such as He, Him, etc.
- Sunday School
- Christian
- The seven "C's," when discussed in the context of them being "C's": Creation, Corruption, Catastrophe, Confusion, Christ, Cross, Consummation

Foreword

Dinosaurs, Dragons, and the Bible is a fascinating book that deals with many of the top questions that are often asked about dinosaurs, dragons, and the Bible. Using the Bible as the absolute authority and foundation for our thinking, these supposedly "difficult" questions suddenly become easy to answer!

Designed for almost all ages, this is the type of book that grips you with answers to questions like:

- *When did God make dinosaurs?*
- *How did dinosaurs fit on Noah's Ark?*
- *Where are they today?*
- *Were there really dragons?*

Most of the answers even keep jr. high readers engaged, as well as scientists, historians, and theologians! The book excites with chapters dealing with dinosaur soft tissue, ichnites (fossil footprints), as well as dragons, serpents, and leviathans in the Bible. There's never been a book produced like this one.

I want to encourage you to grow in your biblical understanding of the connection between dinosaurs and dragons (which are mentioned in the Bible many times) and the Bible. Answering these questions really helps everyone, including pastors, teachers, and the average person in the church to have answers for this skeptical generation that has been overwhelmed with evolutionary views imposed on them by secular schools, media, and museums.

Ken Ham
CEO Answers in Genesis, Creation Museum, Ark Encounter

1

Introduction: Why Is the Subject of Dinosaurs Important for Christians?

Dinosaurs. They are arguably one of the hottest topics in today's culture. Kids love them, teens adore them, adults are fascinated by them, and the academic community can't get enough of them. But strangely, Christians rarely discuss them. Why?

In general, the biblical understanding of dinosaurs has primarily escaped Christians the world over! Most of the time, Christians simply ignore the subject all together. In the past 50 years, how often has a preacher or a Sunday School teacher focused on the biblical view of dinosaurs? Most church leaders and their congregations would say *never*. Obviously, there are exceptions, but largely, Christians are simply outside of the discussion of dinosaurs. But should they be? Not at all.

Meanwhile, the secular world is pumping out media and literature — technical articles, books, textbooks, TV shows, movies, cartoons, and an immense number of kids' books on dinosaurs — that teach a view of dinosaurs that is blatantly *unbiblical*. Christians, it is time to be discerning and beware. If you or your kids and grandkids were anything like I was, you can easily get sucked into this false understanding about dinosaurs — which can lead to *eternal* problems!

Before we dive into the subject throughout the book, there are a few preliminary things that can help us gain a better understanding of the topic. These include a proper definition of what a dinosaur is and what it isn't. And more importantly, point out some key highlights in the Bible.

And lastly, I want to make sure you know what is going on inside of the church (by and large across the Western World) so that you can spot a serious error that many (especially leaders) within the church have made. I'm going to be right up front about this — some Christians are happy to ignore what the Scriptures say on the subject, and merely accept what the secular world says about dinosaurs. This error is permeating the church and causing divisions between people that shouldn't be there (Romans 16:17–18[1]).

So, let's go on an adventure to understand dinosaurs from a biblical viewpoint, putting God and His Word first to properly understand these truly incredible creatures.

---

1. "Now I urge you, brethren, note those who cause divisions and offenses, contrary to the doctrine which you learned, and avoid them. For those who are such do not serve our Lord Jesus Christ, but their own belly, and by smooth words and flattering speech deceive the hearts of the simple" (Romans 16:17–18).

2

How Is a Dinosaur Defined?

If we are going to be discussing dinosaurs, we need to know what the definition of a "dinosaur" is. The word *dinosauria* means "terrible or terrifying lizard." It was coined by a Christian man named Sir Richard Owen in 1841 from the Greek word *deinos* which means "fearfully great." This is where we get "terrible" and *sauros* which means lizard.

As researchers were digging up dinosaurs in the 1800s, these lizards, which were identified as reptiles, quickly became a hot item due to some of them having an immense size. But the question arose regarding their definition (i.e., what exactly were these creatures?). After all, researchers had found mainly bones, teeth, some skin imprints of scales (technically scutes, which are shield-like scales), and some egg fossils.

Initially, researchers thought these large reptiles were merely scaled-up versions of smaller reptiles seen today. But Richard Owen was the one who showed, by their fossils, that they were not. They were indeed unique creatures not seen running around anymore.

Despite some people incorrectly labeling certain reptiles as dinosaurs, not all reptiles are dinosaurs — which brings us to a defining moment — literally!

Defining a Dinosaur

This may surprise you, but dinosaurs do not include crocodiles, alligators, nor komodo dragons. And many dinosaurs are not big either. So how do we know what a dinosaur is? There are a number of factors, but the primary factors have to do with their hip structures.

Sir Richard Owen

Dinosaurs are land animals (consider Genesis 1:24–25[1]), specifically reptiles, that have one of two hip structures that allow them to stand upright or erect, whereas reptiles like crocodiles, alligators, and komodo dragons have hip structures that have their legs come out to the side, which forces their belly to naturally rest on the ground. Crocodiles and other land reptiles with legs extending out to the side can stand up for shorter periods of time, but not like dinosaurs.

Dinosaur hips have their legs placed underneath their body (underslung). This means they normally stand up (erect) on either two legs or four legs. This is how Richard Owen originally defined a dinosaur in the 1800s. L.B. and Jenny Halstead write in their book called *Dinosaurs*:

> It was not until 1841, when Richard Owen in his Report on British Fossil Reptiles presented to a meeting of the British Association for the Advancement of Science, that the concept of the dinosaur was first introduced to the public. Owen showed that it was not possible simply to scale up fossil reptiles on the basis of living forms as that would have produced 60m (200ft) long lizards. From his study of the vertebrae and limb bones he was able to establish beyond any shadow of a doubt that these animals, for which he coined the name Dinosauria, held their limbs beneath their bodies in exactly the same way as mammals, that they were the reptilian equivalent of the pachyderms — the rhinoceroses, elephants, and hippopotamuses. Owen stressed the fact that the dinosaurs were the peak of the reptilian creation and since their day the history of the reptiles had been one of degeneration rather than progressive evolution.[2]

For the more detailed definition, Paul S. Taylor points out how dinosaurs have technically been defined since then. He writes:

---

1. Then God said, "Let the earth bring forth the living creature according to its kind: cattle and creeping thing and beast of the earth, each according to its kind"; and it was so. And God made the beast of the earth according to its kind, cattle according to its kind, and everything that creeps on the earth according to its kind. And God saw that it was good (Genesis 1:24–25).

2. L.B. Halstead and Jenny Halstead, *Dinosaurs* (New York: Sterling Publishing Co., Inc., 1987), p. 10.

1. underslung legs that gave dinosaurs an erect posture
2. a large hole in the bottom of their basin-shaped hip-socket
3. a secondary palate (uncharacteristic of reptiles) that permits dinosaurs to eat and breathe at the same time
4. a fairly straight thigh bone with an in-turned head
5. two pairs of holes in the temporal region of the skull (diapsid skull)
6. backward-pointing knees (or elbows) of the front legs
7. forward-pointing knees of the rear legs (rather than pointing sideways)
8. front legs shorter and lighter than the rear legs (in almost every case)
9. a special bone (predentary) at the chin that capped the front of the bottom jaw in some dinosaurs (the ornithischians)
10. land-dwelling creature, rather than marine or airborne[3]

Even if you didn't quite understand all ten of these points, the main takeaway is that it eliminates a number of reptiles from being labeled dinosaur, besides crocodiles, alligators, and komodo dragons. With this more technical definition in mind, this means marine (sea) reptiles and flying reptiles are not dinosaurs. More specifically, this means creatures like the plesiosaur (sea reptile), ichthyosaur (sea reptile), pteranodon (flying reptile), kronosaurus (sea reptile), pterodactyl (flying reptile), and so on are not actually dinosaurs either.

In a layman sense, these unique flying and sea reptiles are sometimes lumped with dinosaurs because, as far as we know, they are all groups of extinct reptiles. But being more precise, the flying and sea reptiles are not dinosaurs per definition.

Changing Definitions

Now that you better understand the definition of a dinosaur, it's important you also understand its arbitrariness. Ultimately, it's a man-made definition to lump certain creatures based on certain features (sorry for the rhyme!). This also means there will be issues with this definition.

Over the years, the definition of a dinosaur has essentially whittled down to a land reptile having 1 of 2 hip structures, with a hole in it, so that the creature stands upright or erect. Traditionally, people classify dinosaurs using the ten-point definition, but in more recent times with fossil discoveries, these "definitions" have been changing with more exceptions.

---

3. Paul S. Taylor, *Dinosaur!*, Films for Christ, *Christian Answers*, Accessed 9/15/17, http://www.christiananswers.net/dinosaurs/dinodef.html.

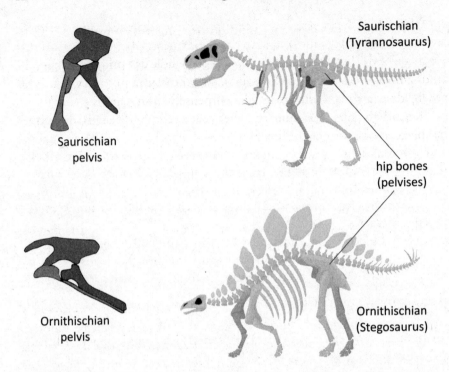

Saurischian
(Tyrannosaurus)

Saurischian
pelvis

hip bones
(pelvises)

Ornithischian
pelvis

Ornithischian
(Stegosaurus)

For example, there *was* a creature defined as a dinosaur called *Teleocrater rhadinus* that had the dinosaur head depression feature. However, it didn't have the hip structure. So, the decision was finally made that this creature is not a dinosaur anymore and thus one of the defining features (dinosaur head depression), is no longer a major factor in defining a dinosaur.[4] Interestingly with all the exceptions, we are almost back to defining dinosaurs as merely having underslung legs, like Richard Owen did in the first place.

Are Birds Defined As "Avian Dinosaurs"?

Those with an evolutionary worldview try to redefine dinosaurs in drastic ways. Did you know there are people who call birds "avian dinosaurs"? *Avian* means bird. A large building or cage for holding birds is called an *aviary*.

Why is this "definition" (idea) put forth? Because of the secular religious belief that some dinosaurs ultimately evolved into birds. We will get into substance of this in much greater detail in appendices that deal with the allegation that dinosaurs changed into birds. But in brief, birds and dinosaurs are distinctively different — birds have feathers, avian/bird lungs, and other anatomical features that are very different from dinosaurs.

---

4. Carolyn Gramling, "New Fossils Are Redefining What Makes a Dinosaur," *New Scientist,* February 21, 2018, https://www.sciencenews.org/article/new-fossils-are-redefining-what-makes-dinosaur.

Major bird types have also been found buried in the same sediment layers as dinosaurs.[5] Not to mention that God informed us in Genesis 1, that He made birds (Day 5 of Creation Week) one whole day prior to making the land animals (this included dinosaurs). Thus, the idea put forth that birds are the descendants of dinosaurs falls immensely short.

Regardless, this evolutionary belief that dinosaurs changed into birds has plagued our current culture. Some researchers have foolishly gone so far as to try to re-define birds as dinosaurs. However, it's clear from God's design that birds are birds and dinosaurs are dinosaurs.

This effort of trying to lump birds as dinosaurs under terms like "avian dinosaurs" is simply trying to force the evidence to "fit" the religious view that dinosaurs evolved into birds, which not only is unscientific and illogical but also deceitful. The fact is, unlike bird fossils, dinosaur fossils do not have evidence of feathers.

As a result, evolutionists attempt to redefine birds as dinosaurs, and then try to point to actual birds and say, "We found feathered dinosaurs." This fallacious way of thinking opens a door for artists to start making images of "dinosaurs" with feathers on them (as commonly seen at secular museums and artwork today).

However, birds are simply birds, not dinosaurs. Other than trying to push an evolutionary agenda, there is no justification for putting feathers and other bird features on dinosaurs or vice-versa. So, beware of this "redefinition" of birds as dinosaurs. Just remember, when you read about an "avian dinosaur," it is simply a bird — nothing more. However, let me add a caveat to that. Because dinosaurs and birds are being convoluted together, there may be instances where a dinosaur is being called an avian dinosaur but is really a dinosaur, so one must be discerning in some instances. (See Appendix 2 for more on this subject). As for true birds, their ancestors were on the Ark of Noah and extend back to Day 5 of creation (Genesis 1:20–23[6]).

---

5. Besides archaeopteryx, see also Thomas Stidham, "A Lower Jaw from a Cretaceous Parrot, *Nature*, November 5, 1998, V. 396, p. 29–30, doi:10.1038/23841.

6. Then God said, "Let the waters abound with an abundance of living creatures, and let birds fly above the earth across the face of the firmament of the heavens." So God created great sea creatures and every living thing that moves, with which the waters abounded, according to their kind, and every winged bird according to its kind. And God saw that it was good. And God blessed them, saying, "Be fruitful and multiply, and fill the waters in the seas, and let birds multiply on the earth." So the evening and the morning were the fifth day (Genesis 1:20–23).

3

Does the Secular World Teach a Biblical View of Dinosaurs?

In the Western World, there exists an immense number of resources available on dinosaurs, especially for kids, with various books, shows, and movies. There's a ton of information about dinosaurs in classrooms, technical articles, textbooks, museums, and so much more! But do these sources give a biblical view of dinosaurs? Rarely, if ever. They usually start off with introductory statements like "65–66 million years ago...." Sound familiar?

For thousands of years, people believed and taught that man and animals of the past lived together at the same time. So, if animals were no longer around, then they must have gone extinct — even those in the fossil record. For instance, everyone agrees that *Wooly Mammoths, Aurochs* (a type of cattle), dodo birds, and *Irish Elk* once lived with man but went extinct at some point in the past, usually from excessive hunting, habitat destruction, or natural disasters.

A great example is from a Greek historian, over 2,400 years ago, named Herodotus, who mentioned small flying reptiles in Arabia.[1] These creatures have obviously gone extinct since his time.

But then something strange happened. In the late 1700s and early 1800s, a select few scholars *who rejected the Bible* began to arbitrarily redefine the age of the earth to longer and longer ages. This eventually led many people to buying into the false idea of "millions of years."[2] In this new viewpoint,

---

1. Herodotus, *The History of Herodotus*, Book 2.
2. Bodie Hodge, "How Old Is the Earth?" in *The New Answers Book 2*, Ken Ham, gen. ed. (Green Forest, AR: Master Books, 2008), p. 41–52; Terry Mortenson, *The Great Turning Point* (Green Forest, AR: Master Books, 2004).

some creatures were separated from co-existing with man and were alleged to have lived millions of years before man. Dinosaurs are probably among the most famous creatures to have been separated from co-living with man — by a whopping 65–66 million years!

Today, dinosaurs stand as the leading "icon for evolution and long ages." This relatively new idea (yes, this is a new idea) has become so ingrained in our culture mainly by being imposed on unsuspecting children (and their parents) for generations — even me in my youth! Now many adults who had been indoctrinated into believing man and dinosaurs were separated by "millions of years" go about their lives without thinking twice about it. And on top of that, anyone who actually thinks that dinosaurs and man lived side-by-side is ridiculed and deemed "unscientific." Evolution and dinosaurs have been intertwined by the secular world. Leading creationists Drs. Henry and John Morris once wrote,

> Dinosaurs have been so glamorized as denizens of the long-ago, prehistoric past that they have almost become synonymous with evolutionism in the public mind — and evolutionists feel emotionally attached to them, afraid that if they yield on this point, the whole evolutionary structure will crumble.[3]

Dinosaurs Changed into Birds?

Nevertheless, even with long ages, the predominant view was that dinosaurs had gone extinct. But then another view began to pop up — supposing some dinosaurs evolved into birds and didn't go extinct! Dr. Philip Currie, an evolutionary paleontologist and museum curator, and paleobotanist Professor Eva Koppelhus co-wrote:

> Because birds are dinosaurs, dinosaurs have not died out. . . . Nevertheless, dinosaurs are still alive and very successful. Birds are the direct descendants of small meat-eating dinosaurs, and in modern biological classification are considered to be a subset of the Dinosauria. In this sense, dinosaurs are still very successful because there are more than 8,000 species alive today.[4]

This "dinosaur-to-bird" belief is totally ingrained in our culture today. Ironically, by this view, man and "dinosaurs" (equated with birds in this view)

---

3. Henry Morris and John Morris, *The Modern Creation Trilogy*, Book 2, *Science and Creation* (Green Forest, AR: Master Books, 1996), p. 122.
4. Philip J. Currie and Eva B. Koppelhus, *101 Questions about Dinosaurs* (Mineola, NY: Dover Publications, 1996), p. 59–60.

live together side-by-side and anyone who disagrees is ridiculed. I guess you can't win sometimes!

In the late 1800s, an agnostic[5] (who didn't believe in God or His Word) named Thomas Henry Huxley (May 4, 1825–June 29, 1895) was the first to propose the false idea that dinosaurs changed into birds after studying a small theropod dinosaur called *Compsognathus* (due to its alleged "many bird-like features").[6]

Although Huxley's idea of dinosaur-to-bird evolution was a bit different from what evolutionists believe today, it still set the stage. Of course, movie series like *Jurassic Park* and *Jurassic World* capitalize on these ideas.

A Secular Understanding

The secular world is obviously teaching its own secular (unbiblical) view of dinosaurs. But what do I mean by "secular"? The secular worldview is a view of looking at and interpreting past and present things, assuming God doesn't play any part in this universe in creating or sustaining it, but rather the universe itself is all that there is.

Secularism can be categorized as a form of paganism, specifically called pantheism. There are two major forms of paganism:

1. Polytheistic (a whole bunch of petty "gods")
2. Pantheistic (the universe/cosmos/nature is all there is, i.e., godlike)

So, rightly, secularism can be called paganism — they just don't have a bunch of little pagan gods like some forms of paganism. A secular religious view operates like an atheistic or naturalistic (nature is all that there is) viewpoint where the basic worldview assumption is that man is the measure of all things (the ultimate standard) — not God (consider Colossians 2:8[7]). This is why secular views are utterly absent of any positive comment about God or His Word, and any explanation within these views is devoid of God and creation.

The religious view of secularism, or more properly secular humanism (with its variant "denominations" like atheism, agnosticism, naturalism, materialism, etc.), dominates our culture. It has successfully infiltrated into the textbooks that kids use in government schools, the media and news

---

5. In its most basic form, an agnostic is one who claims you can't know if God exists. Most agnostics, including Huxley, then live and practice life as though they were atheists, materialists, and naturalists. Today, Bill Nye is in the same camp where he says he is an agnostic but argues for atheism, materialism, and naturalism.

6. https://dino.lindahall.org/wag1861.shtml.

7. "Beware lest anyone cheat you through philosophy and empty deceit, according to the tradition of men, according to the basic principles of the world, and not according to Christ" (Colossians 2:8).

outlets, government education system, state museums, journals, books, and movies, and even commonly rears its ugly head in politics and legislation.

Humanism's Ancient Roots

Secular humanistic roots extend back to the beginning and is arguably the oldest religion, next to Christianity, which goes back to the very beginning of time, when Christ created everything including the universe and all that is in it and the heaven of heavens (Genesis 1, Nehemiah 9:6, John 1, Colossians 1, and Hebrews 1).

Humanism essentially elevates man's fallible ideas to supersede God and His infallible Word and was the first false religion that had tenets as far back as Adam and Eve. When Eve, and subsequently Adam, elevated their own thoughts to ignore God's command not to eat from the fruit of the Tree of the Knowledge of Good and Evil (Genesis 3), they officially became the first "humanists." Ultimately, by elevating their human thought above God, they committed high treason against God in their defiance against His command.

Adam and Eve admitted their guilt to God in Genesis 3 when God sought after them (knowing they sinned). Nevertheless, they still tried to "pass the buck" instead of owning up to their full responsibility. Adam passed the blame to Eve, and Eve to the serpent whose deceptive cunning was by Satan's influence.

By God's grace, Adam and Eve seemed to have turned from their sin (repented) to return to God (e.g., Eve even praised the Lord for their first child in Genesis 4:1[8] and Seth in Genesis 4:25-26[9]; godly Seth was in Adam's likeness per Genesis 5:3[10]). Nevertheless, the damage had been done. Sin nature was now inherent to all their descendants — including you and me (e.g., Romans 5:12[11]).

All religions that deviate from God and His Word are man-made and ultimately humanistic in that man's ideas are used to take people away from God and His Word. This is true whether Eastern religions (e.g., Hinduism,

---

8. "Now Adam knew Eve his wife, and she conceived and bore Cain, and said, 'I have acquired a man from the LORD'" (Genesis 4:1).

9. "And Adam knew his wife again, and she bore a son and named him Seth, 'For God has appointed another seed for me instead of Abel, whom Cain killed.' And as for Seth, to him also a son was born; and he named him Enosh. Then men began to call on the name of the LORD" (Genesis 4:25-26).

10. "And Adam lived one hundred and thirty years, and begot a son in his own likeness, after his image, and named him Seth" (Genesis 5:3).

11. "Therefore, just as through one man sin entered the world, and death through sin, and thus death spread to all men, because all sinned" (Romans 5:12).

Taoism, New Age, Sikhism, etc.), moralistic/paganist religions (Buddhism, Confucianism, Wicca, Greek mythology, etc.), atheistic religions (humanism, atheism, agnosticism, etc.), or counterfeits of Christianity (Islam/Muhammad, Mormonism/Smith, Jehovah's Witnesses/Russell, etc.). But our culture in the Western World today has placed the secular humanistic/atheistic religions in the forefront.[12]

> ### What Does "Secular" Mean?
>
> Secular means that God, the Bible, and any spiritual aspect is to be removed or left out. In other words, it is a religious perspective that tries to look at the world as if God doesn't exist like an atheistic or naturalistic worldview where all that exists is matter and energy in the universe.

Although secular forms of humanism were largely dormant for millennia, they began to emerge to influence our modern times in the A.D. 1700s. Some precursors were being laid though. This religious undertone is the basis for modern evolutionary thought, particularly surrounding dinosaurs.

Taking It Back

As a child and youth, even I was swayed to lean in the religious direction of dinosaurs either "dying out millions of years ago" or that they "changed into birds." This was in spite of the fact that I grew up in church. It makes sense too because I was pounded with these secular ideas repeatedly through television, movies, books, and school influences (Proverbs 22:6[13]). Yet, there was little to challenge these beliefs in my Sunday School class. If you are in this camp — like I was — prepare to be challenged.

Many Christians (those who believe and start their thinking with the Bible) may already know the answer to this big question about dinosaurs and the Bible, and if you are reading this book, my hope is that this resource will still be a blessing to you to help strengthen your faith.

---

12. For more on these religious deviations see Bodie Hodge and Roger Patterson, *World Religions and Cults* (Green Forest AR: Master Books, Volumes 1–3, 2015–2016).

13. "Train up a child in the way he should go, And when he is old he will not depart from it" (Proverbs 22:6).

4

Does the Church Teach a Biblical View of Dinosaurs?

I Was There "All the Time"!

I grew up in church. I was there all the time — Sunday School, church, and youth programs. When I say "all the time," I mean it (Hebrews 10:24–25[1]). We sang songs, had announcements, refreshments, fellowshipped, and even had a little teaching from time to time. Yep, I was there all the time — around 2–3 hours per week. That doesn't sound like much, does it? Sadly, this is probably more than the typical week for many "churchgoers" today. Maybe you used to be (or still are) in this same camp?

Consider that I also went to state schools, in which I was *there* typically about 40 hours per week. Hence, this translated to the schools having me until adulthood for at least 16,000+ hours, and that's not even including sports and other extracurricular activities or the secular movies and TV and secular peers. On the other hand, I was at Sunday School for a grand total of over 600 hours (calculating missed days which did happen on occasion).[2]

Why is this important? I was taught different things in secular school than what I was taught in church. Not *complementary* mind you. On the contrary, I had textbooks that directly opposed biblical origins. I had teachers (falsely) tell me that God wasn't relevant to history or that God didn't

---

1. "And let us consider one another in order to stir up love and good works, not forsaking the assembling of ourselves together, as is the manner of some, but exhorting one another, and so much the more as you see the Day approaching" (Hebrews 10:24-25).

2. Natasha Crain, "Why Your Kids Can Spend 600-Plus Hours in Church and Not Get Much Out of It," *Renewanation*, June 22, 2020, https://www.renewanation.org/post/why-your-kids-can-spend-600-plus-hours-in-church-and-not-get-much-out-of-it.

even exist. I was taught secular humanistic morality (i.e., forget God, do what you want). I was told to ignore the Sunday School "stories" — that they are all "fairy tales" anyway. I was also taught that dinosaurs didn't live with man, and they "died out millions of years ago" (which is false).

Yet, at church, I heard God did exist but I only heard bits and pieces about Christian morality. I knew about tons of "stories" (the word *story* means myth now!)[3] in the Bible from Sunday School. In the Bible, I read about origins in Genesis, but that wasn't discussed in church. But I wondered, what about dinosaurs from the Bible? We never discussed anything about them from a biblical perspective in church. I never even found the word *dinosaur* in the Bible, especially in my limited grasp of the Bible as a child.

The Stage Was Set

As an impressionable child, I fully trusted my teachers. They told me dinosaurs died out millions of years ago. And like many other children, I fell for it. I was taught that dinosaurs died out millions of years before man ever "appeared" on the scene. But I'd read Genesis, and I realized that God created man and land animals on the same day — Day 6 of creation week (Genesis 1), but I really didn't put "two and two together" to realize what that meant!

So here I was, a kid with little direct knowledge of God or Christianity, being indoctrinated into a different religion (secular humanism) unbeknownst to me at the government schools. I had textbooks on the subject that brainwashed me on the secular humanistic view of dinosaurs. [I still have some of these grade school textbooks today because I happened to buy these exact textbooks when our school had a "delete sale" when they bought new textbooks.] We usually left our textbooks at school in our desk and used them in class. I doubt my parents ever saw them. One textbook states in the context of turtles, snakes, crocodiles, and lizards:

> They are relatives of the dinosaurs which lived on the earth millions of years ago.[4]

Another of my childhood textbooks states:

> About 200 million years ago, large animals such as triceratops roamed about in large numbers. Over millions of years, these

---

3. The word "story" now means myth or fairy tale or something that isn't necessarily true. Yet churches often still teach Bible stories like the "story" of Noah or the "story" of Isaac, etc. This needs to be remedied. See Bodie Hodge, "What's Wrong with the Word *Story*?" Answers in Genesis, August 20, 2019, https://answersingenesis.org/is-the-bible-true/whats-wrong-with-story/.

4. Albert Piltz and Roger Van Bever, *Discovering Science 6* (Columbus, OH: Charles E. Merrill Publishing Co., 1970), p. 345.

animals became fewer and fewer. After a long time, none of these animals were alive. Many millions of years later...."[5]

This is just a small taste of this teaching. Our school also hosted a scholastic reading program, where you could purchase books through an organization for your age level. I bought a book through this program, and I recall it was my favorite childhood book. It was called *Last of the Dinosaurs*.[6] The first line of this book began with *"Millions of years ago...."* On the first page (which was "page 3" by numbering), it also said,

"About 160 million years went by, from the first dinosaur that lived to the last one."[7] This short book of 32 illustrated pages for children is replete with statements about "millions of years" and the supposed "Age of Dinosaurs."

From the ages of 6 to 10 years old, I was thoroughly indoctrinated with this secular religion, particularly about dinosaurs. Dinosaurs were a lure, and I was a fish caught on the hook. Many kids in church homes today are also hooked on this same lure at a very early age.

According to statistics of kids who have actively walked away from the faith, about 43.1% claimed to have made the decision to seriously question the contents in the Bible (particularly in Genesis 1–11) in grade school.[8] I suggest secular humanistic indoctrination as one of the main reasons, such as what I received at state school and from secular media. I fell for the secular dinosaur story (lie) at a very early age — most of my school mates did too. Did you?

By and Large, How *Did* the Church Counter the Secular View of Dinosaurs?

5. Albert Piltz and Roger Van Bever, *Discovering Science 5* (Columbus, OH: Charles E. Merrill Publishing Co., 1970), p. 313.
6. David Eldridge, *Last of the Dinosaurs: The End of an Age* (Mahwah, NJ: Troll Associates, 1980).
7. Ibid., p. 3.
8. Ken Ham and Britt Beemer, *Already Gone* (Green Forest, AR: Master Books, 2009), p. 179 (adding up grades K–9).

How *Should* the Church Have Responded?

Did you notice that the previous section was blank? It isn't a typo. There isn't missing text. It's blank for a reason. In all my years of attending Sunday School, church, and youth programs, I was never taught how to look at dinosaurs from a biblical viewpoint. Never. Not once. Dinosaurs were *never* mentioned. That is why it is blank. There was nothing to report! And sadly, this is still the case with many churches today.

In fact, I was never taught about biblical origins whatsoever in any detail. Historical accounts in Genesis like Creation, Adam and Eve, and Noah and the Flood were mentioned, but they were related to me as merely "stories" or in brief passing comment. I was never given any apologetic (how to *defend and give answers for* the biblical account, 1 Peter 3:15[9]) information or training to defend biblical origins or refute the false origins account of big bang, millions of years, and evolution. I found out later that one of the church elders (leaders) had actually bought into evolutionary ideas and, consequently, was resistant to biblical teachings in Genesis at our local church.

There are several plausible reasons I've been able to ascertain over the years as to why I wasn't taught about dinosaurs from a biblical viewpoint — and how to defend it. Here are the top three:

> 1. My parents were unaware that I was being brainwashed with the secular humanistic view about dinosaurs, so they never even bothered to look into the subject to help me. My parents (like many parents) were under the impression that schools were "neutral" (neutrality is a myth by the way, Matthew 12:30[10]), and they figured schools wouldn't teach something contrary to Christianity in schools.

> 2. The church leadership (e.g., Sunday School teachers, elders, deacons, and pastors) didn't know we were being taught a secular religion at school — ideas like the big bang, millions of years, and evolution, which are subsets of the religion of secular humanism and naturalism.

> 3. Even if the church leadership knew about the secular indoctrination happening at school, I doubt some of them would have

---

9. "But sanctify the Lord God in your hearts, and always be ready to give a defense to everyone who asks you a reason for the hope that is in you, with meekness and fear" (1 Peter 3:15).

10. "He who is not with Me is against Me, and he who does not gather with Me scatters abroad" (Matthew 12:30).

known how to respond themselves, mainly due to their own lack of knowledge about dinosaurs from a biblical viewpoint.

I want to encourage parents and churches to be able to respond biblically to the secular attacks (war) on our children. So, as any good General would do in times of war, *we need to study our opponent and know exactly* what the secular side is teaching our children. Then, get equipped with solid biblical answers from our highest commanding officer (God and His Word) to defend our children against the attacks. Then, teach this knowledge diligently and apologetically to the next generation, like parents and churches are supposed to do (e.g., Ephesians 6:4[11], 2 Timothy 3:16–17[12]).

How *Are* Churches Responding Today?

This may or may not come as a surprise to you, but even with answers readily available today, many churches sadly are still doing nothing to combat the secular attacks on their congregation. They are openly permitting the world to teach their children about dinosaurs from a non-Christian (unbiblical) perspective. There are exceptions of course. Nevertheless, this trend needs to change immediately. As a point of note, despite what the world says, God never instructed His people to send their children to be indoctrinated by false religions of the peoples surrounding us. In fact, God repeatedly warns the church against that very thing!

Praise God, there are some churches that are going back to the Bible (i.e., back to a proper biblical worldview) to get the true framework to properly look at dinosaurs. Many of these churches are rightly going back to Scripture to develop much of their theology, understanding of history, science, and so on. I want to encourage this, by the way. God (and by extension, His Word) is the absolute infallible authority on all matters. I've noticed it's only the healthier (wiser) churches that tend to stand on a solid foundation in the Word of God (Matthew 7:24–27[13]).

---

11. "And you, fathers, do not provoke your children to wrath, but bring them up in the training and admonition of the Lord" (Ephesians 6:4).
12. "All Scripture is given by inspiration of God, and is profitable for doctrine, for reproof, for correction, for instruction in righteousness, that the man of God may be complete, thoroughly equipped for every good work" (2 Timothy 3:16-17).
13. "Therefore whoever hears these sayings of Mine, and does them, I will liken him to a wise man who built his house on the rock: and the rain descended, the floods came, and the winds blew and beat on that house; and it did not fall, for it was founded on the rock. But everyone who hears these sayings of Mine, and does not do them, will be like a foolish man who built his house on the sand: and the rain descended, the floods came, and the winds blew and beat on that house; and it fell. And great was its fall" (Matthew 7:24–27).

In contrast, some churches strangely try to "mix" Christianity with the world's pagan or secular teachings. In other words, they take secular ideas like the big bang, millions of years, and evolutionary ideas as equally authoritative (as ultimate) as God and mix it with the Bible. This is usually done by "reinterpreting" the early pages of Genesis (primarily Genesis 1–11), attempting to accommodate the secular religion and the secular view of dinosaurs.

Thus, many Christian leaders often accept the secular humanistic view when it comes to origins and speak of dinosaurs being "millions of years old." These Christians are often called compromised Christians (i.e., compromise Genesis with the world's teachings) or syncretistic (i.e., mix secular humanism with Christianity).

Compromised Christians will often unashamedly use the Bible as their ultimate authority in matters, but not Genesis 1–11! These chapters are heavily reinterpreted by compromised Christians away from the plain meaning. Consider the following examples of some "church leaders" attempting to "mix" their Christianity with humanism (specifically with evolution and naturalism):

> "These large (and a few small) reptile species appear to have dominated Earth's land and sea life from 250 million to 65 million years ago. Their creation probably belongs to the fifth creation day."[14]

> "God made the reptiles, including dinosaurs, beginning about 230 million years ago."[15]

> "Our testable creation model says God created dinosaurs to roam the Earth roughly 230 million years ago, and many different types of these creatures dominated the landscape. Their time on Earth ended when a 6-mile-wide asteroid impacted Earth 65 million years ago."[16]

> "Discoveries like these amber-preserved feathers provide new insights into the evolutionary history of theropod dinosaurs and early birds, as well as an inkling of their coloration. They also demonstrate the power of evolutionary theory to make accurate predictions about what the fossil evidence will show. But even

---

14. Hugh Ross, *The Genesis Question* (Colorado Springs, CO: Navpress, 1998), p. 48.
15. Don Stoner, *A New Look at an Old Earth* (Eugene, OR: Harvest House Publishers, 1997), p. 176.
16. "Dinosaurs, Reasons to Believe," http://www.reasons.org/rtb-101/dino, 2013.

as these discoveries confirm the evolutionary link between birds and dinosaurs, they continue to reshape our assumptions about dinosaur appearance."[17]

Sadly, these things are being taught in churches (and even some private Christian schools). Clearly, these positions are taking man's fallible and error-prone opinions about the past as "truth" instead of adhering to what we clearly and plainly read in Genesis, which is God's infallible and inerrant Word to man. Alas, many children today (similar to my case) get caught in the dinosaur "crossfire."

17. Sarah Bodbyl Roels, *Biologos*, December 14, 2016, https://biologos.org/blogs/guest/scientists-find-feathered-dinosaur-tail-preserved-in-amber.

5

How Do I Use the Bible as the Framework to Look at Dinosaurs?

An Assuming Introduction

For years, I've encouraged Christians to look at dinosaurs from a *biblical* viewpoint. However, I had people tell me this was a difficult task for them. At first, I assumed they just struggled with the ingrained beliefs that they had been fed about "millions of years" and evolution. But I later realized this assumption was incorrect.

My problem was that I falsely presumed Christians knew their Bible well enough to properly use it as their "lens" to look at dinosaurs. In my past, even as an adult, I did not have a thorough grasp on the Bible. And if people are anything like me, then they share in the same struggles in thoroughly knowing the Bible.

I was never taught the Bible in state schools. For past generations, people were consistently taught the Bible in subjects like history, science, literature, and so on, so they had the basic framework of the Bible, as state schools were originally an outreach of the church. This goes back to Robert Raikes in the late 1700s and early 1800s in England.

Raikes started the Sunday School movement that grew into weekly schools, and it transformed societies for the good. This movement of schools bled over to the States, Canada, and so on as well — similar but different. The government helped fund these Christian schools or even start them because of their good benefits (governments were more "Christianized" in those days, working with the local church schools). But then the government largely took them over as they were funding them; and then came the attacks to remove the creation, prayer, Bible, theology, etc. from the classroom. By the 1960s, the Bible had been attacked enough so that it was finally ripped out of schools.

Today, we live in the fruit of that removal and see the evil fruits that *secular education* has become — being a place to indoctrinate kids with pagan beliefs, like evolution and homosexuality, through government dictums (Luke 6:43–44[1]). Consequently, I had to learn the Bible primarily from my local church or my own study because state schools were no longer an option to learn the Scriptures.[2]

From church, I only knew the basic Bible stories. I heard gospel sermons galore, but I didn't truly grasp the biblical foundation of the gospel, even though I was a believer. I had only read bits and pieces in the Bible from various church activities like Bible studies, youth programs, Sunday School, small groups, and so forth. But I never actually read an entire book or letter in the Bible in one sitting — not even Jude or the short letters of John!

That statement may sound strange since letters are generally meant to be read as one unit in a single sitting. As an analogy, let's say you received a love letter from someone. Would you only read a few bits and pieces here and there, studying it "a little here" and "a little there" (bit by bit), over the next several years until you finally get through it? Not at all! Yet far too often, this is how we read God's love letters to us in the New Testament.

The point here is I still didn't know my Bible, even after all that time. I needed to get a better understanding of the Bible to more properly understand subjects like dinosaurs, history, science, philosophy, etc. Only then would I be in a more capable position to truly understand dinosaurs *within the context of Scripture*. So, as a simple fix when speaking, I prepared Christians with a basic understanding of the Bible's history of the earth and mankind during my lectures. And this preparation allows Christians to apply a "big picture" (biblical) framework to look at dinosaurs. This preparation really helps — not just with dinosaurs but also with many other subjects that we want to look at with a biblical framework.

Basics of a Biblical Worldview

I presume everyone reading this book has not memorized the entire Bible. No worries, I haven't either! Obviously, we need to know a fair

---

1. "For a good tree does not bear bad fruit, nor does a bad tree bear good fruit. For every tree is known by its own fruit. For [men] do not gather figs from thorns, nor do they gather grapes from a bramble bush" (Luke 6:43-44).

2. I tried reading my Bible too. But as a child from western Illinois in the 1970s and 1980s with a dialect similar to what you would read in Mark Twain's *Tom Sawyer* and *Huck Finn*, it was difficult to understand the late modern English of my KJV Bible, let alone grasp deeper theology and historical understandings as a child left alone.

amount of the Bible before we can look at dinosaurs from a biblical viewpoint.

The ministry of *Answers in Genesis (AiG)* gives a few, easy-to-remember highlights in the Bible that can help keep a "big picture" look at the Bible. At AiG, we call these milestones the *Seven C's Of History*. This name obviously plays off the famous "Seven Seas" of ancient times referring to various popular seas, as denoted by ancient cultures. However, these "C's" are reference points in the Bible's plan of history, listed as:

1. Creation
2. Corruption
3. Catastrophe
4. Confusion
5. Christ
6. Cross
7. Consummation

These milestones in the Bible give us a proper framework to look at various historical subjects including dinosaurs. Allow me to discuss these Seven C's in more detail.

> 1. **Creation:** God created all things in six days and rested on the seventh (Genesis 1:1–2:3). These days were normal-length, 24-hour, days (Exodus 20:11,[3] Exodus 31:15-17[4]). And God called His perfect creation very good (Genesis 1:31,[5] Deuteronomy 32:4[6]). The creation was a world with no death, no bloodshed, and no suffering (e.g., Genesis 1:29–30[7]). And since our

---

3. "For in six days the LORD made the heavens and the earth, the sea, and all that is in them, and rested the seventh day. Therefore the LORD blessed the Sabbath day and hallowed it" (Exodus 20:11).
4. "Work shall be done for six days, but the seventh is the Sabbath of rest, holy to the LORD. Whoever does any work on the Sabbath day, he shall surely be put to death. Therefore the children of Israel shall keep the Sabbath, to observe the Sabbath throughout their generations as a perpetual covenant. 'It is a sign between Me and the children of Israel forever; for in six days the LORD made the heavens and the earth, and on the seventh day He rested and was refreshed" (Exodus 31:15–17).
5. "Then God saw everything that He had made, and indeed it was very good. So the evening and the morning were the sixth day" (Genesis 1:31).
6. "He is the Rock, His work is perfect; For all His ways are justice, A God of truth and without injustice; Righteous and upright is He" (Deuteronomy 32:4).
7. "And God said, 'See, I have given you every herb that yields seed which is on the face of all the earth, and every tree whose fruit yields seed; to you it shall be for food. Also, to every beast of the earth, to every bird of the air, and to everything that creeps on the earth, in which there is life, I have given every green herb for food'; and it was so" (Genesis 1:29–30).

Creator is a God of life (John 14:6[8]), the creation truly was a world full of life.

2. **Corruption:** A ruling God made man in His own image. Being a ruling God, He gave man something to rule over — dominion over the world (Genesis 1:26–28[9]). But when the first two people, Adam and Eve, sinned against our Holy God, they committed high treason against Him (Genesis 3). The punishment for sin was both physical and spiritual death (Genesis 2:16–17,[10] Romans 5:12,[11] 1 Corinthians 2:14[12]). God cursed the ground, cursed the animals, and sentenced mankind to the death we deserve. But by God's grace, He sacrificed the first animals to cover Adam and Eve's sin in Genesis 3:21,[13] showing the relationship between human sin and animal death (Hebrews 9:22[14]). Animal sacrifices were required to cover sin until Jesus Christ, the final and perfect sacrifice (Hebrews 10:10[15]), was put to death on the Cross.

3. **Catastrophe:** Man's sin nature was passed from Adam to all his descendants that increased in sin (Romans 5:12[16]). God promised a global Flood to destroy all life over the entire earth (Genesis

8. "Jesus said to him, 'I am the way, the truth, and the life. No one comes to the Father except through Me'" (John 14:6d).

9. "Then God said, 'Let Us make man in Our image, according to Our likeness; let them have dominion over the fish of the sea, over the birds of the air, and over the cattle, over all the earth and over every creeping thing that creeps on the earth.' So God created man in His own image; in the image of God He created him; male and female He created them. Then God blessed them, and God said to them, 'Be fruitful and multiply; fill the earth and subdue it; have dominion over the fish of the sea, over the birds of the air, and over every living thing that moves on the earth'" (Genesis 1:26–28).

10. "And the LORD God commanded the man, saying, 'Of every tree of the garden you may freely eat; but of the tree of the knowledge of good and evil you shall not eat, for in the day that you eat of it you shall surely die'" (Genesis 2:16–17).

11. "Therefore, just as through one man sin entered the world, and death through sin, and thus death spread to all men, because all sinned" (Romans 5:12).

12. "But the natural man does not receive the things of the Spirit of God, for they are foolishness to him; nor can he know them, because they are spiritually discerned" (1 Corinthians 2:14).

13. "Also for Adam and his wife the LORD God made tunics of skin, and clothed them" (Genesis 3:21).

14. "And according to the law almost all things are purified with blood, and without shedding of blood there is no remission" (Hebrews 9:22).

15. "By that will we have been sanctified through the offering of the body of Jesus Christ once for all" (Hebrews 10:10).

16. "Therefore, just as through one man sin entered the world, and death through sin, and thus death spread to all men, because all sinned" (Romans 5:12).

6:11–13[17]). Noah, being found righteous by his faith (Genesis 6:8–9[18]), was told to build an Ark for salvation from the Flood (Genesis 6:14–16[19]). Noah did all that God commanded with godly fear (Genesis 6:22,[20] Hebrews 11:7[21]) and rescued representative land animals and his family from the Flood (Genesis 7:1–3[22]). From these initial animals, on the Ark descended all the land-dwelling and air-breathing animals we have today (Genesis 7:21–23,[23] 8:19[24]).

Although some rock layers have formed since then, most sedimentary rock layers, all over the earth, are testimonies to this global Flood (Genesis 7:19–20).

4. **Confusion:** After the Flood, God told man to be fruitful and multiply and fill the earth (Genesis 9:1,[25] 7[26]). Man tried to defy God's command when they came together to build a city with

---

17. "The earth also was corrupt before God, and the earth was filled with violence. So God looked upon the earth, and indeed it was corrupt; for all flesh had corrupted their way on the earth. And God said to Noah, 'The end of all flesh has come before Me, for the earth is filled with violence through them; and behold, I will destroy them with the earth'" (Genesis 6:11–13).

18. "But Noah found grace in the eyes of the Lord. This is the genealogy of Noah. Noah was a just man, perfect in his generations. Noah walked with God" (Genesis 6:8–9).

19. "Make yourself an ark of gopherwood; make rooms in the ark, and cover it inside and outside with pitch. And this is how you shall make it: The length of the ark shall be three hundred cubits, its width fifty cubits, and its height thirty cubits. You shall make a window for the ark, and you shall finish it to a cubit from above; and set the door of the ark in its side. You shall make it with lower, second, and third decks" (Genesis 6:14–16).

20. "Thus Noah did; according to all that God commanded him, so he did" (Genesis 6:22).

21. "By faith Noah, being divinely warned of things not yet seen, moved with godly fear, prepared an ark for the saving of his household, by which he condemned the world and became heir of the righteousness which is according to faith" (Hebrews 11:7).

22. "Then the Lord said to Noah, 'Come into the ark, you and all your household, because I have seen that you are righteous before Me in this generation. You shall take with you seven each of every clean animal, a male and his female; two each of animals that are unclean, a male and his female; also seven each of birds of the air, male and female, to keep the species alive on the face of all the earth'" (Genesis 7:1–3).

23. "And all flesh died that moved on the earth: birds and cattle and beasts and every creeping thing that creeps on the earth, and every man. All in whose nostrils was the breath of the spirit of life, all that was on the dry land, died. So He destroyed all living things which were on the face of the ground: both man and cattle, creeping thing and bird of the air. They were destroyed from the earth. Only Noah and those who were with him in the ark remained alive" (Genesis 7:21-23).

24. "Every animal, every creeping thing, every bird, and whatever creeps on the earth, according to their families, went out of the ark" (Genesis 8:19).

25. "So God blessed Noah and his sons, and said to them: 'Be fruitful and multiply, and fill the earth'" (Genesis 9:1).

26. "And as for you, be fruitful and multiply; Bring forth abundantly in the earth And multiply in it" (Genesis 9:7).

a tower in an effort to not be scattered (Genesis 11:4–5[27]). So then God confused their languages and forced them to scatter by their family groups, introducing new language families (that continue to change) and isolated family groups. This dispersion event explains why people have distinct appearances in different parts of the world. That is, different gene pools dominated in different areas — but there is only one race of man — the human race, or Adam's race. Meanwhile, animals were dispersing around the globe before and during this event.

5. **Christ:** As we jump forward to the New Testament, we see the Creator God Himself take on flesh to become a man (John 1:1–14, Colossians 1:15–20, Hebrews 1:1–13). He became our relative, being a descendant of Mary (Luke 3:23–38), thus of Noah and Adam. Is this too hard for an all-powerful God (Jeremiah 32:27[28])? Not at all. Jesus, being the promised seed/offspring (Galatians 3:16[29]), is the one to fulfill the messianic prophecies beginning in Genesis 3:15 ("seed/offspring of the woman"). Jesus is called the *Last Adam* because, as the first Adam led us into death, Christ saves us from death (Romans 6:23,[30] 1 Corinthians 15:45[31]).

6. **Cross:** Jesus Christ's death on the Cross was sufficient to achieve salvation for guilty sinners. The punishment from an infinitely and eternally powerful God (literally "the Almighty," e.g., Deuteronomy 33:27,[32] Job 42:2,[33] Psalm 147:5[34]) is by extension, an

---

27. "And they said, 'Come, let us build ourselves a city, and a tower whose top is in the heavens; let us make a name for ourselves, lest we be scattered abroad over the face of the whole earth.' But the LORD came down to see the city and the tower which the sons of men had built" (Genesis 11:4–5).
28. "Behold, I am the LORD, the God of all flesh. Is there anything too hard for Me?" (Jeremiah 32:27).
29. "Now to Abraham and his Seed were the promises made. He does not say, 'And to seeds,' as of many, but as of one, 'And to your Seed,' who is Christ" (Galatians 3:16).
30. "For the wages of sin is death, but the gift of God is eternal life in Christ Jesus our Lord" (Romans 6:23).
31. "And so it is written, 'The first man Adam became a living being.' The last Adam became a life-giving spirit" (1 Corinthians 15:45).
32. "The eternal God is your refuge, And underneath are the everlasting arms; He will thrust out the enemy from before you, And will say, 'Destroy!'" (Deuteronomy 33:27).
33. "I know that You can do everything, And that no purpose of Yours can be withheld from You" (Job 42:2).
34. "Great is our Lord, and mighty in power; His understanding is infinite" (Psalm 147:5).

infinite and eternal punishment (Daniel 12:2,[35] Matthew 25:46,[36] John 3:36[37]). Animal sacrifices from Genesis 3:21[38] through the Old Testament were not sufficient to satisfy God's infinite wrath on sin (Hebrews 10:4[39]). They could only temporarily cover it until Jesus Christ, the perfect and infinite Son of God Himself, was sacrificed on the Cross, where the infinite Son took the infinite punishment from the infinite Father, thus satisfying the wrath of God (e.g., Isaiah 53, Ephesians 5:2,[40] Hebrews 9:26,[41] 1 Peter 3:18,[42] 1 John 4:10[43]). By God's grace and mercy, the blood of Christ makes salvation a free gift from the Lord (Romans 5:9–15; Ephesians 2:4–9). Christ had the power to lay down His life and the power to take it up again (John 10:18[44]).

7. **Consummation:** Those who repent and put their faith in Christ look forward to a final consummation (Revelation 21–22). There will be a new heaven and new earth that are perfect where the curse from Genesis 3 has been removed (Revelation 22:3[45]). There will be no more death, nor suffering, for the former things will have passed away (Revelation 21:4[46]). We will live eternally

---

35. "And many of those who sleep in the dust of the earth shall awake, Some to everlasting life, Some to shame and everlasting contempt" (Daniel 12:2).
36. "And these will go away into everlasting punishment, but the righteous into eternal life" (Matthew 25:46).
37. "He who believes in the Son has everlasting life; and he who does not believe the Son shall not see life, but the wrath of God abides on him" (John 3:36).
38. "Also for Adam and his wife the LORD God made tunics of skin, and clothed them" (Genesis 3:21).
39. "For it is not possible that the blood of bulls and goats could take away sins" (Hebrews 10:4).
40. "And walk in love, as Christ also has loved us and given Himself for us, an offering and a sacrifice to God for a sweet-smelling aroma" (Ephesians 5:2).
41. "He then would have had to suffer often since the foundation of the world; but now, once at the end of the ages, He has appeared to put away sin by the sacrifice of Himself" (Hebrews 9:26).
42. "For Christ also suffered once for sins, the just for the unjust, that He might bring us to God, being put to death in the flesh but made alive by the Spirit" (1 Peter 3:18).
43. "In this is love, not that we loved God, but that He loved us and sent His Son to be the propitiation for our sins" (1 John 4:10).
44. "No one takes it from Me, but I lay it down of Myself. I have power to lay it down, and I have power to take it again. This command I have received from My Father" (John 10:18).
45. "And there shall be no more curse, but the throne of God and of the Lamb shall be in it, and His servants shall serve Him" (Revelation 22:3).
46. "And God will wipe away every tear from their eyes; there shall be no more death, nor sorrow, nor crying. There shall be no more pain, for the former things have passed away" (Revelation 21:4).

with God and enjoy His goodness for all eternity. Unbelievers, those who did not repent of their sin and receive Christ's death and Resurrection, will spend eternity in hell (a place of eternal punishment), where the wrath of God remains on them forever (Daniel 12:2,[47] Matthew 25:46,[48] John 3:36,[49] Romans 10:9[50]).

This brief summary of Christ and His creation from the Bible is used as the foundation for the necessary framework to look at the subject of dinosaurs (as well as all other subjects) from the biblical perspective.

But What About the Other Possible C's?

Well — it doesn't really mesh with the "Seven Seas" approach, but let's insert a few more "C's" to add a few more milestones. Over the years, many people have approached me (including those at AiG) and have said a couple of things. First, we hear, "What about the 'Covenant' with Abraham — that starts with a C?" The other thing people tend to lament is the large gap between Confusion and Christ, like there was a "jump" from Genesis 11 to Matthew 1 (New Testament).

Okay, we (at AiG) understand these things too. One reason we have the Seven C's (which plays off of the "Seven Seas" of old) is because the world tends to primarily attack Genesis 1–11, more than any other part of the Bible, from secular schools, media, museums, etc. So, our main focus (being Answers in GENESIS) is to help people reclaim the history in Genesis 1–11. But, more importantly, we don't want to merely reclaim that history without pointing people to Christ and His work on the Cross. As Christians, sharing the Good News should always be our goal (Matthew 28:18–20[51]).

At the same time, many churches ask how they can incorporate the Seven C's with the rest of the Old Testament like, for example, adding a

---

47. "And many of those who sleep in the dust of the earth shall awake, Some to everlasting life, Some to shame and everlasting contempt" (Daniel 12:2).
48. "And these will go away into everlasting punishment, but the righteous into eternal life" (Matthew 25:46).
49. "He who believes in the Son has everlasting life; and he who does not believe the Son shall not see life, but the wrath of God abides on him" (John 3:36).
50. "That if you confess with your mouth the Lord Jesus and believe in your heart that God has raised Him from the dead, you will be saved" (Romans 10:9).
51. "And Jesus came and spoke to them, saying, 'All authority has been given to Me in heaven and on earth. Go therefore and make disciples of all the nations, baptizing them in the name of the Father and of the Son and of the Holy Spirit, teaching them to observe all things that I have commanded you; and lo, I am with you always, even to the end of the age.' Amen" (Matthew 28:18–20).

few more C's to fill in this gap with more milestones. Obviously, we want to encourage this effort. So, I came up with the "Twelve C's" that I've shared with fellow Christians. I know, it breaks away from the ancient "Seven Seas" phrase that we are playing off of, but bear with me as I mention these milestones:

1. Creation
2. Corruption
3. Catastrophe
4. Confusion
5. *Covenant* (with Abraham, Isaac, and Israel)
6. *Commandments* (with Moses and the onset of the Judges)
7. *Crown* (when the Israelites began their kingly line)
8. *Captivity* (when the Israelites went into Captivity and returned from it)
9. Christ
10. Cross
11. *Church* (when we see the church exploding from Pentecost until today)
12. Consummation

This C's list should be helpful to start to establish a biblical framework to look at dinosaurs.

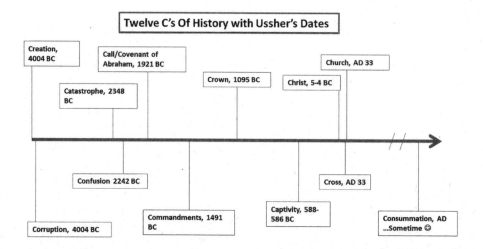

6

When Did God Make Dinosaurs, Pterosaurs, and Plesiosaurs?

 asked my five-year-old daughter (at the time) when God made dinosaurs. Her answer was, "A long time ago." Of course, she's technically correct in that it *was* a long time ago!

But I wanted her to be more specific, because she was watching a TV show for kids that had just mentioned dinosaurs. Since I overheard it, I wanted to make sure that she was being discerning (as much as a five-year-old can be), so this was a perfect time to have a discussion on the subject (e.g., Deuteronomy 6:6–9[1]).

So then I asked her, "On what day did God make man (Adam and Eve)?" And she correctly said, "The 6th day of creation." Then I asked, "What day did God make land animals?" Again, she correctly answered, "The 6th day of creation." [You can see where I'm going with this can't you!] Finally, I asked, "Are dinosaurs land animals?"

She didn't even need to answer that question specifically. She jumped right to the answer with bright eyes and a big smile saying, "Dinosaurs were made on the 6th day, because they are land animals!" Yep, she thought about it and then correctly answered. She just needed a little "nudge" to get there.

Sometimes we are like that with a number of questions surrounding dinosaurs. We just need that little *nudge* because we are not used to thinking about dinosaurs from a biblical viewpoint.

---

1. "And these words which I command you today shall be in your heart. You shall teach them diligently to your children, and shall talk of them when you sit in your house, when you walk by the way, when you lie down, and when you rise up. You shall bind them as a sign on your hand, and they shall be as frontlets between your eyes. You shall write them on the doorposts of your house and on your gates" (Deuteronomy 6:6–9).

Implications of Dinosaurs Being Made on Day 6

Dinosaurs, by definition, are land animals. They are land reptiles with one of two hip structures, allowing them to walk upright on land. So they are land-dwelling creatures made on the 6th day of creation. And since man (Adam and Eve) was also made on the same day, this means dinosaurs lived at the same time alongside humans.

Did they have interactions with humans? It is surely probable. Dinosaurs are definitely inclusive among the "beasts of the earth" (Genesis 1:24–25[2]). Furthermore, if some of them were to be lumped with the "beasts of the field," which is a subcategory of the "beasts of the earth," then Adam may have at least named some of their kinds and interacted with them prior to Eve's creation (Genesis 2:19–20[3])![4]

Adam and his descendants could have potentially interacted with dinosaurs until the time of the global Flood without their fear of man being in effect in Genesis 9:2.[5] After the Flood, their interactions would surely be different.

Nevertheless, representatives of each kind boarded the Ark, where Noah and his family kept them alive during that ordeal. Most of the dinosaur fossils we find are from the ones that died during the Flood. In some rare cases, we find preserved organs and even fossilized stomach contents from their last meal. Along with that, we also sometimes find skin imprints and footprints during their final moments when they were trying to survive by getting to higher ground.

What About Pterosaurs Like Pterodactyls and Plesiosaurs?

There are some creatures, like flying reptiles (e.g., pterodactyls and pteranodons) and sea reptiles (e.g., plesiosaurs and kronosauruses), which were

---

2. "Then God said, 'Let the earth bring forth the living creature according to its kind: cattle and creeping thing and beast of the earth, each according to its kind'; and it was so. And God made the beast of the earth according to its kind, cattle according to its kind, and everything that creeps on the earth according to its kind. And God saw that it was good" (Genesis 1:24–25).

3. "Now out of the ground the LORD God had formed every beast of the field and every bird of the heavens and brought them to the man to see what he would call them. And whatever the man called every living creature, that was its name. The man gave names to all livestock and to the birds of the heavens and to every beast of the field. But for Adam there was not found a helper fit for him" (Genesis 2:19–20; ESV).

4. The serpent that Satan used to deceive Eve in Genesis 3 was also counted among the "beasts of the field" per Genesis 3:1. And although all animals suffer under the curse, this may explain in part why the "beasts of the field" were denoted as being cursed alongside with the serpent specifically in Genesis 3:14.

5. "And the fear of you and the dread of you shall be on every beast of the earth, on every bird of the air, on all that move on the earth, and on all the fish of the sea. They are given into your hand" (Genesis 9:2).

not made on Day 6 of Creation Week, that we often incorrectly link to dinosaurs.

Let me give you a nudge. They are flying and sea creatures (not dinosaurs). What day did God make the flying and sea creatures? It was the day before dinosaurs, which was Day 5 of Creation Week.

Now I want you to consider something fascinating. We are often informed by the secular world that "dinosaurs evolved into birds." Yet, according to the Bible, God created winged creatures, which includes birds, *a day before* the dinosaurs. So, each bird kind (whether flying or not) was in existence before any dinosaur kind was even created. So, did dinosaurs evolve into birds? Nope. When you start your thinking with God and His Word, the secular story falls apart.

It's remarkably easy and not a problem for the all-powerful God of the Bible to create dinosaurs and man the day after He created the flying reptiles, birds, and sea reptiles on Day 5 of Creation Week.[6]

An Authority Issue

In our dark and secularized culture today, the truth and light of the Bible is under constant attack (John 3:18–20[7]) by laymen, scholars, non-Christians, and sometimes even professing Christians too! In light of this fact, consider something much deeper, particularly when you realize that the Bible (God's Word) comes with the authority of God Himself (2 Timothy 3:16–17[8]). *By what authority* (or standard) can someone object to God's authority?

In other words, when someone says, "I don't believe the Bible," on what authority are they standing? That is, they falsely presume they can elevate themselves above God by trying to stand on their own fallible, sinful, imperfect, arbitrary, human authority.

But think about it — by what standard can a fallible, sinful, imperfect, arbitrary, human being (who wasn't there in the past) object to the all-powerful, all-knowing, always existing, absolute authority of the Creator God who

---

6. As a more technical note, the word we often translate as "fowl" or "bird" in Genesis 1 is עוֹף [*owph*] which means *winged creature* and thus it includes bats, birds, flying reptiles, and even winged insects. This is why bats and flightless birds like the ostrich are included as *owph* in Leviticus 11:13–19.

7. "He who believes in Him is not condemned; but he who does not believe is condemned already, because he has not believed in the name of the only begotten Son of God. And this is the condemnation, that the light has come into the world, and men loved darkness rather than light, because their deeds were evil. For everyone practicing evil hates the light and does not come to the light, lest his deeds should be exposed" (John 3:18–20).

8. "All Scripture is given by inspiration of God, and is profitable for doctrine, for reproof, for correction, for instruction in righteousness, that the man of God may be complete, thoroughly equipped for every good work" (2 Timothy 3:16–17).

was there, and eye witnessed what He did? This faulty reasoning is called a *false authority fallacy/faulty appeal to authority fallacy,* which is defined when one appeals to themselves, or other imperfect people, about a past event they didn't witness, in an effort to object to the ultimate authority — God.

To make this point clearer, imagine you have a lump under your arm and instead of making an appointment with a medical doctor, who has 20 years of experience studying cancer, you appeal to a kindergartener who knows virtually nothing about cancer diagnosis. Obviously, no one would make an appointment to grab a random kindergartener instead of seeking out a medical expert. The *medical expert* trumps the *kindergartener* in authority on the subject. The bottom line here is that, in reality, God is the ultimate expert *in all matters*…especially the issues of history and creation.

So the key is God's Word vs. man's word. And God is *always* right!

7

What Did Dinosaurs Originally Eat?

f you've ever watched popular movies that feature dinosaurs, like *Jurassic Park, Jurassic World,* or *Journey to the Center of the Earth,* there's one thing that becomes abundantly clear. When a T-rex comes after you, you need to run! We've been fed this idea that what we define as "meat-eating dinosaurs," if given the chance, would hunt you and eat you.

But was this the case originally — when God *created* dinosaurs? God is a God of life and is perfect. So when God created all life, He created all creatures (including dinosaurs) perfectly. And this perfect creation is what we expect from a perfect God. Deuteronomy 32:4 says:

He is the Rock, His work is perfect; for all His ways are justice, a God of truth and without injustice; righteous and upright is He.

In other words, we received a perfect creation because God's works are perfect. And at the end of the creation week, God saw all that He had made and declared it "very good" (Genesis 1:31[1]). This original world was full of perfect life in harmony, with no death, pain, disease, nor suffering. And the two verses prior to Genesis 1:31[2] (Genesis 1:29–30[3]) indicate that animals and man were initially vegetarian. So animals were not even dying!

---

1. "Then God saw everything that He had made, and indeed it was very good. So the evening and the morning were the sixth day" (Genesis 1:31).
2. Ibid.
3. "And God said, 'See, I have given you every herb that yields seed which is on the face of all the earth, and every tree whose fruit yields seed; to you it shall be for food. Also, to every beast of the earth, to every bird of the air, and to everything that creeps on the earth, in which there is life, I have given every green herb for food'; and it was so" (Genesis 1:29–30).

Again, this is what we expect from a perfect God of life. Logically, since animals weren't dying, then animals weren't eating other animals. This means dinosaurs, which are animals, were *not* eating any other animals or man originally. So they would not have tried to chase Adam and Eve down to eat them.

Did Plants Die?

One might object and say, "But plants were dying!" They argue that since plants were given for food in Genesis 1:29–30,[4] then death did exist originally.

In a biblical sense, plants are not actually "alive," thus they cannot die. I'll explain the true (biblical) definition of life more in a moment. This fallacious reasoning is analogous to saying that rocks died or a star died, but they weren't alive in the first place.

When saying plants "died," this statement is actually an equivocation fallacy and a reification fallacy. People using this fallacious argument are falsely applying the *modern biological definition of life* to the early pages of Genesis, rather than using the *biblical definition of life* as revealed through Scripture. So, first, they are equivocating on the word "life" by using two different definitions (hence, an equivocation fallacy). Second, they are reifying inanimate (non-living) things to be living, then falsely applying those attributes to them (hence, a reification fallacy).

God defines what life is in the early pages of Genesis. For instance, mankind, land-dwelling animals, fish, birds, and winged creatures are alive. In our common vernacular, this equates to humans, birds, mammals, reptiles, amphibians, fish, and so on.

This fact is based on the meaning of the words, *nephesh* and *chayyah*, in Hebrew. *Nephesh* is commonly translated as soul, creature, or being, and *chay/chayyah* as "living" or beast (i.e., living beast).

Chay/chayah is in Genesis in chapter 1, verses 20–21,[5] 24–25,[6] 28,[7]

---

4. Ibid.

5. "Then God said, 'Let the waters abound with an abundance of living creatures, and let birds fly above the earth across the face of the firmament of the heavens.' So God created great sea creatures and every living thing that moves, with which the waters abounded, according to their kind, and every winged bird according to its kind. And God saw that it was good" (Genesis 1:20–21).

6. "Then God said, 'Let the earth bring forth the living creature according to its kind: cattle and creeping thing and beast of the earth, each according to its kind'; and it was so. And God made the beast of the earth according to its kind, cattle according to its kind, and everything that creeps on the earth according to its kind. And God saw that it was good" (Genesis 1:24–25).

7. "Then God blessed them, and God said to them, 'Be fruitful and multiply; fill the earth and subdue it; have dominion over the fish of the sea, over the birds of the air, and over every living thing that moves on the earth'" (Genesis 1:28).

30,[8] and chapter 2, verses 7,[9] 9[10] (regarding the name of the Tree of "Life"),[11] 19–20.[12] *Nephesh* is in Genesis in chapter 1, verses 20–21,[13] 24,[14] 30,[15] and chapter 2, verses 7[16] and 19.[17]

In reading these verses, we clearly see why plants, rocks, air, stars, etc. are not considered living souls. Plants are basically solar and water-powered, self-replicating, biological machines that reduce carbon dioxide gas, which make food and usable oxygen for living creatures.

Humans, unlike animals, are also made differently, being made in the image of an eternal, ruling God. Thus, God gave us something to rule over (dominion) with our souls/spirits lasting forever. So, although the body of man has many physiological similarities to mammalian animals (i.e., we were made to live in the same world by the same God), we are still quite different.

As time passed, however, the definition of "life" changed to include anything that grows using biological processes, reproduces, and so on. Thus,

---

8. "'Also, to every beast of the earth, to every bird of the air, and to everything that creeps on the earth, in which there is life, I have given every green herb for food'; and it was so" (Genesis 1:30).

9. "And the LORD God formed man of the dust of the ground, and breathed into his nostrils the breath of life; and man became a living being" (Genesis 2:7).

10. "And out of the ground the LORD God made every tree grow that is pleasant to the sight and good for food. The tree of life was also in the midst of the garden, and the tree of the knowledge of good and evil" (Genesis 2:9).

11. Not that the Tree of Life is "alive" but that the tree's name uses the word "life," and eating its fruit sustains that which God defines as life (Genesis 3:22–24; Revelation 22:2, 14)

12. "Now out of the ground the LORD God had formed every beast of the field and every bird of the heavens and brought them to the man to see what he would call them. And whatever the man called every living creature, that was its name. The man gave names to all livestock and to the birds of the heavens and to every beast of the field. But for Adam there was not found a helper fit for him" (Genesis 2:19–20; ESV).

13. "Then God said, 'Let the waters abound with an abundance of living creatures, and let birds fly above the earth across the face of the firmament of the heavens.' So God created great sea creatures and every living thing that moves, with which the waters abounded, according to their kind, and every winged bird according to its kind. And God saw that it was good" (Genesis 1:20–21).

14. "Then God said, 'Let the earth bring forth the living creature according to its kind: cattle and creeping thing and beast of the earth, each according to its kind'; and it was so" (Genesis 1:24).

15. "Also, to every beast of the earth, to every bird of the air, and to everything that creeps on the earth, in which there is life, I have given every green herb for food'; and it was so" (Genesis 1:30).

16. "And the LORD God formed man of the dust of the ground, and breathed into his nostrils the breath of life; and man became a living being" (Genesis 2:7).

17. "Out of the ground the LORD God formed every beast of the field and every bird of the air, and brought them to Adam to see what he would call them. And whatever Adam called each living creature, that was its name" (Genesis 2:19).

the modern classification system now includes plants. Even so, God did not define these as living souls (life). Obviously, the process of applying this modern definition to the created order is fallacious — especially when interpreting Scripture.

So the claim that plants are "alive" and can "die" is illogical. Plants originally served their purpose perfectly at the beginning of creation when death was not reigning. Death is the punishment for sin (Geneiss 2:16–17,[18] Ezekiel 18:20[19]; Romans 6:23[20]) so it cannot have existed until sin entered the creation. It was at the *Corruption* — the second "C" of History. This means "meat-eating" dinosaurs didn't exist initially! And this brings us to our next question: What caused some dinosaurs to become meat eaters? For those paying attention, you may not need a nudge but probably already know the answer.

---

18. "And the LORD God commanded the man, saying, 'Of every tree of the garden you may freely eat; but of the tree of the knowledge of good and evil you shall not eat, for in the day that you eat of it you shall surely die'" (Genesis 2:16–17).

19. "The soul who sins shall die. The son shall not bear the guilt of the father, nor the father bear the guilt of the son. The righteousness of the righteous shall be upon himself, and the wickedness of the wicked shall be upon himself" (Ezekiel 18:20).

20. "For the wages of sin is death, but the gift of God is eternal life in Christ Jesus our Lord" (Romans 6:23).

8

What Caused Some Dinosaurs to Become Meat Eaters?

n an originally perfect world, dinosaurs were all vegetarian, as per Genesis 1:30.[1] But because of man's sin (Genesis 3), death and suffering reigned in a now broken world, thus allowing the first *possibility* for animals to eat meat. Yet, prior to this, there was no death. And obviously you must have death to have meat to eat![2]

Furthermore, we do not know how long before dinosaurs and other meat-eating animals first began eating animal flesh as food. This switch to eating meat could have been immediate, or possibly more gradual, after the curse in Genesis 3. Yet some representatives of various kinds could have remained vegetarian, while other members of a kind became meat eating.

We know that some dinosaurs indeed ate meat prior to the Flood of Noah's day (consider Genesis 6:12[3]), based on the snapshots of these dinosaurs (and other meat-eating critters) buried and fossilized in Flood sediment (i.e., most of geological rock layers). In some instances, these dinosaurs' last meals, before being buried, were preserved in their stomach contents

---

1. " 'Also, to every beast of the earth, to every bird of the air, and to everything that creeps on the earth, in which there is life, I have given every green herb for food'; and it was so" (Genesis 1:30).
2. Some may argue that lizard tails are designed to fall off in evading a predator and this would allow for meat without death; however, this is still the result of suffering, which came with sin and in violation of the ordinance that animals were to be eating *green herbs* — vegetarian foods in Genesis 1:30.
3. "So God looked upon the earth, and indeed it was corrupt; for all flesh had corrupted their way on the earth" (Genesis 6:12).

throughout the Triassic, Jurassic, and Cretaceous rock layers (these are where dinosaurs are found or otherwise classified).

Those fossilized stomach remains are often identified as the bones of another animal, thus showing some animals ate meat by the time of the Flood. But I want to add a caveat here by pointing out that these dinosaurs, which were buried and fossilized in the Flood, ate their last meal(s) while fleeing and trying to survive the Flood. This point is important to consider when defining their true *normal* diet prior to the Flood.

According to the Bible, all the land-dwelling, air-breathing animals over the whole earth died by the 150th day of the Flood (Genesis 7:21–24[4]). Between the 40th and 150th day of the Flood the waters had reached their peak maximum. As the waters rose, animals could have moved to higher ground to avoid dying, creating a crowded situation. Some dinosaurs, along with other animals and even some people, could possibly have survived until Day 150 before they drowned (or otherwise died). The few gleanings we can learn from this are as follows:

- Footprints from walking land dwelling creatures ceased to exist by Day 150.

- Any animal eaten by a dinosaur (or other "meat-eating" animal) took place prior to Day 150.

- Unless an animal was rapidly buried at the onset of the Flood, the normal diet of the dinosaurs and other animals was likely disrupted or altered, from the beginning stages of the Flood until Day 150.

So, from these three points, we can conclude that certain pre-Flood dinosaurs may not have eaten meat as part of their *normal* diet. Rather, their last meal (or last few meals) may have been simply a result of scavenging and eating whatever other animals they could find, while fleeing and trying to survive the Flood during those last few months of life.

Genesis 6:12[5] indicates that all flesh had become corrupted on the earth. Both animals and humans were originally commanded to be vegetarians but

---

4. "And all flesh died that moved on the earth: birds and cattle and beasts and every creeping thing that creeps on the earth, and every man. All in whose nostrils was the breath of the spirit of life, all that was on the dry land, died. So He destroyed all living things which were on the face of the ground: both man and cattle, creeping thing and bird of the air. They were destroyed from the earth. Only Noah and those who were with him in the ark remained alive. And the waters prevailed on the earth one hundred and fifty days" (Genesis 7:21–24).

5. "So God looked upon the earth, and indeed it was corrupt; for all flesh had corrupted their way on the earth" (Genesis 6:12).

had corrupted their flesh in many ways. Some of these corrupt ways of man are given in Scripture, such as sexual immorality (e.g., wickedness per Genesis 6:5[6]), eating meats (also in that every intent of thought in a man's heart was evil continually, thus surely going against Genesis 1:29[7]), and other forms of violence, murder, and child sacrifice (per Genesis 6:13[8]). Obviously, animals also deviated into violent ways and ate meat, which included them next to man as "corrupted" flesh as well.

We can be sure that animals ate other animals by the time of the Flood. To give you a "taste," here are just a few examples of Flood burial fossils and what they ate for their last meal, as recorded in their fossilized stomach contents:

1.   An ancient crocodile ate a juvenile ornithopod dinosaur.[9]
2.   *Sinocalliopteryx gigas* (theropod dinosaur) ate birds.[10]
3.   A large *T-rex*, named Sue, ate a juvenile *Edmontosaurus* dinosaur and a young adult *T-rex*.[11]

This is just a small sampling of what can be found on the subject.

The key takeaway here is that eating meat only became a possibility because of sin. And although eating meat was not permitted until after the Flood (Genesis 9:3[12]), there were many people and animals that likely ate meat in defiance of God's original command, until the Flood washed them all away. So, the bottom line here is meat-eating dinosaurs couldn't have existed until sin, but after sin, it became a possibility. And from certain fossil evidences from the Flood, we know some animals feasted on other animals.

---

6. "Then the LORD saw that the wickedness of man was great in the earth, and that every intent of the thoughts of his heart was only evil continually" (Genesis 6:5).

7. "And God said, 'See, I have given you every herb that yields seed which is on the face of all the earth, and every tree whose fruit yields seed; to you it shall be for food'" (Genesis 1:29).

8. "And God said to Noah, 'The end of all flesh has come before Me, for the earth is filled with violence through them; and behold, I will destroy them with the earth'" (Genesis 6:13).

9. Carolyn Gramling, "Fossils show a crocodile ancestor dined on a young dinosaur," *Science-News*, February 21, 2022, https://www.sciencenews.org/article/crocodile-ancestor-ate-dinosaur-fossil-stomach.

10. L. Xing, P.R. Bell, W.S. Persons, S. Ji, et al. (2012) "Abdominal Contents from Two Large Early Cretaceous Compsognathids (Dinosauria: Theropoda) Demonstrate Feeding on Confuciusornithids and Dromaeosaurids," PLoS ONE 7(8): e44012. doi:10.1371/journal.pone.0044012, http://www.plosone.org/article/info:doi/10.1371/journal.pone.0044012.

11. Lenny Flank, "'Sue': The Most Complete T Rex Skeleton Ever Found," *Daily Kos*, April 23, 2014, https://www.dailykos.com/stories/2014/4/23/1250848/--Sue-The-Most-Complete-T-Rex-Skeleton-Ever-Found.

12. "Every moving thing that lives shall be food for you. I have given you all things, even as the green herbs" (Genesis 9:3).

9

Dinosaur "Defense or Attack Structures" Like Teeth and Claws...in a Perfect World?

When people see animals with sharp teeth, they most commonly interpret this to mean that the animal is a meat-eater. When scientists find fossils of creatures with sharp teeth, they also interpret this to mean that the animal was a meat-eater. But is this a proper interpretation? Not really. Sharp teeth in animals indicate only one thing: the animal has sharp teeth.

Let's start at the beginning. Since the world God created was originally very good, meaning there was no death or suffering of man or animals (Genesis 1:29–31[1]) in this perfect world since God's works are perfect (e.g., Deuteronomy 32:4[2]), an interesting question gets brought up from time to time. "Why do animals, like many dinosaurs, have features on their body that seem very well-designed to kill, attack, or protect itself from being eaten or attacked?"

This question is an insightful one, and I appreciate those who ask it, because it shows they are thinking more deeply about the subject of dinosaurs and the Bible. Although many are sincere in questioning, there have been

---

1. "And God said, 'See, I have given you every herb [that] yields seed which [is] on the face of all the earth, and every tree whose fruit yields seed; to you it shall be for food. Also, to every beast of the earth, to every bird of the air, and to everything that creeps on the earth, in which there is life, I have given every green herb for food'; and it was so. Then God saw everything that He had made, and indeed it was very good. So the evening and the morning were the sixth day" (Genesis 1:29–31).
2. "He is the Rock, His work is perfect; For all His ways are justice, A God of truth and without injustice; Righteous and upright is He" (Deuteronomy 32:4).

some who ask the question in a mocking fashion. In these instances, they try to refute the biblical creation account by pointing out the supposed "contradiction" between what we see in the world *today* and what the Bible says about the original, perfect creation.

Notice how I italicized "today"? I did this for a reason. This type of argument that attacks Scripture is commonly known as a part-to-whole fallacy. *Today*, we can see "defense" and "attack" structures in animals. Using this limited knowledge, which exists in *the present*, they presume the entire creation of the past has always been this way (hence, part-to-whole fallacy).

But the original, very good, creation is not what we live in today. All that changed when sin entered creation in Genesis 3, where man (Adam) sinned against a perfect and holy God by committing high treason against Him.

Consequently, God cursed the ground, sentenced man to die (both physically and spiritually), and cursed all of creation, including all the animals (Genesis 3). In one instance, the prime animal involved — the serpent — being used as a vassal for Satan, was cursed to crawl on its belly and eat dust[3] all the days of its life. In parallel, the curse to the ground resulted in some plants now having thorns and thistles (Genesis 3:17–18[4]). The point is that the curse, in Genesis 3, caused *physical* changes in the world, which we now experience today.

With this fact in mind, let's evaluate two particular biblical models or positions that can further answer this question.

Model 1: Animals Originally Used Present Features for a Different Purpose

Regarding defense or attack structures, animals like dinosaurs may simply have used those features for a different purpose or thrust prior to the fall into sin (Genesis 3). This model has animals with these features, such as sharp teeth, claws, venom, webs, or protective shells, protective blowers (e.g., skunks, Bombardier Beetles, etc.) and so on, present before sin, but used in different (yet still "very good") ways.

---

3. This may relate to the fact that snakes and many lizards/reptiles have a Jacobson's Organ/vomeronasal organ inside their mouth that requires their tongue to collects dust particles like pollen and other particulates and insert it into that organ as a means of detecting scent/pheromones for chemoreception. So they literally eat dust. Other animals (e.g., many mammals and amphibians) have a Jacobson's organ and detection methods, but not like this in their mouth where they have to use their tongue to activate it.

4. "Then to Adam He said, 'Because you have heeded the voice of your wife, and have eaten from the tree of which I commanded you, saying, "You shall not eat of it": Cursed is the ground for your sake; In toil you shall eat of it All the days of your life. Both thorns and thistles it shall bring forth for you, And you shall eat the herb of the field'" (Genesis 3:17–18).

Panda bear

Squirrel

- There are many animals today with sharp teeth whose primary diet is not meat. For example, bears, who have sharp teeth and claws, primarily eat plant-based material for most of their diet. Pandas and fruit bats also have very sharp teeth, yet only eat bamboo and fruit, respectively. Likewise, a dinosaur with big, sharp teeth should have no problem tearing through food like coconuts, watermelons, or any sort of hard plant matter.

- Furthermore, squirrels use their *vicious-looking claws* to climb trees and hold nuts. By the way, squirrels really are vicious with their claws. I grew up on a farm and made the mistake of grabbing a wild squirrel once....I'll have you know, that I've never done it since! Its claws tore into me, and it bit me too!

- Mosquitoes eat plant sap and pollen with their proboscis (i.e., their "jabber"). Adult male and female mosquitos can get enough nourishment to survive from only feeding on nectar or honeydew from a wide variety of plants.[5]

- Spiders are known to catch pollen in their webs for food. Jumping spiders actually get about 90% of their nutrition from plant material. Some spiders feed on plant nectar, sugar solutions. While under captivity, common house spiders often feast on milk, marmalade, and bananas.[6]

- Turtle shells are not purely for defense. Their shells are both beautiful and useful for other reasons, such as digging and burrowing prior to

5. "What Do Mosquitoes Eat?" *Mosquito Reviews*, accessed April 26, 2022, https://mosquitoreviews.com/learn/what-mosquitoes-eat.
6. Waleed Khalid, "What Do Spiders Eat?" *Animals Time*, accessed February 7, 2020, http://animalstime.com/what-spiders-eat-what-house-spiders-eat/.

hibernating. Their shell also does a good job of helping keep a healthy balance to protect the turtle (and tortoises) from bacterial and fungal problems similar to what skin does for us. In rare cases in a broken world, when shells get compromised like a crack, or otherwise subjected to too much fungus or bacteria, it can infect the creature. This is called *Turtle Shell Rot* or even *septicemic cutaneous ulcerative disease.*[7]

- The venom of snakes is actually produced from their salivary glands. Prior to sin, when snakes were originally vegetarian, it's possible this venom was used to break down fruits and vegetables, making them easier to digest. Even in modern times, we still sometimes see of "a taste" of the original (Edenic) diet for snakes. For instance, *whip snakes* have been caught on video eating grapes.[8] Today, snakes are typically referred to as "obligate carnivores," which means they eat virtually all meat, as well as eggs. Perhaps snakes no longer had access to their primary vegetarian food sources as a result of the Flood or degeneration since sin and the curse. Regardless, snakes today generally (with some exceptions) have a propensity for meat, insects, eggs, etc.

- Blowers, like skunks, use their ability to mark territory for breeding.

There are many other examples we can list here, but the main takeaway is that these defense/attack functions we see today could have served an *entirely different purpose* prior to sin. That is the basis for this model.

Model 2: Present-Day Animal Features Are the Result of "Cursed-Design"

This next position relates to the curses in Genesis 3. When Adam and Eve sinned, everything changed. Both biblical models agree on that. In this model, after the curse, God changed some of the *designs* of plants and animals into what is called "cursed design."

The serpent is the obvious example. God cursed the serpent by sentencing it to crawl on its belly and eat dust (Genesis 3:14[9]). Interestingly, snakes and other lizards (except for dinosaurs, which are lizards that remained

---

7. Hunter Briggs, "Turtle Shell Rot: Symptoms, Causes & Treatments," *Reptile Direct*, June 7, 2020, https://www.reptiledirect.com/turtle-shell-rot/.

8. "Whip Snake Eating Grapes," accessed February 7, 2020, https://www.bing.com/videos/search?q=video+of+a+snake+eating+a+fruit&&view=detail&mid=-32CEEDC92B433A4281EC32CEEDC92B433A4281EC&&FORM=VRD-GAR&ru=%2Fvideos%2Fsearch%3Fq%3Dvideo%2Bof%2Ba%2Bsnake%2Beating%2Ba%2Bfruit%26FORM%3DHDRSC3.

9. "So the LORD God said to the serpent: 'Because you have done this, You are cursed more than all cattle, And more than every beast of the field; On your belly you shall go, And you shall eat dust All the days of your life'" (Genesis 3:14).

standing erect) now crawl on their belly and eat dust (e.g., the Jacobson's Organ in their mouth for dust particulates).

This model affirms that the original serpent in the Garden stood more upright prior to this curse. But the Bible simply doesn't tell us whether the serpent originally had limbs, legs, wings, or other appendages that were lost or merely reduced.[10]

Many people overlook the fact that the serpent was cursed *more than* all the other animals. This may be indicative that certain other animals were cursed *more* or *less* as well. A small list of other animals is mentioned in Genesis 3:14[11] (such as cattle and beasts of the field); but in Romans 8, we find the entire creation has been cursed and is groaning, which will not be relieved until the New Heavens and New Earth are established (e.g., Romans 8:22,[12] Revelation 22:3[13]) at the Consummation — the seventh and eternal "C" of history.

Again, the Bible doesn't tell us any specific details about the serpent. Some people have suggested the serpent was a dinosaur, but I'm not convinced. Recall that dinosaurs remained standing erect and did not crawl on their belly.

For better clarity, let's look at this perspective from another angle. The Bible says that Christ *is* the seed or offspring of the woman (Genesis 3:15[14]; Galatians 3:16–19[15]). Yet the offspring or seed of the serpent was there to strike/bruise Christ's heel with a crucifixion (e.g., John 19:6–18). But who was this spiritual offspring of the serpent attacking Christ?

---

10. For a discussion on the subject of the serpent and its possible appendages prior to the curse please see: Bodie Hodge, *The Fall of Satan* (Green Forest, AR: Master Books, 2011), p. 33–40.

11. "So the LORD God said to the serpent: 'Because you have done this, You are cursed more than all cattle, And more than every beast of the field; On your belly you shall go, And you shall eat dust All the days of your life'" (Genesis 3:14).

12. "For we know that the whole creation groans and labors with birth pangs together until now" (Romans 8:22).

13. "And there shall be no more curse, but the throne of God and of the Lamb shall be in it, and His servants shall serve Him" (Revelation 22:3).

14. "And I will put enmity Between you and the woman, And between your seed and her Seed; He shall bruise your head, And you shall bruise His heel" (Genesis 3:15).

15. "Now to Abraham and his Seed were the promises made. He does not say, 'And to seeds,' as of many, but as of one, 'And to your Seed,' who is Christ. And this I say, that the law, which was four hundred and thirty years later, cannot annul the covenant that was con- firmed before by God in Christ, that it should make the promise of no effect. For if the in- heritance is of the law, it is no longer of promise; but God gave it to Abraham by promise. What purpose then does the law serve? It was added because of transgressions, till the Seed should come to whom the promise was made; and it was appointed through angels by the hand of a mediator" (Galatians 3:16–19).

In John 8:38–44, Jesus spoke to some of the Jewish people and leaders who opposed Him (per John 8:22,[16] 31,[17] 48,[18] 52,[19] and 57[20]) and pointed out that they are of their father the devil. John the Baptist and Jesus both affirmed the leaders of the Jews (i.e., the scribes, Pharisees, and Sadducees) were a brood (i.e., offspring) of vipers and serpents (obviously not literally, but rather in a spiritual sense) in verses, such as Matthew 3:7,[21] Matthew 12:34,[22] Matthew 23:33,[23] and Luke 3:7.[24] Jesus even says they are of their father the devil in John 8:44.[25]

It's interesting to note that of all the types of serpents currently in the world, the Bible repeatedly uses "a brood of VIPERS" to describe those lashing out at Christ. So, is it possible that the initial serpent in the Garden was actually a type of viper?

We can't know for certain, but it is something to consider; after all, vipers are among the most vicious types of snakes. Though not the most venomous, the aggressive *Saw-scaled viper* (also called *Echis* or *Carpet viper*) leads the way (by far) with the most human kills per year for snake bites.[26]

But what we do know for certain is that the serpent was cursed and physically changed. So the (obvious) follow up question is…*what* was the curse to other animals? Recall that this model has sharp teeth, claws, and

---

16. "So the Jews said, 'Will He kill Himself, because He says, "Where I go you cannot come"'?" (John 8:22).

17. "Then Jesus said to those Jews who believed Him, 'If you abide in My word, you are My disciples indeed'" (John 8:31).

18. "Then the Jews answered and said to Him, 'Do we not say rightly that You are a Samaritan and have a demon?'" (John 8:48).

19. "Then the Jews said to Him, 'Now we know that You have a demon! Abraham is dead, and the prophets; and You say, "If anyone keeps My word he shall never taste death"'" (John 8:52).

20. "Then the Jews said to Him, 'You are not yet fifty years old, and have You seen Abraham?'" (John 8:57).

21. "But when he saw many of the Pharisees and Sadducees coming to his baptism, he said to them, 'Brood of vipers! Who warned you to flee from the wrath to come?'" (Matthew 3:7).

22. "Brood of vipers! How can you, being evil, speak good things? For out of the abundance of the heart the mouth speaks" (Matthew 12:34).

23. "Serpents, brood of vipers! How can you escape the condemnation of hell?" (Matthew 23:33).

24. "Then he said to the multitudes that came out to be baptized by him, 'Brood of vipers! Who warned you to flee from the wrath to come?'" (Luke 3:7).

25. "You are of your father the devil, and the desires of your father you want to do. He was a murderer from the beginning, and does not stand in the truth, because there is no truth in him. When he speaks a lie, he speaks from his own resources, for he is a liar and the father of it" (John 8:44).

26. James Bruce, "Which Snake Kills the Most Humans?" *Snake Info — All About Snakes*, accessed April 4, 2022, https://www.alongtheway.org/all-about-snakes/which-snake-kills-the-most-humans-solution.html.

other defense or attack structures originating from *cursed design.* Therefore, the defense and attack structures, which help animals survive in a sin-cursed world, originated in the same way that thorns and thistles came about at this point in history.

But now another question pops up — *How* did these changes happen? Obviously, it was by the hand of God, but specifically how did it occur? This second model now deviates into two different semi-technical directions. Bear with me for a moment while I briefly define these two subsidiary positions.

1. God, by His sovereign will, providentially placed the information for sharp teeth, claws, and other defense or attack structures in the animals' DNA that remained latent/hidden until He declared the curses in Genesis 3 and was allowed to be expressed when God called down the curses in Genesis 3.

2. God, by His sovereign will, immediately redesigned the creatures and the original information in the animals' DNA upon the declared curses in Genesis 3. The defense and attack structures, then, either immediately or gradually, became expressed from that point.

We won't go into much more detail from this point. But suffice to say, be aware there are likely many minor distinctions in these models. Overall, the main point for this model, with its variations, is that animals may have looked different prior to the curse. Yet, obviously, we can only study the descendants of these animals living today, along with dead ones we find in the fossil record (e.g., Flood sediment), in ancient images, etc.

Combination of the Two Models

Is it possible that God utilized (at least) some aspects of both biblically based models? We should readily leave open this ("Model 3") option too.

In other words, it is possible that God utilized aspects of Model 1 for some animals and perhaps used aspects of Model 2 for other animals. For example, squirrels may have always had those ("vicious looking") claws for its original design to better climb trees, whereas black widow spiders may have received their deadly venom as part of the cursed design. This is one possible situation with the combination of the two models.

Conclusion

From a biblical worldview we can properly understand why dinosaurs, like other animals, have defense or attack structures in our sin-cursed world. The biblical foundation for both models is that everything in our world changed as a result of sin. The models only differ on the specific details and technicalities.

Finally, these models give us an idea of what transpired from the original, perfect creation to today. Of course, Christians look forward to a time in perfection with Christ of a New Heavens and a New Earth where there will be no more death and no more suffering and the curse has been removed. What a glorious ending we have in God.

10

Were Dinosaurs on Noah's Ark (and Did Any Go Extinct Before the Flood)?

For years, I affirmatively answered this question during lectures, conferences, and web articles. During those years, the reaction was always the same — "Wow, I didn't know and have never heard this in my church before." But then we opened the Ark Encounter on July 7, 2016.

Since then, reactions from people asking this question have never been the same. I still point out that dinosaurs were on Noah's Ark, and sometimes I get the response above. But now I usually get responses like, "Yeah, I saw dinosaurs when I went through the Ark Encounter" or "Of course dinosaurs were on the Ark, our family saw them when we visited the Ark Encounter." Don't get me wrong, I'm thrilled to get answers like this for several reasons.

First, it gives me confidence that the message about dinosaurs and the Bible is reaching more Christian circles. Second, it shows the success of the Ark Encounter. For both reasons, I'm ecstatic.

Were Dinosaurs on Noah's Ark?

Yes! Remember, dinosaurs are defined as land animals and were in existence with man from Day 6 onward. Therefore, when God commanded every kind of land-dwelling/dependent, air-breathing animals to go on the Ark, as per Genesis 7:21–23,[1] this included dinosaurs and flying reptiles too. The Bible says,

---

1. "And all flesh died that moved on the earth: birds and cattle and beasts and every creeping thing that creeps on the earth, and every man. All in whose nostrils was the breath of the spirit of life, all that was on the dry land, died.... Only Noah and those who were with him in the ark remained alive" (Genesis 7:21–23).

> And of every living thing of all flesh you shall bring two of every
> sort into the ark, to keep them alive with you; they shall be male
> and female. Of the birds after their kind, of animals after their
> kind, and of every creeping thing of the earth after its kind, two of
> every kind will come to you to keep them alive (Genesis 6:19–20).

Notice in verse 20 that the qualification for birds, animals, and creeping
things is "*of the earth.*" This obviously *excludes* sea creatures. Genesis 7:21–23[2]
confirms that sea creatures were not on the Ark, but rather only land creatures, like dinosaurs, would have been on the ticket to board the Ark. Hence,
two of each kind of dinosaur and flying reptile[3] went on board the Ark.

Did Any Dinosaurs Go Extinct Prior to the Flood?

This is an excellent question that few have considered. When the Bible
says *two of "every" kind* in Genesis 6:20, it is implied that *every* kind is still
alive, although we can't be completely certain in this implication. The Bible
simply doesn't provide us a definitive answer. But there is a hint from the
Bible that we can consider.

Death Reigned

We know that death reigned from Genesis 3, with the intrusion of sin
and the curse, onward — so it is possible that certain creatures, including
dinosaurs, went extinct. The first recorded death of a creature (or of anything for that matter) was in Genesis 3:21[4] when God sacrificed animals
to makes tunics of skins for Adam and his wife. This direct relationship
between man's sin and animal death were closely related ever since that
point in history.

Abel offered fat portions in his sacrifice to God — an acceptable sacrifice by the way, unlike Cain's firstfruits. Because the punishment for sin
is death (Genesis 2:17[5]), the sacrificial solution had to involve death. This
is why Noah (who offered sacrifices after the Flood), Abraham, and his
descendants (the Israelites) ritually offered sacrifices to God. Ultimately, this

---

2. Ibid.
3. Though some have suggested that unclean flying creatures also went in by "seven each"
   (Genesis 7:3) or even 14 by some reckoning, Hebrew and Old Testament scholars of the
   past have typically pointed out the grammar of Genesis 7:3 is tied to the backdrop and
   context of Genesis 7:2 that indicates that 7 meant of the clean winged creatures only. This
   is discussed in detail in the following chapter.
4. "Also for Adam and his wife the LORD God made tunics of skin, and clothed them" (Genesis 3:21).
5. "…but of the tree of the knowledge of good and evil you shall not eat, for in the day that
   you eat of it you shall surely die" (Genesis 2:17).

all pointed to Jesus Christ, the ultimate and final sacrificial Lamb of God (i.e., the supreme Passover; Exodus 12).

Man, being made in the image of our ruling God, gave us something to rule over. Adam and Eve's dominion fell when they sinned in that it affected their whole dominion — not that they forfeited it (Genesis 3), which is when animal death became a reigning reality — even for dinosaurs. By the time of the Flood, man's sin had peaked, and judgment was nigh (Genesis 6:11–13[6]). Consequently, man's dominion, including animals, once again felt the brunt of it. And we see the record of this judgment from God by the Flood in the numerous fossil layers (e.g., from the Cambrian to the Miocene).[7]

Extinction And Fossilization

So now back to our question: Did any dinosaurs go extinct before the Flood? If their kinds were alive at the time of the Flood, representatives would have been on board the Ark and rescued. Some of those that died were preserved as fossils. So, if a kind had gone extinct *prior* to the Flood, then we may not have any evidence for it existing at all.

Rarely do creatures fossilize when they die. The remains usually get scavenged and rot away. A special process needs to happen to fossilize a creature — like a watery rapid burial. Rapid burial seals out the oxygen, which then prevents the quick and complete decay of the dead creature. For example, it allows minerals to be exchanged through water transport, which removes organic molecules, and be replaced with limestone molecules.

Prior to the Flood, processes that allowed for fossilization existed. But the Flood was the mechanism that allowed these processes to kick into full speed and on a grand scale!

Even if we grant that some fossils were made prior to the Flood, some (if not most) of those fossil remnants were likely destroyed by the Flood. If any pre-Flood fossil were to survive, it would be the things at the lowest level covered immediately at the onset of the Flood — assuming that the soil and rock surrounding said fossils were not stirred up, dissolved, or otherwise destroyed by the Flood waters and deposited.

Fossils are quite fragile and require special care to keep them from disintegrating. So it's quite improbable that an intact dinosaur fossil, that had

---

6. "The earth also was corrupt before God, and the earth was filled with violence. So God looked upon the earth, and indeed it was corrupt; for all flesh had corrupted their way on the earth. And God said to Noah, 'The end of all flesh has come before Me, for the earth is filled with violence through them; and behold, I will destroy them with the earth'" (Genesis 6:11–13).

7. Bodie Hodge and Ken Ham, *A Flood of Evidence* (Green Forest, AR: Master Books, 2016), p. 181–192.

been fossilized prior to the Flood would have survived the Flood's devastation. But, since the pre-Flood layers (including all the dirt, mud, sediment, etc. in those layers) were the first to get ripped up by the Flood, it's very possible we could find some pre-Flood fossils that may have been immediately deposited and kept from harm during the Flood — as mentioned before at the lowest levels like stromatolites for instance.[8]

Pre-Flood and Post-Flood World

God designed the original world perfectly. Continental structures were perfect, environments were in perfect harmony, animals were created in proximity to their ideal food sources and play areas and with the ability to get them, and so on. After the Fall, God cursed the ground, and everything in the world was no longer upheld in a perfect state. But the world's arrangements were still ideal.

The key point is that we are living in a post-Fall, post-Flood world where we see many disasters and catastrophes today. This is because the Flood caused continental forces, which completely rearranged the earth's crust.[9] We're still seeing these forces active today (on a lesser scale) with disasters, such as volcanoes, earthquakes, and extreme weather (e.g., avalanches, rapid local flooding, hurricanes, cyclones, and tsunamis).

These factors increase the probability for catastrophes that can cause fossilization. So, it's unwise to assume that the pre-Flood world was like ours is today. The likelihood of fossilization prior to the Flood was probably far less than what we have today.

The main takeaway here is that due to this lack of fossilization and fossil preservation before the Flood, we shouldn't expect to have much evidence to evaluate if a dinosaur went extinct prior to the Flood.

When animals were originally created on the earth, there were likely *quite a few* of each kind — unlike man, where God created only two people. That is, God created enough animals to be plentiful, yet still with enough room to be fruitful and multiply (e.g., Genesis 1:21–22,[10] where the winged creatures were to be fruitful and multiply).

---

8. Andrew Snelling, "Stromatolites — Rare Reminders of a Lost World," *Answers* Magazine, September 1, 2017, https://answersingenesis.org/fossils/stromatolites-rare-reminders-lost-world/.

9. Andrew Snelling and Bodie Hodge, "Did the Continents Split Apart in the Days of Peleg?" *New Answers Book 3* (Green Forest, AR: Master Books, 2010), p. 219–228, https://answersingenesis.org/geology/plate-tectonics/did-the-continents-split-apart-in-the-days-of-peleg/.

10. "So God created great sea creatures and every living thing that moves, with which the waters abounded, according to their kind, and every winged bird according to its kind. And God saw that it was good. And God blessed them, saying, 'Be fruitful and multiply, and fill the waters in the seas, and let birds multiply on the earth'" (Genesis 1:21–22).

Essentially, unlike the post-Flood animals, which generally started out with only a pair (or a few clean pairs), there was a much higher number of pre-Flood animals that were *living* in their perfect environments (albeit that was cursed). So the odds of them possibly going extinct prior to the Flood were far less than the odds today. In other words, it became much easier and more common for animals to go extinct after the Flood.

Fear of Man in the Animals

After the Flood, with fewer animals around, extinction became a more probable reality for certain kinds of animals. At this time, God placed the fear of man into all the animals, including the dinosaurs (Genesis 9:2[11]). As a result, this could have amplified the aggressions between man and some animals. And this in turn would have caused man to try to eradicate certain beasts like dinosaurs that people were uncomfortable around (or even for food or sport).

God Himself was even involved in taking out a sea reptile (e.g., Leviathan per Psalm 74:14,[12] Isaiah 27:1[13]). Dinosaurs were likely a target for removal from inhabited land due to expansion; certain dinosaurs were likely counted with other beasts of the field (Exodus 23:29,[14] Isaiah 43:20[15]). And a final factor to consider is the lack of ideal food sources after the Flood, which may have contributed to some animals developing a taste for blood and becoming carnivorous. This, in turn, could increase the likelihood of certain animals going extinct quicker (lack of natural food sources on one end of the spectrum to being hunted by new blood-loving animals on the other end of the spectrum).

Conclusion

So, all this to say, using the Bible as our starting point, we can confidently conclude each of the representative kinds of dinosaurs (living at the time) were indeed present on Noah's Ark. Again, there is a slight possibility

---

11. "And the fear of you and the dread of you shall be on every beast of the earth, on every bird of the air, on all that move on the earth, and on all the fish of the sea. They are given into your hand" (Genesis 9:2).

12. "You broke the heads of Leviathan in pieces, And gave him as food to the people inhabiting the wilderness" (Psalm 74:14).

13. "In that day the Lord with His severe sword, great and strong, Will punish Leviathan the fleeing serpent, Leviathan that twisted serpent; And He will slay the reptile that is in the sea" (Isaiah 27:1).

14. "I will not drive them out from before thee in one year; lest the land become desolate, and the beast of the field multiply against thee" (Exodus 23:29; KJV).

15. "The beast of the field shall honor me, the dragons and the owls: because I give waters in the wilderness, and rivers in the desert, to give drink to my people, my chosen" (Isaiah 43:20; KJV).

certain dinosaur kinds went extinct prior to the Flood; however it's likely that most kinds did survive the Flood. So, biblically and logically speaking, we can conclude the dinosaurian gradual demise happened after the Flood, and not before.

11

How Many Kinds of Animals, Including Dinosaurs, Were on the Ark?

Of the birds after their kind, of animals after their kind, and of every creeping thing of the earth after its kind, two of every kind will come to you to keep them alive (Genesis 6:20).

The first order of business is to point out that it was only land-based creatures that were placed on the Ark, meaning no marine creatures, like fish or trilobites, or marine reptiles, like plesiosaurs, were on the Ark. Much of the sea life that was living at that time died in the Flood. This was a violent, global-wide Flood after all. But representatives of *water*-based creatures could survive the *watery* Flood to preserve their kinds without the necessity of an Ark.

Kinds vs. Species

To understand how many dinosaurs went on the Ark, we first need to go over some preliminary information, which brings us to the question, "What is a kind?" We discussed dinosaur kinds in the previous chapter but didn't define it yet.

Kinds are not assigned to a specific level in our modern classification system, such as species, genus, family, or order, although, in a general sense, it is usually *close* to the family level in many instances. But a few can still be at a species (like humans), genus, or even order level, depending on the kind of creature.

Examples of kinds are like the dog kind (including wolves, coyotes, dingoes, domestic dogs, etc.) or the cat sort (including lions, tigers, cougars,

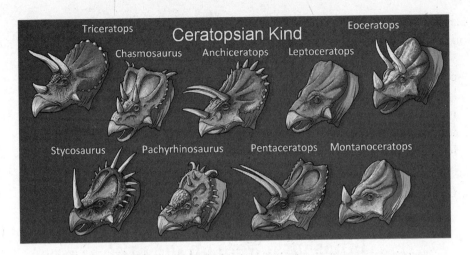

bobcats, domestic cats, etc.), or the horse sort (ponies, Clydesdales, donkeys, zebras, etc.), and so on. There is variation within these kinds, especially since the Flood. But note, this variation is not in the sense of one kind changing into another kind over long periods of time as required in evolution storytelling, which is not observed anyway (e.g., amoebas via evolution over millions of years evolving into dogs). That is, dogs remain dogs, cats remain cats, horses remain horses, and so on.

A nice rule of thumb to remember is that if animals can interbreed or hybridize, they are part of the same kind. For instance, zebras can interbreed with horses and get a *zorse* or a *hebra*. Another instance is lions can interbreed with tigers and get a *liger* or a *tigon*. Usually the male gets the first part of the name and the female gets the last part of the name for the offspring.

Species is an arbitrary "dividing line" and is a paradox, hence the famous *"Species Problem"* when trying to define it. The popular belief is that if creatures can interbreed, then they are the same "species," but clearly that is not always the case. For instance, various species of dogs can and do interbreed (e.g., coyote and wolf, or domestic dog with a coyote) — yet they are considered different species.

The same is true of cats. For instance, we have a blinx (bobcat father with a linx mother hybrid). And, as previously mentioned, there's also ligers (lion father-tiger mother mix) and tigons (offspring of a male tiger and female lion). This is just a small sampling of the cat kind.

Again, most kinds are closer to a family level, but in some cases, they could be at the genus, species, or even order level, as is likely with the elephant kind (such as the extinct families of elephants such as mammoths and mastodons).[1]

The point of all of this is that one should not try to tally the total number of *species* on board Noah's Ark or they will have a gross exaggeration. All the land-dwelling, air-breathing *species* we have today are the descendants of the representative *kinds* that were aboard the Ark. And remember that sea creatures were not required on the Ark (e.g., trilobites or ichthyosaurs). But now let's look at other information in Scripture that further limits what went on board Noah's Ark.

Flesh, Insects, Land-Dwelling, and Air-Breathing...What?

> And all flesh died that moved on the earth: birds and cattle and beasts and every creeping thing that creeps on the earth, and every man. All in whose nostrils was the breath of the spirit of life, all that was on the dry land, died. So He destroyed all living things which were on the face of the ground: both man and cattle, creeping thing and bird of the air. They were destroyed from the earth. Only Noah and those who were with him in the ark remained alive (Genesis 7:21–23).

Genesis 7:21–23 teaches us that the criteria for animals aboard the Ark was limited to *air-breathing (through the nostrils), land-dwelling* creatures. Naturally, creatures that are air-breathing, yet lived in the ocean, were not required to be on the Ark (e.g., whales and dolphins). These representative kinds can survive outside the Ark.

Insects use tubes in their exoskeleton to take in oxygen, not nostrils. Therefore, many creation researchers do not have insects onboard Noah's Ark in their models.[2] Furthermore, they could have easily survived on driftwood, or, at the very least, their eggs could have survived on rafted wood and debris.

We also learn that all *flesh* that moved on the earth had died (e.g., Genesis 7:21,[3] see also Genesis 6:13–19). The Hebrew word for flesh is *basar*. Insects were never considered flesh or *basar* in the Bible, which is a further confirmation their residence wasn't required on the Ark during the Flood.

---

1. For more information on Mammoths and their relationship to the Ice Age, please see: Mike Oard, *Frozen in Time* (Green Forest, AR: Master Books, 2004).

2. Even if insects were on the Ark, due to their extremely small size, they could have easily fit. If a million individuals were taken, it would still be a small footprint in the Ark.

3. "And all flesh died that moved on the earth: birds and cattle and beasts and every creeping thing that creeps on the earth, and every man" (Genesis 7:21).

Furthermore, the Hebrew terms used for *behemah* and *remes*[4] in Genesis 6:19–20[5] were never used of insects in the Bible.

Bear in mind that many insects could survive on driftwood or their eggs could last on drifts and hatch after the 150th day of the Flood when land reappears. The Ark raised off the ground on the 40th day of the Flood so really this is only 110 days of survival time without land. Many insect eggs go longer than this through winter with freezing and thawing conditions.

With honey bee hives, which are more fragile and intricate, I can see them being brought on the Ark because they are a food producer — honey — and Noah and his family were to bring foods of all sorts onboard (Genesis 6:21[6]). Other bees, ants, and wasps such as the stingless bee (Meliponini or stingless bees, Mexican Honey Wasps, Honeypot Ant, Aphids, etc.) are also known to make and store honey by processing flower nectar. Some produce less like bumblebees do but they produce it nonetheless. So it is possible these types of colonies were included on the Ark, but I wouldn't be adamant.

All in all, only land-dwelling, air-breathing (through their nostrils) animal kinds that were considered flesh or *basar* were present on the Ark. And this includes dinosaurs and flying reptiles. Now to the next questions: What were the overall numbers on the Ark? And specifically how many of that number were dinosaurs?

Lower Estimates

What minimum figure of animals on the Ark have creation researchers historically used in their models? Researcher Arthur Jones, writing in the *Creation Research Society Quarterly* in 1973, basically put these qualifications at a family level and did the numbers.[7] He arrived at about 1,000 families (which he equated with the number of kinds). This means a total of about 2,000 individuals were taken on the Ark by his calculations.

---

4. The *Theological Wordbook of the Old Testament* says of *remes*: "The root encompasses all smaller animals but seems to exclude the large grazing animals, whales, birds, and insects" (R. Laird Harris, Gleason L. Archer, and Bruce K. Waltke. Chicago, IL: Moody Press, 2004).

5. "And of every living thing of all flesh you shall bring two of every sort into the ark, to keep them alive with you; they shall be male and female. "Of the birds after their kind, of animals [*behemah*] after their kind, and of every creeping thing [*remes*] of the earth after its kind, two of every kind will come to you to keep them alive" (Genesis 6:19–20).

6. "And you shall take for yourself of all food that is eaten, and you shall gather it to yourself; and it shall be food for you and for them" (Genesis 6:21).

7. Arthur J. Jones, "How Many Animals in the Ark?" *Creation Research Society Quarterly*, Volume 10, Number 2, September 1973, p. 102–108.

This total also includes the number of clean animals that came in by seven (Genesis 7:2[8]). Even so, this is likely a minimum figure since some kinds, in a few instances, are at a genus or a species level. Also, we have more documentation and readily accessed information on animals compared to the 1970s. And this information today shows there are many kinds that do belong to the family level but not all. Thus, at best, Jones' numbers represent a minimum figure.

Higher Estimates

Researcher John Woodmorappe decided to go a different route in 1996. He estimated the *maximum* figures for the total number of animals on the Ark. On top of that, he also estimated the required amount of food and even water that was needed for the animals on board Noah's Ark.[9]

For this model, Woodmorappe used the smaller-sized Ark (based on the shorter cubit of 18 inches). This translates to an Ark about 450 feet long, instead of the older/longer cubit's 510-foot-long vessel. Then, instead of using *family* levels for each kind (although he recognized that most kinds are closer to the family level), he used a *genus* level for all the kinds! So, for instance, instead of one dog kind, there would be more than ten dog "kinds" represented in his numbers. (There are more than ten genus levels within the dog classification.)

And, for the sake of maximum figures, John Woodmorappe assumed 14 (i.e., pairs of 7) *of each genus* of the clean animals, which again was still not that many! In the end, he estimated less than 8,000 kinds (about 15,745 individuals) for a maximum figure, based on this *genus* level and calculations. Using the smaller-sized Ark and this maximum number of animals in his model (plus accounting for their required floor space/cages/rooms), he estimated only 46.8% of the Ark was required to hold all the animals! Remember, this is a maximum figure. But Woodmorappe didn't stop there. As previously mentioned, Woodmorappe also calculated the total amounts of foodstuffs that would have been required on the Ark to feed this maximum number of animals for the entire voyage. His calculated numbers are listed in the following table:

8. "You shall take with you seven each of every clean animal, a male and his female; two each of animals that are unclean, a male and his female" (Genesis 7:2).

9. John Woodmorappe, *Noah's Ark: A Feasibility Study* (Dallas, TX: ICR Publications, 2009).

	Foodstuff	Ark space required
1	Lightly compressed dried hay pellet	16.3 %
2	Doubly compressed hay pellet	12.5%
3	Pelleted horse food	7.0%
4	Dried fruits/vegetables	6.8%

It's unlikely that Noah took *loose hay* (which takes a lot of space) but, for the sake of having a truly maximum number, let's assume the highest reasonable number here (16.3%) is accurate. Even though Noah and his family could have harvested water for part (if not most) of their duration on the Ark, Woodmorappe decided to calculate the total amount of required fresh water needed for storage on board the Ark. He found that it would take up about 9.4% of the Ark.

Putting all this together, about 72.5% of the (smaller-sized) Ark would be required to hold the maximum number of animals with the maximum required amount of food and water. Keep in mind, this number depends on the types of foodstuffs that Noah brought onboard the Ark, as well as the cubit standard he used (Noah likely used the longer one) and the total number of animals, which was likely much fewer in number than Woodmorappe's estimation. Let's now dive into the *Ark Encounter* numbers.

Ark Encounter Estimates

The Ark Encounter is using the Lovett design,[10] which utilizes the older/ longer cubit (20.4 inches), and naturally, this makes a longer and bigger Ark (510 feet long, by 85 feet wide, by 51 feet high). So this Ark has much more space than the smaller-sized Ark (used by Woodmorappe). This needs to be kept in mind with Ark Encounter figures.

When it comes to the animals on board, the Ark Encounter uses "reasonable maximums." In engineering this is basically equated with having a *safety factor* on a product (i.e., being *over engineered)!* The project intentionally errs on the high end of animals, yet not to the degree that Woodmorappe did with a *genus* level. The purpose is to avoid being accused of using lower numbers so all the animals can "fit" on the Ark.

So the Ark Encounter is using 14 of each kind of clean animal and 14 of each kind of *every* winged creature (not just clean ones) instead of only 7 of

---

10. Based on Australian Ark researcher Tim Lovett, M.Sc. He is an engineer who has researched and studied ancient shipbuilding techniques and archaeological finds.

each kind. But a few discussion points need to be understood prior to giving the tentatively final Ark Encounter numbers.

2 or 4 and 7 or 14?

Let's discuss the actual number of pairs of animals on the Ark in more detail. That is, was it 2 or 4 of each unclean kind that went on the Ark? Was it 7 or 14 of each clean kind that went on the Ark?

> You shall take with you seven each of every clean animal, a male and his female; two each of animals that are unclean, a male and his female; also seven each of birds of the air, male and female, to keep the species alive on the face of all the earth" (Genesis 7:2–3).

Furthermore, the animals went on the Ark by pairs, a male and its mate, and in some cases (i.e., the clean animal kinds and clean winged kinds[11]) seven went on board. To learn more about the biblical definitions for what constitutes clean, in the Old Testament, see Leviticus 11 and Deuteronomy 14 for example.[12]

The Ark Encounter is erring on the side of caution by having 14 of each clean animal and *all* birds/winged creatures to maximize the number of animals on the Ark, yet with only 2 of each unclean animal. However, this may not be the *actual* case.

The reason for the confusion is the way "2" or "7" is worded in our Bibles today. Genesis 7:2,[13] 7:9,[14] and 7:15[15] use wording that is uncommon in English. When the word is translated as *two* or as *seven*, the Hebrew behind it is literally ["two two"] or ["seven seven" in Genesis 7:2]. This type of construct is not normally used in English, though it is common in Hebrew.

In other words, the Hebrew used here is essentially "two two" and "seven seven," which is translated as "two" and "seven," denoting that they are paired when possible — bearing in mind that Noah sacri-

---

11. See below for a more extensive discussion on this.
12. Clean animals in the New Testament now differ in that Christ declared all foods clean by His power (e.g., Mark 7:19). This was demonstrated by both Peter (Acts 10:9–16) and Paul (e.g., 1 Corinthians 6:12–13, 1 Timothy 4:1–4, and Colossians 2:16), thus returning essentially to the diet given in Genesis 9:3 not by merely going backwards to eat all foods clean *and unclean*, but by eating *only clean* foods, as all food is now made clean.
13. "You shall take with you seven ["*seven, seven*"] each of every clean animal, a male and his female; two each of animals that are unclean, a male and his female" (Genesis 7:2).
14. "Two by two ["*two, two*"] they went into the ark to Noah, male and female, as God had commanded Noah" (Genesis 7:9).
15. "And they went into the ark to Noah, two by two ["*two, two*"], of all flesh in which is the breath of life" (Genesis 7:15).

ficed some of every clean animal including clean birds after the Flood (Genesis 8:20[16]).[17]

In English, this is akin to saying *"pair of two,"* which still indicates only 2 (not two plus two). Therefore, [two two] would be 2 in the form of a pair. Likewise, it would be 7 in the form of pairs when possible. So it isn't doubled or multiplied.

Consider the immediate context called out (2 of each kind) twice in Genesis 6:20[18] and Genesis 7:2 in reference to the same critters that are also denoted as "two two." Thus, we know that two two is merely 2 in a paired form. Both "two" and "two two" were in reference to the same pair, male and female (a pair that was a male and its mate) of unclean creatures.

Furthermore, Scripture elsewhere uses the construct of [two two] as 2 (not doubled) as well. For instance, Exodus 36:29–30[19] also discusses pairs or couples of sockets under a board. So, for maximum figures, use 14 and 4. Otherwise, it's more precise to use 2 and 7. Famed commentator and Old Testament expert and professor H.C. Leupold concurs when he writes:

> The Hebrew expression "take seven seven" means "seven each" (Koenig's *Syntax* 85; 316b; Gesenius' *Grammatik* rev. by Kautzsch 134q). Hebrew parallels support this explanation. In any case, it would be a most clumsy method of trying to say "fourteen." Three pairs and one supernumery makes the "seven." As has been often suggested, the supernumery beast was the one Noah could conveniently offer for sacrifice after the termination of the Flood.[20]

It would have been very easy to say 14 in Hebrew (*arba*) if that were meant — or more precisely in paired form would be *arba arba*. Interpreting this

---

16. "Then Noah built an altar to the LORD, and took of every clean animal and of every clean bird, and offered burnt offerings on the altar" (Genesis 8:20).

17. John Calvin writes: "Moreover, the expression, by sevens, is to be understood not of seven pairs of each kind, but of three pairs, to which one animal is added for the sake of sacrifice." (John Calvin, *Commentaries on the First Book of Moses called Genesis*, translated by John King, reprinted by Baker Books, Grand Rapids, MI, 2003, commentary notes on Genesis 7:2, p. 267.)

18. "Of the birds after their kind, of animals after their kind, and of every creeping thing of the earth after its kind, two of every kind will come to you to keep them alive" (Genesis 6:20).

19. "And they were coupled at the bottom and coupled together at the top by one ring. Thus he made both of them for the two corners. So there were eight boards and their sockets — sixteen sockets of silver — two sockets under each of the boards" (Exodus 37:29–30, NKJV).

20. H.C. Leupold, Exposition of Genesis, commentary notes on Genesis 7:2, as quoted by Drs. Henry Morris and John Whitcomb, *The Genesis Flood* (Phillipsburg, NJ: Presbyterian and Reformed Publishing Company, 1961), 44th printing, p. 65.

section of Scripture as 7 of each clean animal has made sense to most commentators throughout the years. Why 7 clean animals? Recall that after the Flood, Noah sacrificed each of the clean animals (the supernumery — the one that was not paired). It's possible this was to leave a breeding stock for Noah's 3 sons. This livestock is vital to reinstating the regular sacrificial system since sin with clean animals (Genesis 3:21,[21] 4:4[22]) and an initial source of value with domestic animals (e.g., Genesis 13:2).

John Calvin, the famed reformer and commentator points out where the interpretation of 14 comes from. He says in his commentary notes on Genesis 7:2:

> "…or rather fourteen, seven couple, an equal number of male and female, as Aben Ezra and Ben Gersom, that there might be enough for propagation; since a large number of them would be consumed, both for food and sacrifice."[23]

bird

bat

pterodactyl

The reason for 14 was not due to grammar or context but because two unbelieving rabbis suggested it — Aben Ezra and Gershom Ben Judah living about 1,000 years after the New Testament was written. They felt there should be more animals initially to produce a food and sacrifice supply.

7 of *All* Birds/Winged Creatures or 7 of the *Clean* Birds/Winged Creatures?

Another debate that commonly presents itself at the Ark Encounter is the question of how many birds or winged creatures — including pteranodons and pterodactyls?

The Hebrew word *owph*, that we normally translate as "bird" in Genesis 1 and Genesis 7, means creatures with wings. This obviously includes birds (the predominant type here) but also other winged creatures — such as bats, flightless birds, flying reptiles, etc. For example, ostriches and bats are included under this word *owph* in Leviticus 11.

---

21. "Also for Adam and his wife the LORD God made tunics of skin, and clothed them (Genesis 3:21).
22. "Abel also brought of the firstborn of his flock and of their fat. And the LORD respected Abel and his offering" (Genesis 4:4).
23. John Calvin, Commentary Notes Genesis 7:2, *Online Bible*, 2022.

Most commentators recognize that Genesis 7:3 (see above), "seven each of the birds of the air," is tied to the backdrop of *clean* creatures in Genesis 7:2 (see above). Verse 2 lists all animals coming onboard the ark in two categories — clean and unclean — and how many of each. When verse 3 immediately after that lists 7, it is discussing a subgroup of the clean animals, otherwise, verse 2 is in error. However, contextually, this doesn't mean *all* winged/flying creatures came by 7 but instead limited to 7 of the *clean* ones. Pteranodons and pterodactyls are not among the clean creatures defined per the Bible (Leviticus 11 and Deuteronomy 14). For instance, Leupold writes:

> In v. 3 the idea of "the birds of the heavens" must, of course, be supplemented by the adjective "clean," according to the principle laid down in v. 2.[24]

Likewise, Dr. John Gill, who agrees when discussing the birds, writes:

> That is, of such as were clean; seven couple of these were to be brought into the ark, for the like use as of the clean beasts, and those under the law.[25]

Commentator Matthew Poole also agrees, who writes:

> Of clean fowls, which he leaves to be understood out of the foregoing verse.[26]

Even so, the Ark Encounter is still inserting 14 of each winged creature, regardless of whether it was clean or unclean. This increases the number dramatically to help maximize the numbers on the Ark.

Ark Encounter Final Numbers

Without going into much more detail, the Ark Encounter numbers yield a total of about 1,400 kinds. This number translates to just under 7,000 individuals on the Ark, which helps *maximize* the animals — particularly flying creatures. However, this total number is a little fluid where it can decrease as more research into new hybrids comes to light or increase as we find new potential kinds, particularly in the fossil record.

Precise Figures Are Much Less

But, as previously explained, the precise numbers are likely much lower. For example, having only 7 of the *clean* birds and winged creatures would

---

24. Ibid.
25. John Gill, "Genesis 7 Bible Commentary," Christianity.com, https://www.christianity.com/bible/commentary/john-gill/genesis/7
26. Matthew Poole, Commentary Notes on Genesis 7:3, *Online Bible*, 2014.

rapidly reduce the number of total birds and other winged creatures on the Ark. Combining certain animals together that are likely the same kind, like the various sauropod families or families of bats, would reduce the number too. Also, having 2, instead of 14, of the unclean winged creatures (birds/bats/pteranodons, etc.) would reduce the number of kinds and *significantly reduce* the number of *individuals* on the Ark. The number could be as low as 3,200 individual creatures on the Ark.

Jones' minimum number of about 1,000 kinds and the Ark Encounter's maximum number of about 1,400 kinds gives a decent range for researchers to narrow down, somewhere between the two, more precise numbers.

So How Many of These Are Dinosaurs Kinds?

In the past, many researchers loosely held to about 50 different kinds of dinosaurs. The Ark Encounter numbers yielded a maximum of 85 kinds of dinosaurs. How did they arrive at these numbers? After all, we don't have dinosaurs around today to see what interbreeds to make hybrids.

Ark researchers define each of the dinosaur kinds based on their assigned "family" classification. This works for maximizing numbers because it involves assumptions based on the religion of secular humanism and its evolutionary worldview. Essentially, Ark researchers are at the mercy of secular researchers and how they lump dinosaurs into their families — though they recognize that the secular researchers may have errors in their methods.

But do secularists have it correct? Not exactly. For example, they believe there are several families of sauropods, when there is likely one family — hence there is a good reason to believe there is just a single kind. When we study sauropods at a *cognitum* level (i.e., the way their bone structures *look* across the spectrum), they are very similar. Why do secularists break sauropods into several families? Because of their *evolutionary* beliefs (worldview). Let me explain.

Found in Different Places

For instance, when a sauropod in South Africa (e.g., *Melanorosaurus*) was found and another one in South America (e.g., *Riojasaurus*), both in Triassic sediment, they believed both of them to be over 210 million years old (i.e., geological evolution). Yet, because of their differing locations, they put them in different families (Melanorosauridae and Riojasauridae, respectively).

Nevertheless, both sauropod fossils are very similar in "age" and physical features, such as minor bone and teeth variations. In other words, both are clearly sauropods. But secularists still distinguished them from other sauropods by calling them *Prosauropods* (alleged early precursors to sauropods).

Massospondylus

Barosaurus

Titanosaurus

Riojasaurus

Melanorosaurus

Brachiosaurus   Diplodocus   Camarasaurus

Sauropods and *Prosauropods* Likely Variations in One Kind

This was essentially an attempt to make them evolutionary links (as part of the *biological evolution story*) to other later sauropods (as part of the *geological evolution story*). So, in addition to location, secularists falsely put these sauropods into separate families based on geological and biological evolution beliefs.

Different Rock Layers

Another reason for these distinct families is when a sauropod is found in the same general area but vertically separated by alleged millions of years of rock layers; thus, that dinosaur gets separated into a different family by evolutionary standards. But, again, this is all based on geological evolution beliefs.

For example, another sauropod found in South Africa was the *Massospondylus*. But instead of lumping it with *Melanorosaurus* (found in South

Africa in Triassic sediment) and putting it in the family Melanorosauridae with *Melanorosaurus*, they put it in another family called Massospondylidae. Why? Because it was found in Jurassic sediment (which is relatively only a little bit higher in the rock record). Consequently, they lumped this *Massospondylus* as a *Late Prosauropod* (alleged late precursors to sauropods).

Yet likely, there is one sauropod kind, just as there is one dog kind, one cat kind, one equine kind, and so on. Evolutionary assumptions cause the Ark numbers to be maximized even further. Ark researchers, who already knew this, decided to permit this over-exaggerated number in order to further maximize the total numbers on the Ark. Overall, based on these reasons, it is safe to say that 85 dinosaur kinds is a reasonable and yet flexible maximum figure on the Ark.

But What Are More Precise Numbers?

We can start to come up with more precise numbers when we realize that Triassic, Jurassic, and Cretaceous sediment are all from the same Flood. That is, everything buried in these layers was laid down in the same global catastrophe and likely in various phases while the Flood settled to form each of the unique layers.

Biblically and scientifically speaking, all the sauropods we find in any layer (Triassic, Jurassic, Cretaceous) at any location (Europe, Africa, or Americas) were living at the same time. And they were not precursors but contemporaries to others buried in the same Flood. The only actual "precursors" would be immediate ones, such as father/mother or grandfather/ grandmother to offspring, where specific bigger ones would be the precursors to the juveniles or younger ones we find!

When you subtract evolutionary limitations, then we can accurately unite certain families based on similar features (called a "*cognitum*" level). As a result, we then have only one sauropod family/kind (or, if we still wanted to be generous, perhaps a few at most). This situation is also similar for other dinosaur families that were falsely split via evolutionary beliefs of the fossil record. Overall, researchers have concluded there are as few as 36 dinosaur kinds.

This number is the *minimum* number of dinosaur kinds but is likely closer to the precise number on the Ark. Nevertheless, we can confidently say that the range is 36–85 total dinosaur kinds. Therefore, the range of individual dinosaurs, which are unclean animals, on the Ark was somewhere between 72–170.

12

How Did Huge Dinosaurs Fit on the Ark?

Bathtub Arks Lead to Misconceptions

Far too often, children (as well as teens and adults) have been influenced by the dreaded... "*bathtub ark.*" In case you're not familiar with the *bathtub ark,* its (obvious) name comes from the fact that it looks like the old-fashioned bathtubs of the past.

Sadly, over the last several decades, the image/artwork of a *bathtub ark* has been commonly inserted into kid and teenage books on the Flood to represent Noah's Ark.

Truthfully, using "kid-friendly" (cute/cuddly) images of *bathtub arks* introduces big problems. First, it lumps the historical account of the Flood and the Ark with fairy tales and make-believe stories. That is, this artwork strongly suggests that the Flood is nothing more than a mere fictional story.

Second, these images of *bathtub arks* influence our minds to think that the true Ark was very small. And consequently, this subtle false concept creeps into the young minds of children, which if not dealt with, causes problems later on. This misconception leads to questions, which sometimes cause people to doubt, such as:

> How could all the required animals fit on that little (bathtub) Ark?

> How could all the big dinosaurs (like T-Rex or Brachiosaurus) fit on the Ark?

This brings us to our chapter topic — "huge" dinosaurs fitting on "little" Noah's Ark. Here's a clue to the answer — this is actually back-to-front. Let's reverse this statement and ask, how do we fit those "little" dinosaurs on that "huge" Ark?

First, Noah's Ark was huge. Second, why would Noah choose to take the huge dinosaurs onto the Ark rather than the smaller juveniles? All of a sudden, this question is no longer imposing. Let's explore this further.

Size of the Ark

Noah's Ark was a huge vessel. God tells us the dimensions of Noah's Ark:

> And this is how you shall make it: The length of the ark shall be three hundred cubits, its width fifty cubits, and its height thirty cubits (Genesis 6:15).

Most people today are not familiar with the measure of cubits since most of us either use a metric/S.I. system (e.g., *decimal*-based like centimeters, meters, kilometers, liters) or English/Imperial/US Customary system of units (e.g., *fraction*-based like inches, feet, miles, gallons).[1] So, in order for us to get a good picture of how big the Ark was, according to the dimensions from the Bible (300 cubits long, 50 cubits wide, 30 cubits high), we must first ask, "How long is a cubit?"

The answer, however, is not so precise. Ancient people groups usually assigned different lengths to the term "cubit" (Hebrew word אמה [*ammah*]), which was the primary unit of measure in the Old Testament. Examples include the Ark of the Covenant (Exodus 25:10[2]), the Altar (Exodus 38:1[3]), Goliath

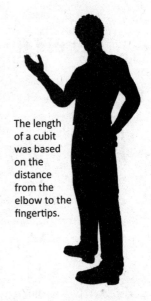

The length of a cubit was based on the distance from the elbow to the fingertips.

---

1. For example, a mile is 5,280 feet, and although that sounds like a strange number, it is evenly divisional by 1, 2, 3, 4, 5, 6, 8, 10, 11, 12, 15, and 16; an inch is 1/12 of a foot and 1/36 of a yard, etc. A foot is evenly divisible by 1, 2, 3, 4, and 6. A measure of a foot is used in Scripture in Acts 7:5 which says, "Yet he gave him no inheritance in it, not even a foot's length, but promised to give it to him as a possession and to his offspring after him, though he had no child" (ESV). Many of these ancient measures were naturally found on the human body. A foot is a foot length, a short cubit is from the elbow to fingertip (~ a foot and a ½), a span is from thumb to little fingertip (~¾ of a foot), a handbreadth is ~¼ of a foot, and a fathom is about the height of an average male being ~ 6 feet.
2. "And they shall make an ark of acacia wood; two and a half cubits shall be its length, a cubit and a half its width, and a cubit and a half its height" (Exodus 25:10).
3. "He made the altar of burnt offering of acacia wood; five cubits was its length and five cubits its width — it was square — and its height was three cubits" (Exodus 38:1).

(1 Samuel 17:4[4]), and Solomon's Temple (1 Kings 6:2[5])?

By definition, the length of a cubit was based on the distance from a man's elbow to his fingertips, which means it varied between different ancient groups of people. To add to the problem, there is a long cubit and a short cubit! Here are some samples from Egypt, Babylon, and ancient Israel.[6]

When Noah came off the Ark, naturally it was his cubit measurement

Culture	Inches (Centimeters)
Hebrew (short)	17.5 (44.5)
Egyptian	17.6 (44.7)
Common (short)	18 (45.7)
Babylonian (long)	19.8 (50.3)
Hebrew (long)	20.4 (51.8)
Egyptian (long)	20.6 (52.3)

that existed — the length he used to construct the Ark. Unfortunately, the exact length of his cubit is unknown. After the nations were divided, years later at the Tower of Babel (Genesis 11), different cultures (people groups) adopted slightly different sized cubits. Thus, some logical guesswork (based on historical research) is required to reconstruct the most likely length of the original cubit (used by Noah).

Since the Babel dispersion was relatively soon (about 100 or so years) after the Flood, we can reasonably assume the builders during that time still used the same cubit length as Noah. Moreover, we can assume the people who settled near Babel retained or remained close to the original cubit. Yet, cubits from that region (near the ancient Near East) are generally either a common (short) or a long cubit. So now the question is, which one did Noah likely use?

In large-scale construction projects, ancient civilizations typically used the long cubit (about 19.8–20.6 inches [52 cm]). For instance, the Bible, in 2 Chronicles 3:3,[7] reveals that Solomon used the older (long) cubit in construction of the Temple.

Most archaeological finds in Israel are not as ancient as Solomon's Temple. More modern finds consistently reveal the use of a short cubit,

---

4. "And a champion went out from the camp of the Philistines, named Goliath, from Gath, whose height was six cubits and a span" (1 Samuel 17:4).

5. "Now the house which King Solomon built for the LORD, its length was sixty cubits, its width twenty, and its height thirty cubits" (1 Kings 6:2).

6. Bodie Hodge, "How Long Was The Original Cubit?" *Answers* Magazine, April 1, 2007, https://answersingenesis.org/noahs-ark/how-long-was-the-original-cubit/.

7. "This is the foundation which Solomon laid for building the house of God: The length was sixty cubits (by cubits according to the former measure) and the width twenty cubits" (2 Chronicles 3:3).

such as confirmed by archaeologists while measuring Hezekiah's tunnel.[8] However, in Ezekiel's vision of the altar in the Temple, an angel used "a cubit plus a handbreadth," which is an unmistakable definition for the long cubit (Ezekiel 43:13[9]). Thus, the long cubit appears to be God's preferred standard of measurement for these ancient projects.

Again, the original cubit length is uncertain. Logically, it was within the range of the other typical long cubits (about 19.8–20.6 inches). Thus, the Ark was actually bigger than the size described in most books today (prior to the opening of the Ark Encounter), which usually use the common short cubit (18 inches).

Using the shorter cubit (18 inches), Noah's ark would have been about:

- 450 feet (137 meters) by 75 feet (22.9 meters) by 45 feet (13.7 meters)

Using the longer cubit of about 20.4 inches, Noah's Ark would have been about:

- 510 feet (155 meters) long by 85 feet (25.9 meters) by 51 feet (15.5 meters)

Again, the older (longer) cubit was likely used by Noah, meaning the real Ark was likely around this larger size (give or take a little). Also, note that these dimensions for length and width are to be measured from the water level, which is called the "draft level." Overall, the main takeaway here is that Noah's Ark was indeed huge.

Size of the Dinosaurs

When many people think of dinosaurs, they tend to think of the large ones like *Tyrannosaurus Rex* (~15–20 feet/4.6–6 meters high!) or *Brachiosaurus* (~60–70 feet/18–21 meter in length!). But in reality, most dinosaurs were not that big.

One popular small dinosaur was *velociraptor*. Full-sized *velociraptors* were less than waist high, usually around 20 inches tall (~50 cm). This may come as a surprise to you, especially if you've been influenced by popular culture and movies series like *Jurassic Park* and *Jurassic World*. These Hollywood movie makers greatly exaggerate the height of the *velociraptors* being nearly 7 feet tall (2.1 meters).

---

8. Wayne Jackson, "Hezekiah's Tunnel," ChristianCourier.com, Accessed August 18, 2022, https://www.christiancourier.com/articles/101-hezekiahs-tunnel.

9. "These are the measurements of the altar in cubits (the cubit is one cubit and a handbreadth): the base one cubit high and one cubit wide, with a rim all around its edge of one span. This is the height of the altar" (Ezekiel 43:13).

Yet, there is a larger variation of raptors — the *Utahraptor strommaysi.* If these movies had used these dinosaur-raptors, then they could have justified the larger raptors in the movies!

Furthermore, many dinosaurs are even smaller than *velociraptors, such as heterodontosaurus* whose height was about 12 inches (~31 cm) with some only reaching as high as 20 inches (~ 50 cm). The key point here is that there were both large and small dinosaurs, with the average size about as big as an American bison.[10]

But again, regarding dinosaurs on the Ark, why take the full-grown ones rather than juveniles or even just the eggs? The largest dinosaur egg we've ever found is a *T-rex* egg — which is about the size of a football. So, of course, this means even the largest dinosaurs were once much smaller in their past.

It makes more sense that God sent the smaller, younger dinosaurs — perhaps juveniles — of each representative kind on board the Ark. Obviously, they require less food, less waste, and less space in the Ark. Plus, they are more vigorous for survival, and better able to repopulate the earth after the Flood.

T-rex egg

But please note, this does not mean eggs were taken on the Ark. Instead, it makes better sense to put the juveniles on the Ark — those that are old enough and yet durable enough to live on their own.

Hopefully you can now see the answer to our initial question, "How do we fit huge dinosaurs on that little Ark?" is simply the reverse of this question! That is, the true Ark was huge and the onboard dinosaurs were relatively small. So, this means the 72–170 individual dinosaurs on the Ark, averaging about the size of a bison, was merely a small footprint in that huge Ark.

10. Timothy Clarey and Jeffrey Tompkins, "Determining Average Dinosaur Size Using the Most Recent Comprehensive Body Mass Data Set," *Answers Research Journal* 8 (2015): 85–93, https://answersresearchjournal.org/determining-dinosaur-body-mass/.

13

What Happened to the Dinosaurs Outside of Noah's Ark During the Flood?

t's an easy answer — they died! The Bible says:

> The waters prevailed fifteen cubits upward, and the mountains were covered. And all flesh died that moved on the earth: birds and cattle and beasts and every creeping thing that creeps on the earth, and every man. All in whose nostrils was the breath of the spirit of life, all that was on the dry land, died. So He destroyed all living things which were on the face of the ground: both man and cattle, creeping thing and bird of the air. They were destroyed from the earth. Only Noah and those who were with him in the ark remained alive. And the waters prevailed on the earth one hundred and fifty days (Genesis 7:20–24).

Yes, dinosaurs died, but there is much more to learn.

Death and Fossilization

Every land animal (or even man!), including birds and other flying creatures, that lived up until the 150th day of the Flood (Genesis 7:24) likely ate food that was not part of their normal diet. With the environment all over the earth in flux, their normal habitats were disrupted. Due to massive flooding, which forced animals to flee to higher grounds (as the waters rose and the land sank) and even swim in certain locales to get to solid places, they surely ate whatever they could find just to survive — even rotting carcasses and other floating material.

Higher ground

By the 150th day of the Flood, all the land-dwelling, air-breathing animals had died, including the dinosaurs and flying reptiles. As a result, land animals stopped making footprints by this date. So, if you find a set of fossil footprints in Flood sediment, it would have been made prior to the 150th day. After this point, there was no more "fleeing to higher ground." It was not until after animals exited the Ark that animals started making footprints again.[1]

Fossilization of a specimen requires rapid burial to seal out oxygen. On the 150th day of the Flood, the Ark struck the mountains of Ararat (Genesis 8:4[2]) and became more stable ("rested") once again by having earth beneath it — although the earth was likely shaking from time to time up until their exit with mountainous uplifts, residual continental shifting, ocean valleys sinking, and so on. The earth's crust is still slightly moving, even today, with earthquakes and settling of continents (just with less frequency and magnitude). Hence, Noah and his family remained in the Ark far after the 150th day, until God called them off the Ark.[3]

Nevertheless, that same day (150th day), we see a shift in the stage of the Flood, from a prevailing stage to a recessional stage. So, by about this point,

1. I understand that a dead carcass can have the rare possibility of making an imprint of its foot/feet depending on the right conditions as it is being buried or washed along, but it would not be a normal "trail" of prints or other standing, and then "walking around" type of step pattern.
2. "Then the ark rested in the seventh month, the seventeenth day of the month, on the mountains of Ararat" (Genesis 8:4).
3. Bodie Hodge, "Biblical Overview of the Flood Timeline," *Answers in Genesis*, August 3, 2010, https://answersingenesis.org/bible-timeline/biblical-overview-of-the-flood-timeline/.

flood layers from the inundation stage should be laid down, while recessional layers began to be deposited. These were layers that took sediment downward with them as they ran off the rising continents and mountains into gorges, valleys, and finally rivers and streams. Bear in mind that some of these massive rock layers from the Flood were continental in scale as the mountains rose and valleys sank down (Psalm 104:8–9[4]).

Due to rising and sinking elevations in the latter parts of the Flood stage, water begins to run off the continents. Initially, there are massive amounts of "sheet erosion" of water, then channeling of water in valleys that become rivers and creeks and so on. Of course, there can be natural dams that hold water in places, where lakes can form — or even breached dams where sudden carving of areas (gorges) are more devastating.

This runoff and drainage from the Flood also caused much cave formation[5] in subterranean places. Moving water acts on the minerals where the cave would ultimately be formed. Limestone rock layers (e.g., calcium carbonate and calcite), which are dissolvable in water (particularly when it is acidic) for instance, are ideal for exiting underground water to make the newly forming caves. With saturated water making its way out of limestone layers, this makes the initial cave formation "extremely active." As the "extremely active" cave slows down water

4. "The mountains rose, the valleys sank down to the place that you appointed for them. You set a boundary that they may not pass, so that they might not again cover the earth" (Psalm 104:8-9; ESV).

5. Of course, we have had some cave formation after the Flood as well.

transport it becomes merely an "active cave," and if water transport stops entirely, then it becomes an "inactive cave."

One set of famous mountains that formed during the Flood were the mountains of Ararat. The mountains of Ararat were made out of Flood sediment that had settled, formed into rock layers, and pushed upward due to continental shifting. The mountains of Ararat are intricate and intertwined rock layers containing Miocene, Eocene, Cretaceous, Triassic, and Permian rock (listed from the upper layers to the lower layers).

The Cretaceous, Jurassic, and Triassic are *dinosaur* rock layers, where the Jurassic rock, when present, typically sits between the Triassic and the Cretaceous. However, in the case of the mountains of Ararat, Jurassic is largely missing.

While it's possible that some dinosaurs and other land creatures were still being washed into places for burial, we can be certain that the dinosaurs were largely buried by the 150th day of the Flood.

Many of the carcasses likely rotted and decayed while others were rapidly buried. However, it was only the rapidly buried animals that were actually fossilized. This is primarily because an animal's organic material (e.g., carbon-based molecules) can be replaced by the movement of water. That is, the organic material moves out with the water and pools in lower rock layers, while non-organic rock material, such as dissolved limestone from the water, can precipitate in place of the previous organic material. This process can quickly turn any dead animal or plant into a fossil.

In other words, fossil formation is a rapid event. And, with the right amount of heat, pressure, and minerals, this process can even be duplicated in a laboratory in a mere 24 hours.[6] So it is not a slow and gradual process over long ages, which is commonly taught in secular sources.

Various sources push this idea of slow gradual fossil formation over long ages. In a quick glance at my own bookshelf, I found:

- Peter Wellnhofer, *The Illustrated Encyclopedia of Prehistoric Flying Reptiles* (New York, NY: Barnes & Noble Books, 1996), p. 10.

- Christopher Brochu et al with consulting editor Michael Brett-Surman, *A Guide to Dinosaurs* (San Francisco, CA: Fog City Press, 1997–2002), p. 19.

- Arthur Busbey et al, *A Guide to Rocks & Fossils* (San Francisco, CA: Fog City Press, 1997–2002), p. 97.

---

6. Ben Coxworth, "Lab-made Fossils Cram 1000s of Years into 24 Hours," NewAtlas.com, July 25, 2018, https://newatlas.com/lab-made-fossils/55619/.

The dinosaur dies in the river.

The body is slowly covered with sediment. The meat decomposes. The dinosaur becomes a fossil over millions of years.

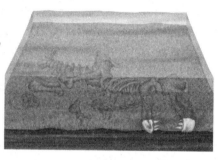

The sediments become rock. The skeleton is compressed.

The earth's movements raise the layers of rock to the surface.

The rock erodes, exposing the fossil.

- Dougal Dixon, *The Complete Book of Dinosaurs* (London, England: Hermes House, 2006), p. 60–61.
- Steven Gould, *The Book of Life* (New York, NY: W.W. Norton & Company, 2001), p. 34.

In each of these five secular instances, they push for long ages of slow, gradual changes to form fossils in the context of their discussions. And this is but a taste of secular books that push these ideas. Do we observe fossils form like this? No. Has fossil formation ever been observed over long ages to verify this? No. Animals die, rot, and decay without fossilization on lake and ocean beds, in the wild, and so on.

It takes a catastrophe to make fossils naturally and rapidly by burying the specimen quickly in the right conditions to form a fossil. An abundance of heat, pressure, and minerals, using the mechanism of water movement from the Flood, were the exact conditions needed for worldwide fossilization. Interestingly, Dr. Wellnhofer comments on the majority of flying reptile fossils by saying: "By far the most frequent pterosaur finds are made in marine strata, that is to say in rocks which originated in prehistoric marine deposits."[7]

Thus, Dr. Wellnhofer presumes pterosaurs were living on the edges of coastal regions but failed to realize the implications of this regarding the global Flood of Noah's day that put them to death. He acknowledges that few flying reptiles died of old age and natural causes, which is what we have long predicted in the biblical model — animals of every age died in the Flood.

Keep in mind that the brutality of the Flood likely tore many dead animals' bodies apart, which means only certain pieces of them were washed into place to become fossils. Some animals may have only consisted of a single bone left as a candidate by the time they were buried! When bones are separated from the rest of the body, it is called *disarticulation*.

Most fossils are *disarticulated*. Even when a fossil is considered complete, it is still usually missing many bones. We have found some rare fossils where the entire, complete fossil is preserved. Those are the exciting ones!

So What Happened to the Organic Materials?

A lot of people don't think about this question and its implications. When the water from the Flood removed the organic material — from the animals, vegetation, and so on — and left other rock material in its place, where did the organic material go?

It obviously went with the water and followed paths down through rock cracks (called *striations*) via gravity that then gets trapped at a lower level. This process of organic material getting trapped and accumulating is called *pooling*. In these areas, the organic hydrocarbons pool together and then separate from the water. This is where we find *crude oil*.

---

7. Peter Wellnhofer, *The Illustrated Encyclopedia of Prehistoric Flying Reptiles* (New York, NY: Barnes & Noble Books, 1996).

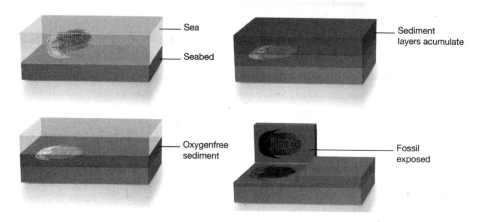

Crude oil is made up of hosts of bioorganic materials all mixed together — even with some remnant water, nitrogen, sulfur, oxygen, etc. It can be processed to get diesel fuel, gasoline, plastic, and hosts of other materials. It is basically organic material, largely from the Flood, but some could have been made and pooled since the time of the Flood too.

14

Are Dinosaur Fossils in the
Cretaceous, Jurassic, and *Triassic* Rock
Millions of Years Old or from the Flood?

hen evolutionists are looking for transitional forms (i.e., from dinosaurs to birds), they tend to look at the rock layers that are just above the three main geological rock layers that contain dinosaurs (Cretaceous, Jurassic, and Triassic) in hopes of finding these "intermediate" fossils. On the other hand, Christians who believe the Bible rarely think twice about their alleged finds for a pretty big reason — God's Word!

God created birds a day before dinosaurs, so having dinosaurs turn into birds is obviously in contradiction with God's Word, therefore it's false. If someone wants to object by saying God's Word is wrong, then they have bigger problems. That is, God, and by extension His Word, provides the only absolute basis for the concepts of "right" and "wrong." So this means the Bible must be true for someone to even make an argument! In other words, without the Bible, the idea that something can be "wrong" would not even exist. So the secular view is self-refuting from the start.

Furthermore, by what authority can someone object to God's absolute authority? Once again, this is a *faulty appeal to authority* fallacy because God's infallible Word always trumps fallible (man-made) opinions. But there is another reason why Bible believers don't flinch when people claim there is a "missing link" found in these particular dinosaur rock layers or above. Let's take a look.

Evolutionary Diggings . . . in the Wrong Place Too?

Each year, there are many headlines, books, technical articles, and videos about another "missing link" — a supposed link between a land mammal and whale,[1] a dinosaur and bird,[2] an ape and human,[3] and so forth. Usually, these are quite easy to refute by anatomical features.

The fossils that are claimed to be "missing links" have always been proven false (or a lie). For example, the alleged "ape-man" missing links for apes and humans are normally proven to be either just an ape fossil or just a human fossil, or sometimes even a fake (e.g., Piltdown man[4]), but never an actual "transitional" fossil.[5] The same applies for the so-called "missing links" for dinosaurs — being either a dinosaur, bird, or a fake (e.g., Archaeoraptor[6]).

Nevertheless, these alleged missing links rarely make biblical creationists cringe or seldom even bat an eye. This frustrates some evolutionists because they think they have found some sort of "knock-out" evidence, which they interpret as undeniable support for evolution.

Well, I'm going to let you in on a secret as to why creationists, in general, rarely take notice of these alleged missing links. It is because evolutionists are digging in the wrong place! When you don't have the correct information (wrong assumptions), you can miss the mark significantly (wrong conclusions).

What Do You Mean by "Digging in the Wrong Place"?

Before I go further into these rock layers, there is a misconception I want to clear up. Many mistakenly think the rock layers' names denote *eras* or geological *time*. But they don't, they are merely *rock layers*. Believe it or not everyone largely agrees on these rock layers.

Many of these names may seem strange, but they are named for places that they outcrop.

- For example, **Cambrian** is named for the old name of Wales (Cambria) where this rock layer can be found at the surface.

1. Terry Mortenson, "Fossil Evidence of Whale Evolution?" *Answers in Genesis*, March 25, 2014, https://answersingenesis.org/aquatic-animals/fossil-evidence-of-whale-evolution/.
2. David Menton, "Did Dinosaurs Turn into Birds?" *Answers Book 1*, Ken Ham, gen. ed. (Green Forest, AR: Master Books), p. 296–305, https://answersingenesis.org/dinosaurs/feathers/did-dinosaurs-turn-into-birds/.
3. David Menton, "Did Humans Really Evolve from Apelike Creatures?" *Answers Book 2*, Ken Ham, gen. ed. (Green Forest, AR: Master Books, 2008), p. 83–94, https://answersingenesis.org/human-evolution/ape-man/did-humans-really-evolve-from-apelike-creatures/.
4. Monty White, "The Piltdown Man Fraud," *Answers in Genesis*, November 24, 2003, https://answersingenesis.org/human-evolution/piltdown-man/the-piltdown-man-fraud/.
5. In some cases, it could be a mixture of human and ape fossils (not a real creature) which is still just human or ape fossils, or in some odd cases another animal altogether, like a lemur as in the case of "Ida."
6. Editors, "Archaeoraptor Hoax Update — National Geographic Recants!" *Answers in Genesis,* March 2, 2000, answersingenesis.org/dinosaurs/feathers/archaeoraptor-hoax-update-national-geographic-recants/.

- Two other regions in Wales are named for ancient Celtic peoples that lend their title to **Ordovician** and **Silurian**.

- **Devonian** is named for Devonshire, England.

- **Permian** is named for a region in Russia.

- **Jurassic** is named for Jura Mountains in Switzerland that border France.

- Coal is primarily made from carbon, hence the **Carboniferous** layers contain a lot of coal. The Carboniferous is broken into two — Mississippian and Pennsylvanian — and these are obviously named for two states in the USA.

- *Creta* is the Latin name for chalk and thus is used of the chalk layers of the **Cretaceous.**

- **Triassic** is named for trinity because it has three primary layers in it.

- **Tertiary** (from Eocene to Miocene) was named for *Montes tertiarii* meaning sediments at the foothills of the Alps in Northern Italy.

Evolutionists generally look for alleged dinosaur-to-bird missing links in the Cretaceous and Paleocene geologic rock layers/strata (bolded in the accompanying table). This is because they misrepresent the Flood rock as long eras and then they expect to find evolutionary intermediates trapped in the rock layers. The table also shows the biblical timescale of the geologic layers.

But here's the problem. The rock layers from the Triassic (10) to the Miocene (4) are mapped in the mountains of Ararat (Genesis 8:4), which were from

	Rock layer	Timeline
1	Recent	Post-Flood
2	Pleistocene	Post-Flood
3	Pliocene	Post-Flood
4	Miocene	**Flood**
5	Oligocene	Flood
6	Eocene	**Flood**
7	Paleocene	Flood
8	Cretaceous	**Flood**
9	Jurassic	Flood
10	Triassic	**Flood**
11	Permian	Flood
12	Pennsylvanian	Flood
13	Mississippian	Flood
14	Devonian	Flood
15	Silurian	Flood
16	Ordovician	Flood
17	Cambrian	Flood
18	Precambrian	Pre-Flood

the Flood.[7] Also, the Miocene (4), and Eocene (6) rock layers are intricately part of the makeup of the mountains of Ararat, as is the Cretaceous and Triassic (many times inverted, above the Miocene and Eocene). Since that time, the upper strata are post-Flood strata — such as Ice Age layers[8] and recent volcanic flows[9]. I understand there are ongoing (sometimes heated!) debates among creationists about the tertiary sediment (Paleocene through Miocene) and I encourage you to study this further.[10]

So, when evolutionists say they found a transitional form between an ape and a human in Pliocene rock, biblical creationists hardly flinch, since in the biblical timeline, humans were around long before that rock layer was ever laid down. This obviously means evolutionists are incorrectly looking at the rock strata *and* the age of the earth![11] Furthermore, humans existed when the Cambrian rock was laid down during the Flood. And on top of that, mankind had dominated the earth for over 1,600 years[12] *before* the Cambrian rock was even laid down!

So, again, when someone says they found a "transitional form" between a dinosaur and a bird in the Paleocene rock layer, creationists hardly think twice. Both specimens died the same year in the same Flood[13] and thus

---

7. I'm denoting these bolded layers as Flood because Miocene, Eocene, Cretaceous, and Triassic sediments are found in the makeup of the mountains of Ararat (formed by the 150th day of the Flood), so these *specific* layers were indeed Flood layers. Even if other Miocene-Paleocene were post-Flood layers, the article's same point is made. Though there is debate on tertiary sediment elsewhere in the world being Flood or post-Flood, it is not for this article (see footnote 4). Y. Yilmaz, "Alochthonous Terranes in the Tethyan Middle East: Anatolia and the Surrounding Regions," *Philosophical Transactions of the Royal Society,* A 331 (1990): 611–624; G.C. Schmidt, "A Review of Permian and Mesozoic Formations Exposed Near the Turkey/Iraq Border at Harbol," *Bulletin of the Mineral Research and Exploration Institute* 62 (1964): 103–119.
8. Mike Oard, "Where Does the Ice Age Fit?" *Answers Book 1*, Ken Ham, gen. ed. (Green Forest AR: Master Books, 2006), p. 207–219, https://answersingenesis.org/environmental-science/ice-age/where-does-the-ice-age-fit/.
9. Andrew Snelling, "Volcanoes — Windows into Earth's Past," *Answers In Genesis*, July 1, 2010, https://answersingenesis.org/geology/natural-features/volcanoes-windows-into-earths-past/.
10. The debate over the Flood/Post-Flood boundary is an ongoing debate in creationist literature. I suggest starting with the discussion here: Andrew Snelling, *Earth's Catastrophic Past* (Green Forest, AR: Master Books, 2010), https://answersingenesis.org/store/sku/10-3-124/; and the Institute for Creation Research's Column Project led by Dr. Tim Clarey including http://www.icr.org/article/10779/.
11. Bodie Hodge, "How Old Is The Earth?" *Answers Book 2*, Ken Ham, gen. ed. (Green Forest AR: Master Books, 2008), https://answersingenesis.org/age-of-the-earth/how-old-is-the-earth/.
12. Bodie Hodge, "Ancient Patriarchs in Genesis," *Answers in Genesis*, January, 20, 2009, https://answersingenesis.org/bible-characters/ancient-patriarchs-in-genesis/.
13. For more about the Flood, see Ken Ham and Bodie Hodge, *A Flood of Evidence* (Green Forest, AR: Master Books, 2016).

are not related. This is why finding feathers in the rock layers "before the dinosaurs" is not a problem for creationists.[14] Nor is it a problem when we find theropod dinosaurs (which supposedly evolved into birds in the evolutionary story) that had eaten birds in a lower region in the Cretaceous rock layer.[15] Nor is it a problem when we find a parrot jaw buried in Cretaceous rock.[16] But it's a major problem for evolutionists (again, because they have the wrong starting point).

Birds were made on Day Five of Creation Week, which is a whole day before the dinosaurs (land animals, like dinosaurs, were made on Day Six[17]). Thus, finding both birds and dinosaurs buried in Flood sediment isn't a big deal and is actually expected in the biblical worldview.

Indeed, Digging in the Wrong Place . . .

If evolutionists want to get creationists to take notice (and make any sort of impact), then they need to find alleged transitional forms in the Precambrian (pre-Flood) rock layers.[18] But keep in mind that we had over 1,600 years of erosion and rock strata where people and animals *did coexist* before the Flood.

Consider the evolutionary position for a moment. Imagine if a researcher hypothetically found a body of a person preserved from the Mount St. Helens eruption[19] and claimed it was the earliest human ancestor. Would the evolutionist be convinced? Not at all, because they would know that sediment came from a catastrophe that happened well *after* people were around. It is the same with the Flood and post-Flood sediment, which was formed *after* people, birds, whales, and all other creatures were around.

---

14. Jeff Hecht, "Reptile Grew Feather-Like Structures Before Dinosaurs," *New Scientist* 2857 (2012), 8. When these feathers were found, the researchers arbitrarily and without warrant said they attach to a pre-dinosaur reptile (in the evolutionary view). However, the feathers would have attached to this reptile in an anatomically impossible way. This proves the feathers were not part of the reptile.

15. Lida Xing, et al., "Abdominal Contents from Two Large Early Cretaceous Compsognathids (Dinosauria: Theropoda) Demonstrate Feeding on Confuciusornithids and Dromaeosaurids," *PLOS*, August 29, 2012, doi:10.1371/journal.pone.0044012.

16. Thomas Stidham, "A Lower Jaw from a Cretaceous Parrot," *Nature* 396, 29–30 (1998), https://doi.org/10.1038/23841.

17. Ken Ham, "What Really Happened to the Dinosaurs?" *Answers Book 1* (Green Forest, AR: Master Books, 2006), p. 149–177, https://answersingenesis.org/dinosaurs/when-did-dinosaurs-live/what-really-happened-to-the-dinosaurs/.

18. Cambrian rock is from the sea floor. This is yet another problem with which the long ager has to deal!

19. Steve Austin, "Why Is Mount St. Helens Important to the Origins Controversy?" *Answers Book 3*, Ken Ham, gen. ed. (Green Forest, AR: Master Books, 2010), https://answersingenesis.org/geology/mount-st-helens/why-is-mount-st-helens-important-to-the-origins-controversy/.

So when evolutionists find a creature buried in sediment, it is from a recent disaster — a global Flood about 4,300 years ago. In the same way, the Mount St. Helens sediment is also recent (just much more recent from two eruptions in A.D. 1980–1982).

The point is that evolutionists keep digging in the wrong place, yet they wonder why we hardly take notice. Well . . . this is why.

So Why Don't Evolutionists Look at Flood Rock and Recognize it as "Flood Rock"?

Biblical creationists presuppose the Bible's truth and, subsequently, the true history of the earth — including the global Flood of Noah's day. But note that evolutionists have presuppositions too (albeit false ones). This is why, when evolutionists look at rock layers laid down by the Flood, they unwittingly believe that the rock layers were laid down slowly and gradually over long ages, rather than seeing geological sediment as a result of major catastrophe (the Flood).

This is because they have been indoctrinated to believe in the story of gradual rock accumulation over millions of years (which, of course, has never been observed or repeated). Thus, the concept of "millions of years" is not in the realm of science but rather interpretation. Nevertheless, we and kids of the next generation are constantly bombarded with the evolutionary *Geological Time Scale* (see below).

Era	Period		Succession of Life
Cenozoic recent life	Quaternary	2.6 Million Years–Today	
	Tertiary	66–2.6 Million Years	
Mesozoic middle life	Cretaceous	145–66 Million Years	
	Jurassic	201–145 Million Years	
	Triassic	252–201 Million Years	
Paleozoic ancient life	Permian	299–252 Million Years	
	Pennsylvanian	323–299 Million Years	
	Mississippian	359–323 Million Years	
	Devonian	419–359 Million Years	
	Silurian	444–419 Million Years	
	Ordovician	485–444 Million Years	
	Cambrian	541–485 Million Years	
	Precambrian		

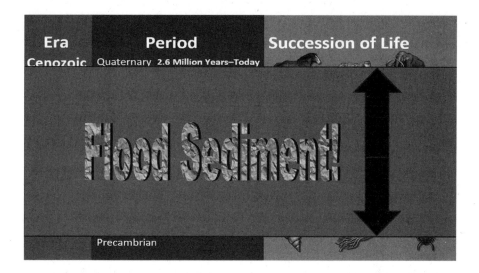

We look at the same rock layers and realize the global Flood of Noah's day is what accounted for most of those rock layers. We observed some layers form since the Flood with local catastrophes for instance. But most are from the Flood.

Nevertheless, God and His Word are the ultimate standard. And any standard (man's opinion) that opposes God and His Word is a lesser standard (a false authority fallacy/faulty appeal to authority fallacy). Take notice that the battle is not over evidence. It is a battle of *worldviews!* The evolutionist has a false worldview about the rock layers, which were laid down by the Flood. And it is this false worldview that drives their conclusions in hopes of finding "missing links."

A correct worldview — the biblical worldview — can help researchers get back on the right track of having the correct understanding of rock layers and evidences. Let God be true and every man be found a liar (Romans 3:4[20]).

---

20. "Certainly not! Indeed, let God be true but every man a liar. As it is written: 'That You may be justified in Your words, and may overcome when You are judged'" (Romans 3:4).

15

How Far Back Do Dinosaurs Go — "Thousands" or "Millions" of Years?

nterestingly, yet also unsurprisingly, we are living in a culture today where people will give you two starkly different answers to this question! But usually, they range from *millions of years* to *thousands of years* ago. The answer depends on which religious view of the past you believe.

Naturalistic/Secular View

The **naturalistic view** (i.e., nature or the cosmos is all that exists; no God, for instance) holds that dinosaurs first began to exist somewhere around 243 million years ago and 231 million years ago. So, there is an openly admitted error of about 12 million years in the naturalistic (i.e., secular humanistic, atheistic, materialistic) view. According to the naturalist, the dinosaurs supposedly came about by natural processes, from "lower" reptiles.

More specifically, as the secular religious story goes ("once upon a time..."), somewhere around 243 to 231 million years ago, reptiles around that time evolved into dinosaurs to have under-slung legs from an archosaur. An archosaur has hips for sprawling legs (that extend out to the side), and those hips would have evolved into a different type of hip (to sit under the creature) — either (1) Erect or (2) Pillar Erect to properly become a dinosaur.[1] Finally, the dinosaurs supposedly went extinct about 65–66 million years ago (however, the theropod line allegedly survived by evolving into modern bird lines).

---

1. *Erect* means the leg bones come out slightly on the shoulders and hip sockets *and then go down,* where *pillar erect* have the bones basically going straight down from the shoulder or hip socket. Don't let it confuse you. In either case, the dinosaurs stand upright, unlike other reptiles that had sprawling legs.

This "millions of years" concept is based on the false assumption that each geological rock layer was laid down slowly and gradually over millions of years. This assumption was made popular based on the uniformitarian beliefs of a lawyer (not a scientist) named Charles Lyell, who largely ignored the Flood of Noah's Day.

Lyell held to a belief in "uniformitarianism" where slow, gradual accumulations of dirt, rock, and sediment — with no major catastrophes — laid down the rock layers that contained fossils. He developed this idea in detail in the 1830s, in his book series called the *Principles of Geology*. Since then, most naturalists, without question, blindly start their thinking with this belief. There were quite a few people prior to Lyell, like James Hutton for instance (see table below), who held similar views. However, Lyell gets the credit for making this view popular and widespread in academic circles. As seen in the following table, the date for the age of the earth has been in flux, in the secular view, over the last few hundred years.

Summary of the Old-earth Proponents for Long Ages

Who?	Age of the Earth	When Was This?
Comte de Buffon	78 thousand years old	1779
Abraham Werner	1 million years	1786
James Hutton	Perhaps eternal, long ages	1795
Pièrre LaPlace	Long ages	1796
Jean Lamarck	Long ages	1809
William Smith	Long ages	1835
Georges Cuvier	Long ages	1812
Charles Lyell	Millions of years	1830–1833
Lord Kelvin	20–100 million years	1862–1899
Arthur Holmes	1.6 billion years	1913
Clair Patterson	4.5 billion years	1956

Although, this (relatively new) idea of refusing to believe that significant sediment was laid down, or carved out, by any major catastrophe(s) is rather laughable, especially considering that localized disasters we see today lay down sediment very quickly (such as Mt. St. Helens volcano). Nevertheless, modern-day naturalists, because of their religiously held belief, widely assume there were no major catastrophes in the past that produced the rock layers, which contain dinosaurs (Triassic, Jurassic, and Cretaceous), but instead believe the rock layers were laid down slowly over "long ages."

This is why the secular world *REFUSES* to publish technical papers in their journals about a global (i.e., worldwide) Flood on earth. A global

Flood totally destroys their "millions of years" story! Again, it's because this naturalistic view rejects the massive worldwide Flood of Noah's day, which accounts for most of the rock layers that contain fossils.

Biblical View

Per the **biblical view,** God created every kind of land animal, which obviously included dinosaurs, on Day 6 of *Creation Week,* about 6,000 years ago. This, of course, is contrary to any secular or naturalistic religious view of the past.

Granted, the Bible doesn't explicitly say, "The earth is 6,000 years old" or "Dinosaurs first existed 6,000 years ago." But that's actually a good thing! Otherwise, the Bible would be immediately "out of date" by the following year. We shouldn't expect an all-knowing God to make that kind of a mistake.

Rather, God gave us something better. In essence, He gave us a "birth certificate." For example, using a personal birth certificate, a person can calculate how old they are at any point. Similarly, in Genesis 1, we read that the earth was created on the first day of creation (Genesis 1:1–5). Using this as our starting point, we can begin to calculate the age of the earth.

Let's do a rough calculation to show how this works. The age of the earth can be estimated by taking the first five days of creation (from the creation of the earth to Adam), then by using the genealogies from Adam to Abraham (in Genesis 5 and 11) one can add up the time from Adam to Abraham. Then merely add in the time from today back to Abraham.

Adam was created on Day 6, so there were five days before him (which is essentially negligible in this calculation). If we add up the dates from Adam to Abraham, we get about 2,000 years, using the Masoretic Hebrew text of Genesis 5 and 11.

Most Christian and secular scholars would agree that Abraham lived around 2,000 B.C. (which is 4,000 years ago). So, based on these numbers, a simple calculation would look like this:

~2,000 years (from Creation to Abraham)
+ ~4,000 years (from Abraham to today)
= ~6,000 years total[2]

Quite a few people have done this calculation using an original language text like the Masoretic Hebrew text of Genesis (which is what most modern translations are based on). With careful attention to the biblical details, they

---

2. B. Hodge, "About 6,000 Years or 10,000 Years — Does It Matter?" *Answers in Genesis,* April 15, 2017, https://answersingenesis.org/why-does-creation-matter/about-6000-years-or-10000-years-does-it-matter/.

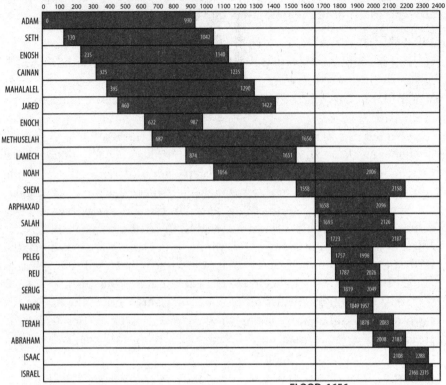

YEARS AFTER CREATION

	FLOOD 1656

also have arrived at the same time frame of about 6,000 years (about 4000 B.C.[3]) This author has also done the calculation as well from creation to the captivity of the Israelites by Babylon and Nebuchadnezzar II.[4] Just about everyone agrees on that date within a year or two (~586-588 B.C.).

So, then who is right? Should we trust God or trust (fallible) people who are merely guessing about the past? When you start with the Bible, dinosaurs are made on Day 6 of Creation Week about 6,000 years ago. God, being the absolute authority on all matters, is always right, and this means the naturalistic view is suspect and untrustworthy.

3. B. Hodge, "How Old Is the Earth?" Answers in Genesis, May 30, 2007, https://answersin-genesis.org/age-of-the-earth/how-old-is-the-earth/.

4. B. Hodge, "Age of the Earth as Tallied from Creation to the Captivity using Biblical References, Biblical Authority Ministries, August 14, 2020, https://www.biblicalauthorityminis-tries.org/2020/08/creation-to-captivity.html.

16

Why Don't We Find the Word "Dinosaur" in the Bible?

Go to a search program or concordance for most Bible translations and "dinosaur" simply doesn't exist.[1] It's just not there. You also don't find the word "mammal" in most Bible translations either.[2] So why don't we find the word *dinosaur*?

Early Bible Translations into English

Early translations of the Bible into English began in the A.D. 1500s, with the exception of John Wycliffe's translation in A.D. 1382, which was actually a translation of a translation (to English from the Latin Vulgate). Wycliffe was denounced by the Roman Catholic Church, so most of his works, including Bible translations, were largely burnt. During that time, translating the Bible into ordinary language (for the layman to read) was illegal according to the Catholic elite of the day.

However, in the 1500s, scholars were still gaining access to copies of the Masoretic text of the Old Testament Hebrew, which was done by the Masoretes (scribes) up until about the 11th century A.D.

The New Testament became more widely available through the work of Catholic Dutchman Desiderius Erasmus. Erasmus relied on 6 partial (poor quality) Greek New Testament texts together with a little help from the Latin Vulgate in a few places to make his first edition Greek New Testament. It was published and available to the public in 1516 with multiple edited versions later on when he had access to further Greek texts.[3]

---

1. I say *most* simply being conservative because I've never seen "dinosaur" in any translation yet.
2. Ibid., "mammal."
3. James White, *The King James Only Controversy* (Minneapolis, MN: Bethany House Publishers, 1995), p. 54.

This was all made possible by Johannes Gutenberg, a goldsmith who had invented a printing press in 1440. In ten years' time, the presses were being sold and distributed commercially. This allowed the New Testament text to be published and available without a handwritten copy.

William Tyndale translated the full New Testament in 1526 and, while working on the Old Testament, was arrested and later put to death in 1536 by church officials. As mentioned, getting the Bible into English was a dangerous task — sadly because of the religious leaders of that day opposing God's Word. Miles Coverdale, who had helped Tyndale on some of the Old Testament translation, finished Tyndale's work and published it in 1535 with a dedication to King Henry VIII. Tyndale may have had the blessing of knowing that his work finally reached the world prior to his death while he was imprisoned.

Other Bible translations were produced in the 1500s as well — the Great Bible (1539), the Geneva Bible (1560), and the Bishops' Bible (1568–1572). The Great Bible was authorized and commissioned by King Henry VIII and led by Lord Thomas Cromwell. It is sometimes called the Cromwell Bible. Miles Coverdale was heavily involved in that translation as well. And interestingly, it is extremely similar to Tyndale's version. It could almost be seen as an update of Tyndale's work.

The Pilgrims famously brought the Geneva Bible with them to the New World. Then, in the early 1600s, the King James Version (KJV) was produced. The KJV of 1611 is about 80% of Tyndale's version.[4] Even with many updates, the KJV translation has gone on to influence most translations even into recent times.

Still No Dinosaurs!

None of these early translations have the word "dinosaur." The reason is simple, yet often overlooked. The word dinosaur was coined by a Christian man named Sir Richard Owen, who first used this term in 1841, which is about 200–300 years *after the Bible had been put into English*.

Richard Owen was a famous comparative anatomist, biologist, and paleontologist from England and was the founder and first superintendent of the British Museum of Natural History (now called the *Natural History Museum* in London due to a name change in 1992). The British Museum (Natural History) was originally a spinoff of the famous British Museum.

Owen used two Greek words to make the word Dinosauria and hence variations like dinosaur and dinosaurian. It is a mixture of *deinos* and

---

4. Ronald Mansbridge, "The Percentage of Words in the Geneva and King James Versions taken from Tyndale's Translation," The Tyndale Society, accessed August 3, 2022, http://www.tyndale.org/tsj03/mansbridge.html.

sauros, which means "terrible or terrifying lizard." It was used to denote certain reptilian creatures that had underslung legs. Edwin Colbert wrote in 1984:

> For this group, Owen coined the name Dinosauria — from the Greek *deinos*, meaning terrible, and *sauros*, meaning lizard. (One must not be confused by Owen's choice of a Greek word meaning "lizard" when he devised the name for this group of reptiles; the Greeks did not always have a word for everything, so Owen chose the term etymologically which was the nearest this he could get. Perhaps it is permissible to extend the original meaning of the Greek word, and think of sauros in this connection as meaning "reptile.") The name was proposed by Owen at the meeting of the British Association for the Advancement of Science, convened at Plymouth in 1841. It was published in 1842 in the Proceedings of the association.[5]

Richard Owen was arguably one of the leading researchers on dinosaurs. His works and effort really make him the "godfather" of the field. Owen was highly respected and, as an interesting sidenote, a statue of him graced the Natural History Museum as one entered it until 2009 when his statue was replaced with a statue of Charles Darwin.

One can't help but notice a parallel in the shift of our Western culture from Christian to Darwinian naturalism with the replacement of these statues. Instead of looking at nature and the natural through the lens of God and His Word where God is the sovereign Lord over nature, many in our culture are abandoning God altogether and worshiping nature as though it were all that exists (i.e., the religion of naturalism).

God is the supreme God over both the natural and the supernatural, but in naturalism, God, as well as all things that are not material (e.g., unless they are made of matter and energy), cannot exist in naturalism which is inherently a materialistic philosophy and religion.

Of course, this naturalistic and materialistic religion can easily be refuted by the fact that logic, truth, knowledge, conclusions, science, morality, and so on are not material. Therefore, materialism and naturalism are false. Sadly, these religions (naturalism, and materialism, which are part of a humanistic and Darwinian worldview) are taught in museums, textbooks, government schools, and secular media all across the world.

---

5. Edwin Colbert, *The Great Dinosaur Hunters and Their Discoveries* (New York, NY: Dover Publications Inc., 1984), p. 32.

In summary, the Bible was already in English prior to the invention of the word dinosaur (Dinosauria). So we don't expect it to be in the Bible any more than we expect to find other specifically defined modern words like "mammals."

17

Are Dinosaurs and Dragons the Same Thing?

As we've previously discussed, the word "dinosaur" is a relatively new word. To refresh our memory, it was first coined or invented by Sir Richard Owen, a Christian man, in the year 1841, which, by the way, was the same year that the late Queen Elizabeth II's great grandfather King Edward VII was born. Prior to that, a dinosaur would not have been known as a "dinosaur."

This leads to the question, What were dinosaurs called prior to being called "dinosaurs"? The most obvious name, throughout history, was the word "dragon." Rightly, every *dinosaur* could be called a *dragon*. But dragons were not exclusively dinosaurs. So why is that?

Dragons and Their Relation to "Dinosaurs"

The word dragon has a much broader definition than the *very specific definition* of "dinosaur." Dinosaurs, by definition, were specifically land reptiles with one of two hip structures, whereas dragons can include a variety of land, sea, and water reptiles.

Dragons, in old forms of classification, also included large snakes (i.e., no legs), crocodiles (i.e., creatures with hip structures that had the legs out to the side instead of "under-slung"), and so forth. Again, the definition of dinosaurs is more specific, but still can be lumped into the category of dragons.

Dinosaurs are land reptiles that (by definition) naturally raise themselves off the ground.[1] So, in other words, crocodiles, komodo dragons, alligators, and so on, are not technically dinosaurs since their hip structures have their

---

1. P.S. Taylor, "Dinosaur!" *Christian Answers*, accessed 8/11/2022, http://www.christiananswers.net/dinosaurs/dinodef.html.

legs coming out to the side, which causes their belly to naturally rest on the ground. This also means flying reptiles like pterodactyls, and water reptiles like plesiosaurs are not dinosaurs either.

Simply put: *all dinosaurs are dragons*, but *not all dragons are dinosaurs*. Dinosaurs and other land dragons were made on Day Six (Genesis 1:24–31). Flying dragons and sea dragons were made on Day Five (Genesis 1:20–23[2]), such as pteranodons and plesiosaurs.

It is important to emphasize the newness of the word *dinosaur*. Sir Richard Owen invented the term "dinosaur," and it means "terrifying" or "terrible" lizard. Maybe the controversy could have been avoided if dinosaur fossils were instead simply considered "dragon" bones.

Nevertheless, this means dinosaurs were created and lived at the same time as man (both made on Day Six) and went aboard the Ark of Noah (Genesis 6:20[3]). The dinosaurs that did not go aboard the Ark had died from the Flood (Genesis 7:21–23[4]).

Many of them likely rotted and decayed, while others were rapidly buried by sediment, making them candidates for fossilization. Hence, we find many of these dragon bones (e.g., dinosaur bones, pterosaur bones, etc.) in the rock layers laid down by the Flood. Dinosaurs, along with the other onboard flying and land dragons, have been dying out ever since they came off the Ark (Genesis 8:19[5]).

The image on the following page depicts a non-exhaustive breakdown of *dragon*.

Some Dinosaurs Still Retain the Name "Dragon"

Some dinosaurs even closely resemble common images of dragons, so much to the point that their scientific names often denote a variation of the name

---

2. "Then God said, 'Let the waters abound with an abundance of living creatures, and let birds fly above the earth across the face of the firmament of the heavens.' So God created great sea creatures and every living thing that moves, with which the waters abounded, according to their kind, and every winged bird according to its kind. And God saw that it was good. And God blessed them, saying, 'Be fruitful and multiply, and fill the waters in the seas, and let birds multiply on the earth.' So the evening and the morning were the fifth day" (Genesis 1:20–23).
3. "Of the birds after their kind, of animals after their kind, and of every creeping thing of the earth after its kind, two of every kind will come to you to keep them alive" (Genesis 6:20).
4. "And all flesh died that moved on the earth: birds and cattle and beasts and every creeping thing that creeps on the earth, and every man. All in whose nostrils was the breath of the spirit of life, all that was on the dry land, died. So He destroyed all living things which were on the face of the ground: both man and cattle, creeping thing and bird of the air. They were destroyed from the earth. Only Noah and those who were with him in the ark remained alive" (Genesis 7:21–23).
5. "Every animal, every creeping thing, every bird, and whatever creeps on the earth, according to their families, went out of the ark" (Genesis 8:19).

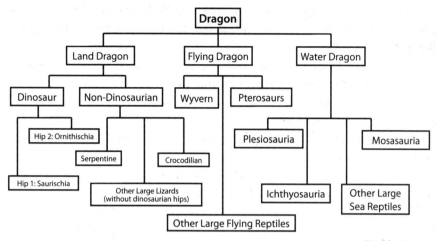

Non-Exhaustive

Dracorex Hogwartsia
Image by Dan Lietha

dragon. An excellent example is *Dracorex Hogwartsia*. Dracorex is a variation of "dragon."

Some readers may also recognize the name *Hogwarts* in the name as well. This particular dinosaur was rediscovered in Flood sediment in 2004. Because this creature looks so similar to a dragon in the fictional movie series *Harry Potter,* they decided to use the name *Hogwarts* — the castle and school in the movies — as part of the scientific name (*Hogwartsia*).

Another dinosaur is called the *Dragon of Qijiang*. This dragon/dinosaur is named for the city Qijiang, China, where its fossil remains were originally found in Flood sediment in 2006. Interestingly, this 50-foot sauropod dinosaur had a neck nearly half the length of its body![6]

A *Dracopelta* is a type of ankylosaurian dinosaur. You may spot the Latin word for dragon (*draco*) in its name. This particular dragon is a dinosaur whose fossil was found in Portugal. Other dragon-based names also appear in certain dinosaur names, such as *Dilong* and *Guanlong*, where "*long*" is a Chinese word for dragon.

---

6. Alyssa Newcomb, "'Dragon' Dinosaur Fossil With Massive Neck Discovered in China," ABC News, January 30, 2015, https://abcnews.go.com/Technology/dragon-dinosaur-fossil-massive-neck-discovered-china/story?id=28609366.

To alleviate confusion, one might be wondering about creatures like komodo dragons. Are they dragons in this classical sense? The short answser is no. Bearded dragons, Australian water dragons, and komodo dragons, and so on, are not dragons in a classical sense. The names given to these creatures are actually modern names from more recent times.

In the 1800s, the bearded dragon was originally called *Amphibolurus barbatus,* and the Australian water dragon was originally called Physignathus lesueurii (later renamed in 2012 to Intellagama lesueurii[7]), which were both named and described by Georges Cuvier.

In 1927, the komodo dragon received its name from the Indonesian island that it inhabits (Komodo) and was originally known as the komodo monitor (lizard). Even the modern flying bug called a *dragonfly* is a name that was adopted in the 1600s for the insect formerly known as *adderbolt.* Obviously, these creatures have little connection to classical dragons, yet the name "dragon" for these creatures has still become widely popular.

7. Australian Water Dragon, Australian Museum, July 28, 2022, https://australian.museum/learn/animals/reptiles/water-dragon/.

18

When Did People Start Believing Dragons Were a Myth?

A Dodo of an Introduction

The dodo was a strange bird, and our understanding of its demise and extinction by 1662 is equally strange. The dodo was a flightless bird that lived on the island of Mauritius in the Indian Ocean. It was easy to catch and provided meat to sailors. There were numerous written accounts, sketches, and descriptions of the bird from the 1500s through the 1600s.

But when the dodo went extinct, no one seemed to notice. And a few years later, scientists began to promote the idea that the dodo was merely a myth. Just look at the evidence:

Drawing by Sir Thomas Herbert of a cockatoo, red hen, and dodo in 1634. Courtesy of Wikipedia Commons, http//en.wikipedia.org/wiki/File:Lopho-psittacus.mauritianus.jpg.

1. It was a very strange creature.
2. No one could find them.
3. They seemed to exist only in the old descriptions, accounts, and drawings!

But at last, in the 19th century, there was vindication that the dodo was real and that it had merely gone extinct. Had it not been for specimens popping up in the recesses of museum collections — and finally found and then brought to light — they could have been labeled as "myth" for as long as the earth endures! Since then, fossils and other portions of specimens have also been identified as dodo.

Parallel to Dragons

So what does this have to do with dragons? Consider the following points:

1. *Dragons* are very strange creatures.
2. No one can find them.
3. They seem to exist only in the old descriptions, accounts, and drawings!

If we don't know our history, are we doomed to repeat the same mistake? Sadly, in recent times, secular scientists have relegated dragons to myths as well.

But unlike the dodo, which is just a particular type of bird, dragons represent a large range of different types of reptilian creatures. Moreover, there exists a *massive* number of descriptions, drawings, and accounts of dragons from all over the world, whereas only a handful of accounts exist of the dodo. And many of these descriptions and accounts are very similar to creatures known by a different name — dinosaurs (as well as other strange reptiles).

When Were Dragons Relegated to Myths?

It was not until the 20th century that dragons were commonly seen as myths. For instance, in 1890, a large flying dragon was reportedly killed in Arizona (a western state in the United States of America), and samples of the creature were sent to universities back east. This event was recorded in a newspaper under "A Strange Winged Monster Discovered and Killed on the Huachuca Desert," *The Tombstone Epitaph*, on April 26, 1890. Few people back then seemed to entertain the idea they were myths (there were some though!).

Even the 1902 edition of the *Encyclopædia Britannica*, while trying to explain away the accounts of sea dragons ("sea serpents"), concluded that they might still exist (as their numbers were few by this time):

> It would thus appear that, while, with very few exceptions, all the so-called "sea serpents" can be explained by reference to some well-known animal or other natural object, there is still a

residuum sufficient to prevent modern zoologist from denying the possibility that some such creature may after all exist.[1]

Yet only eight years later, it was published that dragons are a myth! In 1910, the *Encyclopædia Britannica* stated the following:

> Nor were these dragons anything but very real terrors, even in the imaginations of the learned until comparatively modern times. As the waste places were cleared, indeed, they withdrew farther from the haunts of men, and in Europe their last lurking-places were the inaccessible heights of the Alps, where they lingered till Jacques Balmain set the fashion which has finally relegated them to the realm of myth.[2]

So, aside from the instances of fabled dragons prior to 1910, rather than consider the reality that dragons (which includes dinosaurs) went extinct, Jacques Balmain, who apparently just "couldn't find one," deemed them as a myth.

This idea that dragons are a myth also made it into *Nelson's Loose Leaf Encyclopedia* under the entry of "Dragon" in 1910.[3] So this means dragons were not commonly relegated to a purely mythical status in popular publications, like encyclopedias, until the 20th century!

From the 1500s to the 1900s, due to loss of habitat, being hunted, and other factors, there was a steep decline in real dragon encounters. In several accounts, dragons lived near swamps and marshes. They often lived underground in "lairs" (as commonly called in the past). Consider the dragon/dinosaur Grendel and Grendel's mother in Beowulf that was living underground particularly near swamps.[4]

Historically, during the age of exploration and colonization from the 1400s to the 1900s, many swamps and wetlands were drained and replaced with land that is more suitable and usable for man. (As an example, Chicago, Illinois, was once a swamp that was drained.)

Thus, as expected, people began circulating the idea that dragons were fables or myths due to the lack of actual dragon encounters during this time

1. William Evans Hoyle, *Encyclopædia Britannica*, 9th ed. s.v. "Sea-Serpent" (New York, NY: The Encyclopædia Britannica Company, 1902), http://www.1902encyclopedia.com/S/SEA/sea-serpent.html.

2. Walter Alison Phillips, *The Encyclopædia Britannica*, 11th ed. (New York, NY: The Encyclopædia Britannica Company, 1910), 8:467.

3. *Nelson's Perpetual Loose-Leaf Encylcopædia*, Volume IV, John Finley, Editor-in-Chief, Thomas Nelson and Sons in association with the Trow Press, New York, 1910, p. 116.

4. Beowulf, Lesslie Hall, translator, D.C. Heath & Co., Publishers, https://www.gutenberg.org/files/16328/16328-h/16328-h.htm.

in history. In the 1800s, some Christian scholars like Adam Clarke and Lancelot Brenton began circulating the idea that dragons were a myth (more on this in Chapter 20). Their influence culminated in the late 1800s, and by 1910 this belief had become widespread in the culture.

By the late 1600s, winged dragons had largely disappeared in much of Europe, which resulted in people believing that these creatures were nothing more than mere myth. Yet the scholar and professor, Athanasius Kircher, in his book *Mundus Subterraneus* (his chapter on *Dragons* specifically), still decided that he had to refute this idea, which was starting to become popular in his day. This just further shows the reality that people will generally choose to profess creatures to be myth instead of accepting the simple (straightforward) answer — that they went extinct.

This idea of dragons being myth still defied *Encyclopædia Britannica*'s claim, even into the 1920s, when some scholars were still not eager to make such bold claims. For instance, in 1927, one dictionary still viewed dragons as real but rare, stating:

> A huge serpent or snake (now rare); a fabulous monster variously represented, generally as a huge winged reptile with crested head and terrible claws, and often as spouting fire; in the Bible, a large serpent a crocodile, a great marine animal, or a jackal.[5]

But, again, this makes sense. As people spread out and settled in more lands, dragons, which were largely rare creatures anyway, were pushed to the brink of extinction. As man develops areas, those habitats are destroyed. And just like the case with the dodo, when you can't find them any longer, they are suddenly considered "myth" instead of being seen as extinct.

Sadly, this secular idea has influenced many Christians and, as a result, modern translations rarely use the word *dragon* in the Old Testament.

Why and When Was the Decline?

So *why* did dragons (including dinosaurs) die out? The simple answer is *sin*. When Adam and Eve sinned (Genesis 3) death came into the world. Living

---

5. *The New Century Dictionary* (New York, NY: P.F. Collier & Son Corporation, 1948), p. 456

creatures began to physically die. Dragons, as well as other animals like the dodos, were no exception.

Some specific reasons for their extinction likely included changing environments (e.g., the Ice Age that followed the Flood, the destruction of swamp lands by man, etc.), predation by man (cf. Genesis 10:9[6]), diseases, genetic problems, catastrophic events, etc.[7]

Keep in mind that most dragon legends end with a dragon getting killed, which means man could have been a major factor in the extinction of dragons. Of course, there is the possibility that some still exist in remote parts of the world (or underground) and only come out at certain times. This was actually quite common with old dragon accounts.

However, in the same way that we will not likely find extinct creatures like dodos, it is highly unlikely that we will find any living dragons today.

Dragons in Relation to Satan

There is much to be said about dragons, and this short chapter is just a taste. Dragons were real creatures and have simply gone extinct due to sin, just like so many other extinct animals including the dodo. The land-dwelling, air-breathing dragons survived on the Ark of Noah and have been dying out ever since the end of the Flood (Genesis 6:20[8]; 7:21–22[9]).

While many dragons were surely timid creatures (especially since they are known to have inhabited old ruins — consider Isaiah 34:13[10] in older translations like the KJV, Geneva, Young's Literal Translation, Webster's etc.), others were sometimes known to be real terrors, according to certain old accounts (e.g., Beowulf). And when such conflicts arose, a dragon usually ended up dead by some warrior who could overcome it. Such conquerors were remembered in history with a powerful and strong name.

These types of vicious attacks could be the reason that Satan is metaphorically called a "dragon" in Scripture (e.g., Revelation 12:3[11]); also consider

---

6. "He was a mighty hunter before the Lord; therefore it is said, 'Like Nimrod the mighty hunter before the Lord'" (Genesis 10:9).
7. Ken Ham, gen. ed., *New Answers Book 1* (Green Forest, AR: Master Books, 2006), p. 207–219.
8. "Of the birds after their kind, of animals after their kind, and of every creeping thing of the earth after its kind, two of every kind will come to you to keep them alive" (Genesis 6:20).
9. "And all flesh died that moved on the earth: birds and cattle and beasts and every creeping thing that creeps on the earth, and every man. All in whose nostrils was the breath of the spirit of life, all that was on the dry land, died" (Genesis 7:21–22).
10. "And thorns shall come up in her palaces, nettles and brambles in the fortresses thereof: and it shall be an habitation of dragons, and a court for owls" (Isaiah 34:13).
11. "And another sign appeared in heaven: behold, a great, fiery red dragon having seven heads and ten horns, and seven diadems on his heads" (Revelation 12:3).

Satan's use of a serpent in Genesis 3:1[12] to deceive Eve, which ultimately led to Adam's disobedience that brought sin and death into the whole world (Romans 5:12[13]).

Satan's vicious attacks have left (and continue to leave) many blinded (e.g., 2 Corinthians 2:11[14]; 1 Peter 5:8[15]). But Christ, the "stronger man" in Luke 11:21–22,[16] has conquered Satan (Hebrews 2:14[17]), whose eternal name is above every name (Philippians 2:9[18]). For in Christ, one can have the victory over Satan, the great dragon (1 Corinthians 15:57[19]).

With this in mind, it is good to realize the big picture. Satan, whose goal is to undermine God's authority, *wants* people to accept this idea that dragons were a myth, which is obviously just another attack on the authority of God's Word. That is, Satan wants us to doubt God's Word via the same way he deceived Eve — using a serpent — in the Garden of Eden (Genesis 3:1–6; 2 Corinthians 2:11).

Were dragons a myth or did they simply die out? It's time to trust God's Word over the fallible ideas of man, who was not there, and not in a position of superseding God on the subject (Isaiah 2:22[20]). *Of course dragons were real.*

---

12. "Now the serpent was more cunning than any beast of the field which the LORD God had made. And he said to the woman, 'Has God indeed said, "You shall not eat of every tree of the garden"?'" (Genesis 3:1).
13. "Therefore, just as through one man sin entered the world, and death through sin, and thus death spread to all men, because all sinned" (Romans 5:12).
14. "Lest Satan should take advantage of us; for we are not ignorant of his devices" (2 Corinthians 2:11).
15. "Be sober, be vigilant; because your adversary the devil walks about like a roaring lion, seeking whom he may devour" (1 Peter 5:8).
16. "When a strong man, fully armed, guards his own palace, his goods are in peace. But when a stronger than he comes upon him and overcomes him, he takes from him all his armor in which he trusted, and divides his spoils" (Luke 11:21–22).
17. "Inasmuch then as the children have partaken of flesh and blood, He Himself likewise shared in the same, that through death He might destroy him who had the power of death, that is, the devil" (Hebrews 2:14).
18. "Therefore God also has highly exalted Him and given Him the name which is above every name" (Philippians 2:9).
19. "But thanks be to God, who gives us the victory through our Lord Jesus Christ" (1 Corinthians 15:57).
20. "Sever yourselves from such a man, whose breath is in his nostrils; for of what account is he?" (Isaiah 2:22).

19

Dragons, the Fiery Serpent, and the Leviathan in the Bible

Dragons

To truly settle this issue of the reality of dragons, let us turn to the Word of Almighty God, who knows all things. God's Word repeatedly mentions dragons. Again, since they are not around today (or at least none that we can find), then the obvious answer is that they have gone extinct (we've already established this reality).

Prior to the late 1800s, the Hebrew words *tannin, tannim, tannah/tannot*, or *tanninim*, were historically translated as "dragon(s)" in most translations, in both English and foreign languages. Each of these words is from the same Hebrew root word, *tan*, which is actually unused in the Bible. Of course, there is some variation in the range of meanings of these words.

Tannin and *tanninim* refer to both sea and land creatures, so it is more of an overarching term. Dragon, like our modern words "mammal" or "reptile," is also an overarching term referring to creatures in both the sea and on land. The instances of *tannin* or *tanninim* in the Old Testament are[1]:

- **Genesis 1:21** And God created great whales <u><tanninim></u>, and every living creature that moveth, which the waters brought forth abundantly, after their kind, and every winged fowl after his kind: and God saw that *it was* good.

- **Exodus 7:9** When Pharaoh shall speak unto you, saying, Shew a miracle for you: then thou shalt say unto Aaron, Take thy rod, and cast it before Pharaoh, and it shall become a serpent <u><tannin></u>.

---

1. King James Version.

- **Exodus 7:10** And Moses and Aaron went in unto Pharaoh, and they did so as the LORD had commanded: and Aaron cast down his rod before Pharaoh, and before his servants, and it became a serpent <u><tannin></u>.

- **Exodus 7:12** For they cast down every man his rod, and they became serpents <u><tanninim></u>: but Aaron's rod swallowed up their rods.

- **Deuteronomy 32:33** Their wine is the poison of dragons <u><tanninim></u>, and the cruel venom of asps.

- **Nehemiah 2:13** And I went out by night by the gate of the valley, even before the dragon <u><tannin></u> well, and to the dung port, and viewed the walls of Jerusalem, which were broken down, and the gates thereof were consumed with fire.

- **Job 7:12** Am I a sea, or a whale <u><tannin></u>, that thou settest a watch over me?

- **Psalm 74:13** Thou didst divide the sea by thy strength: thou brakest the heads of the dragons <u><tanninim></u> in the waters.

- **Psalm 91:13** Thou shalt tread upon the lion and adder: the young lion and the dragon <u><tannin></u> shalt thou trample under feet.

- **Psalm 148:7** Praise the LORD from the earth, ye dragons <u><tanninim></u>, and all deeps.

- **Isaiah 27:1** In that day the LORD with his sore and great and strong sword shall punish leviathan the piercing serpent, even leviathan that crooked serpent; and he shall slay the dragon <u><tannin></u> that is in the sea.

- **Isaiah 51:9** Awake, awake, put on strength, O arm of the LORD; awake, as in the ancient days, in the generations of old. Art thou not it that hath cut Rahab, and wounded the dragon <u><tannin></u>?

- **Jeremiah 51:34** Nebuchadrezzar the king of Babylon hath devoured me, he hath crushed me, he hath made me an empty vessel, he hath swallowed me up like a dragon <u><tannin></u>, he hath filled his belly with my delicates, he hath cast me out.

- **Lamentations 4:3** Even the sea monsters <u><tannin></u> draw out the breast, they give suck to their young ones: the daughter of my people is become cruel, like the ostriches in the wilderness.

Young's Literal Translation, done in 1862, draws out Lamentations 4:3 as "Even dragons have drawn out the breast, They have suckled their young ones, The daughter of my people is become cruel, Like the ostriches in a wilderness." Interestingly, I've had people (those that disagree this verse is referring to a dragon) say this verse shows that a mammal is in view because of the "suckling the breast."

The argument is that reptiles today do not suckle their young. However, there's very little known about extinct dragons (an entire class of animals), which means we can't conclusively say if they suckled or not. Furthermore, people once falsely believed some mammals only gave birth to live young until we discovered the platypus and spiny anteaters, which lay eggs, so we need to avoid making "blanket statements" about creature types, based only on what little we know today. Simply put, we do not know many remedial things about these extinct creatures. So, if Lamentations 4:3 does refer to dragons (or dragons of a specific type), then we would know that some *did* suckle.

Furthermore, there have been at least 10 animals, which are not mammals, that have been documented to nurse or suckle their young.[2] For instance, certain birds, fish, insects, sharks, and spiders have been observed to suckle in their physiology, so why assume that certain dragons couldn't? As a result of this belief that dragons couldn't suckle, some have thought this word for dragons is a copyist mistake, concluding that *tannin* should be *tannim* (or something else) and may represent another animal type (e.g., jackal). But there is no textual support for this claim.[3]

Tannim, the plural of tan, is used 13 times in the Old Testament, which, like *tannin,* included both sea and land creatures:[4]

- **Job 30:29** I am a brother to dragons <u><tannim></u>, and a companion to owls.

- **Psalm 44:19** Though thou hast sore broken us in the place of dragons <u><tannim></u>, and covered us with the shadow of death.

---

2. Christina Szalinski, "10 Animals That Make 'Milk' and Aren't Mammals," *Discover* Magazine, June 24, 2021, https://www.discovermagazine.com/planet-earth/10-surprising-animals-that-make-milk-and-arent-mammals.

3. (1) Some point out that the Masoretes believed Lamentation 4:3 should have been *tannim* instead of *tannin* and denoted that in a column next to it, but they didn't have any manuscripts that had the alleged variant. (2) Some suggest that Jerome might have seen a textual variant because of his choice of word used in Latin to translate tannin, but still no actual variants. Some might argue that the Latin word *lamiae* used by Jerome means jackal, but it actually means bloodsucking or devouring monsters (plural of lamia) and was feminine and is usually translated as vampire nowadays. But in more recent times, jackal was added to that definition in Latin. Likely for the very reasons I'm discussing in Chapter 20. (3) Lastly, there is the argument from grammar for the plural and singular. *Tannin* is treated as plural so one suggests maybe *tannim* should have been used (which is a plural form). However, none of these are based on actual variants, just suggestions that there should be variants somewhere.

4. King James Version.

- **Isaiah 13:22** And the wild beasts of the islands shall cry in their desolate houses, and dragons <u><tannim></u> in their pleasant palaces: and her time is near to come, and her days shall not be prolonged.

- **Isaiah 34:13** And thorns shall come up in her palaces, nettles and brambles in the fortresses thereof: and it shall be an habitation of dragons <u><tannim></u>, and a court for owls.

- **Isaiah 35:7** And the parched ground shall become a pool, and the thirsty land springs of water: in the habitation of dragons <u><tannim></u>, where each lay, shall be grass with reeds and rushes.

- **Isaiah 43:20** The beast of the field shall honour me, the dragons <u><tannim></u> and the owls: because I give waters in the wilderness, and rivers in the desert, to give drink to my people, my chosen.

- **Ezekiel 29:3** Speak, and say, Thus saith the Lord GOD; Behold, I am against thee, Pharaoh king of Egypt, the great dragon <u><tannim></u> that lieth in the midst of his rivers, which hath said, My river is mine own, and I have made it for myself.

- **Ezekiel 32:2** Son of man, take up a lamentation for Pharaoh king of Egypt, and say unto him, Thou art like a young lion of the nations, and thou art as a whale <u><tannim></u> in the seas: and thou camest forth with thy rivers, and troubledst the waters with thy feet, and fouledst their rivers.

- **Jeremiah 9:11** And I will make Jerusalem heaps, and a den of dragons <u><tannim></u>; and I will make the cities of Judah desolate, without an inhabitant.

- **Jeremiah 10:22** Behold, the noise of the bruit is come, and a great commotion out of the north country, to make the cities of Judah desolate, and a den of dragons <u><tannim></u>.

- **Jeremiah 14:6** And the wild asses did stand in the high places, they snuffed up the wind like dragons <u><tannim></u>; their eyes did fail, because there was no grass.

- **Jeremiah 49:33** And Hazor shall be a dwelling for dragons <u><tannim></u>, *and* a desolation for ever: there shall no man abide there, nor any son of man dwell in it.

- **Jeremiah 51:37** And Babylon shall become heaps, a dwellingplace for dragons <u><tannim></u>, an astonishment, and an hissing, without an inhabitant.

- **Micah 1:8** Therefore I will wail and howl, I will go stripped and naked: I will make a wailing like the dragons <u><tannim></u>, and mourning as the owls.

Tannah is used one time in Malachi 1:3.[5]

- **Malachi 1:3** And I hated Esau, and laid his mountains and his heritage waste for the dragons <u><tannah/tannot></u> of the wilderness.

Translators for 2,000+ years have largely translated these words as dragons. Only in recent times have translators and scholars deviated from this scholarship.

Leviathan the Dragon!

The Leviathan is also a dragon according to Isaiah 27:1. So each instance of Leviathan in the Bible is technically discussing a dragon. Albeit the Leviathan is a sea dragon so it wouldn't be a dinosaur (by definition). Leviathan is mentioned in four different verses in the Bible, though the entirety of Job 41 discusses this creature in detail — he breathes fire, and spears, darts, lances, javelins, and swords can't pierce him.

- **Job 41:1** Canst thou draw out <u>leviathan</u> with an hook? or his tongue with a cord which thou lettest down?
- **Psalm 74:14** Thou brakest the heads of <u>leviathan</u> in pieces, and gavest him *to* be meat to the people inhabiting the wilderness.
- **Psalm 104:26** There go the ships: there is that <u>leviathan</u>, whom thou hast made to play therein.
- **Isaiah 27:1** In that day the LORD with his sore and great and strong sword shall punish <u>leviathan</u> the piercing serpent, even <u>leviathan</u> that crooked serpent; and he shall slay the dragon that is in the sea.

Twice in the Latin Vulgate, which is a translation from Hebrew and Greek into Latin around A.D. 400, the word Leviathan is simply switched to dragon, draconis, and draco respectively in Psalm 74:14 and Psalm 104:26. The name Leviathan may also be a compound word. Hebraist John Gill writes:

> ...it is not easy to say "Leviathan" is a compound word of *than* the first syllable of "thanni," rendered either a whale, or a dragon, or a serpent, and of "levi," which signifies conjunction, from the close joining of its scales, **Job 41:15–17**; the patriarch Levi had his name from the same word; see **Ge 29:34**; and the name bids fairest for the crocodile, and which is called "thannin," **Eze 29:3,4 32:2**. Could the crocodile be established as the "leviathan"....[6]

---

5. King James Version.
6. John Gill Commentary Notes for Job 41:1. Biblestudytools.com/commentaries/gills-exposition-of-the-bible/.

Note that Gill was not necessarily advocating this claim, but rather pointed out the reality that some scholars have considered it to be true. However, the idea that leviathan is a crocodile clearly presents two main problems. First, why wasn't the word for crocodile (e.g., *thannin*) used? Second, the long description of leviathan in Job 41 doesn't match a crocodile at all. Crocodiles don't breathe fire (whether normal fire or chemical burning spits). Also, people today hunt crocodiles with a bow and arrow (i.e., darts). And swords and javelins (spears) can indeed kill crocodiles.

The fact that it is distinguished from crocodiles means the leviathan is definitely not a croc! So, then, what is it exactly? That is indeed a great question.

Some scholars have suggested it to be a *kronosaurus*. Again, based on the description, the leviathan may or may not be, though it is possible. Others have suggested a *plesiosaurus,* since by its design it can raise itself up and crash back to the water (e.g., Job 41:25[7]). So, this is also a possibility. Leviathan's primary habitat is the great sea (Psalm 104:25–26), but it can also rest near the land, inlets, and rivers to potentially "be stirred up" (Job 41:10[8]). And it has a neck strong enough to be called out by God (Job 41:22[9]). No doubt, the identity of leviathan is a good question to debate, even with creatures like crocodiles being ruled out.

From Scripture, it seems only God was able to humble this beast that had gone wildly astray (Isaiah 27:1). And He killed many of these creatures and gave them to be meat to the people inhabiting the wilderness (Psalm 74:13–14).[10]

- **Psalms 74:13–14** …thou brakest the heads of the dragons in the waters. Thou brakest the heads of **leviathan** in pieces, and gavest him to be meat to the people inhabiting the wilderness (KJV).

Leviathan was also clearly a "fire" breather (Job 41:1–21) along with the fiery serpents in the next section (from Moses and Isaiah). Breathing fire? Impossible, right? It's actually not! For example, there is an insect called the bombardier beetle that shoots chemicals into a chamber called the "pygidial gland" on its hind end, which essentially ignites, superheats, and chemically burns its victim.

In the bombardier beetle, there are twin sets of nozzles attached to the pygidial gland that allows for accurate "firing"! The bug lives on 5 continents

---

7. "When he raises himself up, the mighty are afraid; Because of his crashings they are beside themselves" (Job 41:25).
8. "No one is so fierce that he would dare stir him up. Who then is able to stand against Me?" (Job 41:10).
9. "Strength dwells in his neck, And sorrow dances before him" (Job 41:22).
10. There is debate over the meaning of Leviathan here.

(not Asia or Antarctica). When this beetle feels threatened, like a skunk, it gets ready to "fire" and then (you can even hear it!) a mixture of hot, highly noxious spray of aqueous benzoquinones, oxygen, and steam come shooting out. It stuns all sorts of predators, ranging from insects like spiders to mice, which allows the beetle to easily escape.[11]

A popular argument is that behemoth (large creature described in Job 40) and leviathan were just mythological creatures, but if that's true, then why does God speak of real creatures (lion, raven, donkey, wild ox, ostrich, horse, locust, hawk, and eagle) in the same context as the behemoth and leviathan (Job 38–41)? The behemoth in Job 40 was made alongside of Job (Job 40:15[12]), which means it was a real creature living alongside Job.

Some have suggested the behemoth was an elephant or a hippo, but neither the elephant nor the hippo eat grass in the same way as an ox, nor do they have a tail that "moves like a cedar," which obviously does not include an elephant or a hippo. An elephant has a tail that moves like a weeping willow swatting insects, and a hippo hardly even has a tail!

Fiery Serpents

Some have argued that the fiery flying serpents (and fiery serpents) were also myth. But again, God clearly reveals them as real creatures by listing them with other real creatures, like scorpions, lions, vipers, donkeys, camels, and so on, in the immediate context. Does anyone today think those creatures are myth? Obviously not!

Others have argued that fiery flying serpents were real but were just venomous snakes that would leap into the air. But that would render a portion of the Scriptures redundant, as the viper, which does that very thing, is mentioned immediately before it in Isaiah 30:6 (see below).

Historians often discuss fiery flying serpents, which also no longer exist but are likely extinct. Ancient Greek Historian Herodotus (5th Century B.C.) wrote:

> …here is a place in Arabia not far from the town of Buto where I went to learn about the winged serpents. When I arrived there, I saw innumerable bones and backbones of serpents: many heaps of backbones, great and small and even smaller. This place, where the

---

11. Mark Armitage and Luke Mullisen, "Preliminary Observations of the Pygidial Gland of the Bombardier Beetle, *Brachinus sp.*," *Journal of Creation*, 17, no 1(April 2003): 95-102.2003, https://answersingenesis.org/evidence-for-creation/design-in-nature/pygidial-gland-of-the-bombardier-beetle-brachinus-sp/.
12. "Look now at the behemoth, which I made along with you; He eats grass like an ox" (Job 40:15).

backbones lay scattered, is where a narrow mountain pass opens into a great plain, which adjoins the plain of Egypt. Winged serpents are said to fly from Arabia at the beginning of spring, making for Egypt; but the ibis birds encounter the invaders in this pass and kill them. The Arabians say that the ibis is greatly honored by the Egyptians for this service, and the Egyptians give the same reason for honoring these birds.

Now this is the appearance of the ibis. It is all quite black, with the legs of a crane, and a beak sharply hooked, and is as big as a landrail. Such is the appearance of the ibis which fights with the serpents. Those that most associate with men (for there are two kinds of ibis) have the whole head and neck bare of feathers; their plumage is white, except the head and neck and wingtips and tail (these being quite black); the legs and beak of the bird are like those of the other ibis. The serpents are like water-snakes. Their wings are not feathered but very like the wings of a bat.[13]

First Century Jewish historian Flavius Josephus, who was a prominent Jewish military leader who fought against the Romans during the Jewish-Roman War (A.D. 66–70), which led to the destruction of the Temple, Jerusalem and Judea, around A.D. 70, was commissioned to write a history of the Jewish people for his Roman conquerors. When discussing the exploits of Moses, he wrote:

(245) for when the ground was difficult to be passed over, because of the multitude of serpents, (which it produces in vast numbers, and indeed is singular in some of those productions, which other countries do not breed, and yet such as are worse than others, in power and mischief, and an unusual fierceness of sight, some of which ascend out of the ground unseen, and also fly in the air, and so come upon men at unawares, and do them a mischief), Moses invented a wonderful stratagem to preserve the army safe, and without harm;

(246) for he made baskets, like to arks, of sedge, and filled them with ibis, and carried them along with them; which animal is the greatest enemy to serpents imaginable, for they flee from them when they come near them; and as they flee they are caught and devoured by them, as if it were done by the harts;

---

13. Herodotus, Book II, Lines 76-77, https://www.perseus.tufts.edu/hopper/text?-doc=Perseus%3Atext%3A1999.01.0126%3Abook%3D2&force=y.

(247)but the ibis are tame creatures, and only enemies to the serpentine kind: but about these ibis I say no more at present, since the Greeks themselves are not unacquainted with this sort of bird. As soon, therefore, as Moses was come to the land which was the breeder of these serpents, he let loose the ibis, and by their means repelled the serpentine kind, and used them for his assistants before the army came upon that ground.[14]

Though other historians have also made similar comments on serpents, this should be sufficient to show that, historically, people (at least) did not view these creatures as myth. To give us an idea of how reptilian wings may have been in texture and style we only need to look at the flying draco lizards of today (*Draco volans*). Having four legs and wings, there are several variations of these small lizards that still exist.

Flying dragon
Draco lizard

They use these amazing little wings for gliding and mild flight.

Nevertheless, these instances and other historical examples are an excellent confirmation of what we read in Scripture.

Consider in summary the scriptural references to "fiery serpents" or "fiery flying serpents," "leviathan," and "behemoth":

Table 1: Fiery Serpents, Leviathan, and Behemoth (that Dragon/Dinosaurian-like Creature)[15]

Reference	Verse
Numbers 21:6, 8	And the Lord sent **fiery serpents** among the people, and they bit the people; and much people of Israel died. . . . And the Lord said unto Moses, Make thee a **fiery serpent**, and set it upon a pole: and it shall come to pass, that every one that is bitten, when he looketh upon it, shall live.
Deuteronomy 8:15	Who led thee through that great and terrible wilderness, wherein were **fiery serpents**, and scorpions, and drought, where there was no water; who brought thee forth water out of the rock of flint.

14. Flavius Josephus, *The Revised Works of Josephus*, Book 2, Chapter 10 (War with the Ethiopians), translated by William Whiston, 1960, as ascertained in Online Bible by Larry Pierce.
15. King James Version.

Isaiah 14:29	Rejoice not thou, whole Palestina, because the rod of him that smote thee is broken: for out of the serpent's root shall come forth a cockatrice, and his fruit shall be a **fiery flying serpent**.
Isaiah 30:6	The burden of the beasts of the south: into the land of trouble and anguish, from whence come the young and old lion, the viper and **fiery flying serpent**, they will carry their riches upon the shoulders of young asses, and their treasures upon the bunches of camels, to a people that shall not profit them.
Job 41:1	Canst thou draw out **leviathan** with an hook? or his tongue with a cord which thou lettest down?
Psalm 74:14	Thou brakest the heads of **leviathan** in pieces, and gavest him to be meat to the people inhabiting the wilderness.
Psalm 104:26	There go the ships: there is that **leviathan**, whom thou hast made to play therein.
Isaiah 27:1	In that day the LORD with his sore and great and strong sword shall punish **leviathan** the piercing serpent, even **leviathan** that crooked serpent; and he shall slay the dragon that is in the sea.
Job 40:15–24	Behold now **behemoth**, which I made with thee; he eateth grass as an ox. Lo now, his strength is in his loins, and his force is in the navel of his belly. He moveth his tail like a cedar: the sinews of his stones are wrapped together. His bones are as strong pieces of brass; his bones are like bars of iron. He is the chief of the ways of God: he that made him can make his sword to approach unto him. Surely the mountains bring him forth food, where all the beasts of the field play. He lieth under the shady trees, in the covert of the reed, and fens. The shady trees cover him with their shadow; the willows of the brook compass him about. Behold, he drinketh up a river, and hasteth not: he trusteth that he can draw up Jordan into his mouth. He taketh it with his eyes: his nose pierceth through snares.

20

Why Did "Dragons" Become "Jackals" in Bible Translations?

The A.D. 1800s were some of the darkest days of church history where compromise, cults, reinterpretations of the Bible, and attacks on the text of Scriptures were commonplace, such as:

- Higher criticism (attacks on the infallibility/inerrancy of Scripture, calling the written text of the Bible as untrustworthy)

- Documentary hypothesis (attacks on the authenticity of specific authors of Scripture, specifically the Pentateuch, to be supposed later writers and/or editors)

- Compromise in Genesis (Christians accepted the secular view of geologic long ages, like millions of years, and rejected a global Flood)

- Cult movements (Jehovah's Witnesses, Mormons, Christadelphians, etc.) that twisted the meaning of Scripture to fit their ideas, which began to steadily influence the culture with their heretical teachings

This assault on biblical authority is but a small taste of the significant unbiblical aggression against God and His Word. Let's not forget that *subtle* strikes were also looming. One such "mild attack" was a translation change in the Bible that largely went unnoticed by most people, yet many, including certain scholars, fell "hook, line, and sinker" for it.

When the word "dragon" was changed to "jackals" (or something else other than dragons), precious few comments were given for the change. That is, this change was done with little defense *or rebuttal* against it!

Sadly, many Christians failed to fully realize the implications and the ripples that this change would ultimately cause down the line. To truly grasp the scope of this change, we need to first understand what was happening in the culture at that time — bear with me, it is a long chapter but worth the read!

Dinosaurs Were Largely Extinct by the 1800s

Due to the post-Flood Ice Age, which was triggered by the global Flood of Noah's day, mammals seemed to dominate the planet more than reptiles.[1] Unlike mammals, reptiles do not tend to thrive in colder environments. With this in mind, dragons, including the prominent subset of dinosaurs, would not have been that numerous in many parts of the world.

From the A.D. 1500s to the 1800s, dragon sightings and encounters largely became less common among the general public. Of course, this was for good reason — they were going extinct at that time, likely as a result of being hunted for thousands of years, as evidenced by most dragon legends (which told of a dragon getting killed in the end). More accurate and deadlier guns, like muskets, became common use by the late 1600s, which had a profound effect on the hunting of animals and the prowess of an army or local militia to subdue an area overrun by beasts.

Furthermore, over the past 500 years, many swampland areas in the New World have been destroyed and converted into land for farming and other purposes (e.g., Chicago, Illinois, was originally a swamp). For instance, the land that would become the United States in the 1600s had about 221 million acres of wetlands, which was reduced significantly to about 106 million acres.[2]

Historically speaking, this was actually a short amount of time compared to other parts of the world (e.g., the Old World), such as the Middle East, Europe, and Asia, that were destroying swamps and wetlands for a far longer amount of time. Many ancient dragon accounts often linked swamps (and other similar water sources) as the primary habitat for dragons and dinosaur-like creatures. Thus, these destruction efforts likely impacted dragon territories severely in many parts of the world.

By the A.D. 1500s, dragon sightings and encounters became much rarer in occurrence (very few accounts were around at that time). And by the 1800s, these accounts had all but disappeared, with only a few brief occurrences in that century. For instance, the *Tombstone Epitaph*, in the late 1800s, recorded an account of two ranchers who encountered a large

---

1. Mike Oard, "Where does the Ice Age Fit?" in Ken Ham, gen. ed., *The New Answers Book* (Green Forest, AR: Master Books, 2006), p. 207–219.
2. Thomas Dahl and Gregory Allord, "History of Wetlands in the Conterminous United States," *US Geological Survey Water Supply Paper* 2425, USGS, March 7, 1997, https://water.usgs.gov/nwsum/WSP2425/history.html.

pterosaur-like dragon, which they were able to kill using their rifles, that was witnessed by several townspeople.[3] Samples of this encounter were even sent off to scientists back east. But once again, it appears a dragon was killed, when there may have only been a precious few that still existed at that time.

So what did the academic elite do in response to this lack of dragon sightings, encounters, and the inability to study them, due to their largely extinct nature? Did they do the logical thing and declare them extinct?

No! Instead, they did something very strange… they foolishly assumed dragons never existed at all! They took the odd route of reducing dragons to nothing more than myth. This false assumption then started quickly spreading in academia, especially among certain Christian academics too. And finally, in the early 1900s, dragons were officially and publicly declared mythical in encyclopedias. In both *Nelson's Perpetual Loose Leaf Encyclopaedia*[4] and *Britannica*, dragons were officially declared unreal creatures in their entries under "dragon." *Britannica* states:

> Nor were these dragons anything but very real terrors, even in the imaginations of the learned until comparatively modern times. As the waste places were cleared, indeed, they withdrew farther from the haunts of men, and in Europe their last lurking-places were the inaccessible heights of the Alps, where they lingered till Jacques Balmain set the fashion which has finally relegated them to the realm of myth.[5]

Nevertheless, their alleged mythic status didn't happen overnight. Leading up to this transition, scholars were already discussing dragons behind the scenes, relegating them to myth, in the 1800s before the public was fully aware.

A New Name for Dragons

Then another event happened in the 1800s that was equally odd. Bones of huge reptilian creatures were starting to be discovered and dug up — not that *that* was odd, but we'll get to the oddity in a moment. Some of these bones were relatively small in size, but it was the large ones that caught the attention of both scientists and the general public, with creatures like Megalosaurus, discovered by William Buckland in 1815, and Iguanodon in 1822 in Sussex, England.

---

3. "A Strange Winged Monster Discovered and Killed on the Huachuca Desert," *The Tombstone Epitaph*, on April 26, 1890.

4. John H. Finley (Editor in Chief), *Nelson's Perpetual Loose Leaf Encyclopaedia* (New York: The Trow Press, 1910), p. 116.

5. Walter Alison Phillips, *The Encyclopædia Britannica*, 11th ed. (New York, NY: The Encyclopædia Britannica Company, 1910), 8:467.

These large reptilian creatures were rapidly buried and fossilized by the Flood of Noah's day. In the 1800s, anatomists (scientists who study features of bodies) and paleontologists (scientists who study fossils) like Sir Richard Owen took to their study. Owen, in 1841, coined the name "dinosaur" and "Dinosauria" (as a category) for these reptilian creatures that walked upright in their posture.

Dinosaur means "terrible" or "terrifying lizard." So, *instead of calling these creatures dragons* and analyzing dragon bones, they switched to an entirely different name! Did anyone back then truly realize the implication of this switch? The entirety of dragon fossils that stood erect that were in the ground was now called "dinosaurs." And any living descendant of dragons in the 1800s were the last surviving remnant of creatures, which now have other names such as flying reptiles, sea reptiles, or now "dinosaurs."

So the real *oddity* was (and still is) the blatant neglect of connecting *dragon bones* to *dinosaur bones* simply because of a new name. In other words, dragons went the route of myth, while dinosaurs became a whole new category, or "new creatures," that required further study.

As an analogy, elephants are currently listed as endangered (some even critically endangered) and have been on the edge of extinction for years (some post-Flood variants, like wooly mammoths and mastodons, have already been lost). If not for zoos and circuses, most of the world would have never had the opportunity to actually see these living creatures in the days prior to common photography (and no internet) like in the early part of the 1800s.

Now let's imagine for a moment that elephants went extinct in the early 1800s and scholars back then were discussing if they were even real. Finally, they declare that elephants were a myth. And then they start digging up bones that look very similar to elephants, even finding some in the permafrost (frozen), but assume these creatures must be something other than elephants.

As a result, they name these new finds "Tuskers." In doing so, they completely disconnect these "new creatures" from the original (elephant) creatures. In a nutshell, this imaginary scenario is akin to what happened with dragons (original creatures) and dinosaurs (new creatures). And sadly, this disconnection has affected Bible translations, starting in the 1800s, and still persists today.

Dragon(s) in the Text and Translations until A.D. 1800s

For two thousand years, the Hebrew words that were commonly translated as "dragon(s)" are:

תַּן *tan*

תַּנִּין *tannin*

תנים *tannim*

תַּנָּה *tannah*

From about 300 B.C., the translators of the LXX (a.k.a. the Septuagint, which translated the biblical text from Hebrew to Greek), who were fluent in ancient Hebrew, consistently translated many of these Hebrew words (*tan, tannin, tannim,* etc.) into one of the various words for dragon(s) in Greek.

The word for "dragon(s)" is also seen in early translations, such as the famous Latin Vulgate (done by St. Jerome, around A.D. 400, who translated from the original Hebrew and Greek languages), and was commonly used in languages like French, German, Portuguese, and others, until recent times.

Furthermore, "dragon(s)" was consistently used in early English translations, starting with Wycliffe in the 1300s (translating from the Latin Vulgate), Tyndale/Coverdale (translating from original languages), the 1611 King James Version (KJV), and many others, including revisions up until the KJV revision in 1873.

In 1808, the LXX was translated into English by Charles Thomson, and though it was largely unknown and lacked popularity, it used dragons as well. On top of that, the 1811 Samuel Pike Hebrew lexicon,[6] 1829 John Parkhurst Hebrew and English lexicon,[7] and the 1874 Wigram Hebrew Concordance[8] also still defined these Hebrew words as dragons.

In 1876, Julia Smith's Translation (first female translation) had *jackals* and, in some rare cases, still retained dragons. By 1885, the ERV (English Revised Version, which was the first KJV update that wasn't called the KJV) also largely had jackals. What happened? Let's take a step back to a translation from 1844–1870, done by Sir Lancelot Brenton. This is when things changed for Bible translation (more on this in a moment).

What Led Up to This Major Change?

Adam Clarke (1762–1832) was a respected Wesleyan/Methodist pastor, biblical scholar, and commentator whom I've referenced many times over

---

6. Samuel Pike, *A Compendious Hebrew Lexicon*, Second Cambridge Edition (London, England, 1811), entry for tanin and tanim.
7. John Parkhurst, *An Hebrew and English Lexicon*, Thomas Tegg, London, England, 1829, entry for tanin and tanim.
8. George Wigram, *The Englishman's Hebrew Concordance of the Old Testament*, 1874 version (Peabody, MA, Hendrickson Publishers, 1997), p. 1352–1353.

the past years. Adam Clarke actually mentioned "dragons" several times in his Bible commentary. However, in Ezekiel 29:3[9] he clarifies what he really means by "dragon," saying:

> *The great dragon hattannim* should here be translated *crocodile,* as that is a *real* animal, and numerous in the *Nile;* whereas the *dragon* is wholly *fabulous.* The original signifies any large animal.[10]

When Clarke's commentary was published (by 1826) he viewed dragons as fabulous (i.e., fabled) and mythological. Clarke also comments on Exodus 7:10:[11]

> *tannin.* What kind of a serpent is here intended, learned men are not agreed. From the manner in which the original word is used in; Ps 74:13 Isa 27:1 Isa 51:9 Job 7:12 some very large creature, either aquatic or amphibious, is probably meant; some have thought that the *crocodile,* a well-known Egyptian animal, is here intended. In Ex 4:3 it is said that this rod was changed into a *serpent,* but the original word there is *nachash,* and here *tannin,* the same word which we translate *whale. {Ge 1:21}*
>
> As *nachash* seems to be a term restricted to no one particular meaning, as has already been shown on Gen. iii.; See note on "Ge 3:1" So the words *tannin, tanninim, tannim,* and *tannoth,* are used to signify different kinds of animals in the Scriptures. The word is supposed to signify the *jackal* in; *{Job 30:29} {Ps 44:19} {Isa 13:22} {Isa 34:13} {Isa 35:7} {Isa 43:20} {Jer 9:11}* and also a *dragon, serpent,* or *whale;{ Job 7:12} {Ps 91:13} {Isa 27:1} {Isa 51:9} {Jer 51:34} {Eze 29:3} {Eze 32:2}* and is termed, in our translation, a *sea-monster. {La 4:3}"*[12]

Clarke suggests jackals for *tannim* in his notes for Exodus 7:10,[13] Job 30:29,[14]

---

9. "Speak, and say, Thus saith the Lord GOD; Behold, I am against thee, Pharaoh king of Egypt, the great dragon that lieth in the midst of his rivers, which hath said, My river is mine own, and I have made it for myself" (Ezekiel 29:3; KJV).

10. https://www.sacred-texts.com/bib/cmt/clarke/exo007.htm.

11. "And Moses and Aaron went in unto Pharaoh, and they did so as the LORD had commanded: and Aaron cast down his rod before Pharaoh, and before his servants, and it became a serpent" (Exodus 7:10; KJV).

12. https://www.sacred-texts.com/bib/cmt/clarke/index.htm.

13. "And Moses and Aaron went in unto Pharaoh, and they did so as the LORD had commanded: and Aaron cast down his rod before Pharaoh, and before his servants, and it became a serpent" (Exodus 7:10; KJV).

14. "I am a brother to dragons, and a companion to owls" (Job 30:29; KJV).

and Jeremiah 9:11,[15] but a hippopotamus in Jeremiah 14:6.[16] His justification for "jackals" derived from Archbishop William Newcome, per his comment notes on Micah 1:8:

> *I will make a wailing like the dragons Newcome* translates: — I will make a wailing like the foxes, (or jackals).[17]

Clarke often references Newcome's commentary on Ezekiel, Hosea, Joel, Amos, Obadiah, Jonah, Micah, Nahum, Habakkuk, Zephaniah, Haggai, Zechariah, and Malachi. However, while Newcome's New Testament translation is readily available, I unfortunately have failed to find any of Newcome's Old Testament translations.

In 1844, Sir Lancelot Brenton published an English translation of the Septuagint (LXX) that wasn't quite completed yet (it didn't have the book of Daniel for example). So, later in 1851, Brenton published a more complete version, this time having included Daniel, as well as the Apocrypha. Let's pause for a moment because neither of these publications were that popular. To this day, the 1851 version is still extremely rare to find. Finally, around 1870, Brenton published his LXX with a diglot (i.e., bi-lingual) edition including the Greek Old Testament (from which he was translating).

It was this 1870 version from Brenton that made headway into scholarly circles and became quite influential with its publication in the early 1870s. And to this day, the 1870 version from Brenton is considered his major contribution.[18]

Unlike the previous LXX versions from Thomson or himself, which had little popularity, Brenton's new diglot was very popular. As a result, Brenton became an influencer who then affected other translations from that point forward.

So, did Sir Brenton have dragons in his LXX translation? He retained dragons in a few rare places, which was consistent with the KJV (et al's use of dragons), but largely changed dragons to other creatures. But he didn't use jackals in those instances. In fact, he never used jackals at all! So what did he use? He used "monsters," "hedgehogs," "birds," "serpents," "affliction," "ostriches," "fig trees." And in three cases, he just deleted the word dragon,

---

15. "And I will make Jerusalem heaps, and a den of dragons; and I will make the cities of Judah desolate, without an inhabitant" (Jeremiah 9:11; KJV).

16. "And the wild asses did stand in the high places, they snuffed up the wind like dragons; their eyes did fail, because there was no grass" (Jeremiah 14:6; KJV).

17. Adam Clarke Bible Commentary, Micah 1:8, https://www.bibliaplus.org/en/commentaries/7/adam-clarke-bible-commentary/micah/1/8.

18. Brenton's Translation of the Septuagint, The International Organization for Septuagint and Cognate Studies, accessed June 6, 2022, http://ccat.sas.upenn.edu/ioscs/brenton/.

or its entire accompanying phrase, altogether! Clearly, there was a lack of consistency. But this also means he wasn't drawing information from Adam Clarke who lent toward jackals, crocodiles, and hippos for instance.

Brenton retained dragon in only a handful of instances. In one of those, Psalm 74:13–14,[19] he denoted that it was a "serpent," which clearly demonstrated Brenton's confusion and struggle with consistently translating "dragon." It's like after 2,000 years of scholarship on dragons, he suddenly had no idea how to properly translate "dragon" and instead opted to use a host of differing things.

The word *dragon* was clearly being attacked (and even deleted), and he presumably didn't know what direction to take. He apparently didn't take the route that Clarke had taken with jackal. This leaves two independent scholars relegating dragons to fabulous (i.e., fabled, "make-believe") creatures and thus in need of some other creature.

Why was it so difficult for Brenton? Although he made this change without direct comment, he viewed dragons as symbolic (not real creatures) as a result of buying into the false notion that dragons were merely a myth (more on this in a moment). This error became a problem when some passages were clearly referring to real creatures. So how did he interpret the text that clearly refers to a real creature and can't be interpreted allegorically? He used sea monster (for sea creatures) or birds, ostriches, hedgehogs, etc.

From a big picture, Brenton and Clarke basically "opened a door" to the secular ideas that dragons were not real, which subsequent scholars then pushed open farther. The next thing we know, translations, lexicons, and Bible dictionaries after Brenton's and Clarke's influence are now excluding dragon for other creatures, namely jackals.

Why did Brenton feel the need to deviate from thousands of years of translations to do something different? Why not just use dragon?

Remember what was happening in the academic culture at the time? Dragons were increasingly being relegated to mythic status (because they weren't around anymore). Clarke didn't believe them to be real. Brenton was also in this camp. The new big and popular thing in the culture was dinosaurs that supposedly lived "in long ages past" (according to their secular religion/worldview). Dinosaurs were being totally disconnected from dragons by the secular world. And, sadly, Christian scholars were following the secular world's lead. Brenton was no different.

---

19 . "Thou didst establish the sea, in thy might, thou didst break to pieces the heads of the *{1}* dragons in the water. *{1} Or, serpents}* Thou didst break to pieces the heads of the dragon; thou didst give him *for* meat to the Ethiopian nations" (Psalm 74:13–14 [which is 73:13–14 in the Brenton LXXE]; LXXE by Brenton).

As previously mentioned though, Brenton didn't comment on his change directly. Another scholar (Samuel Davidson) revealed the reason and the driving belief behind this change in the LXX (from 1844–1870). Davidson, on discussing Brenton's new translation of the LXX, points out that symbolism should be "generally" translated. And he then goes on to defend Brenton's idea that dragons are in the symbolic category because a "mythological idea is attached."[20]

In further discussing the new English translation, Davidson goes on to argue for the false understanding of documentary hypotheses (attacking authorship of the biblical authors) and even denies a biblically derived age of the world by instead siding with the secularists' (shifting) opinions on the age of the world (i.e., long ages). He writes:

> It is impossible to settle the age of the world with any approach to probability. It is certainly much older than six thousand years. It is equally impossible to determine the period of man's creation. The chronology of the first chapter in Genesis, who can tell?[21]

So, because Brenton was directly influenced by the secular humanistic view of origins (regarding the age of the earth and dinosaurs), he regarded dragons as symbolic/myth, thus causing him to disconnect dinosaurian creatures from dragons.

Clarke and Brenton were surely not alone in their influence by secular ideas. As a consequence of Clarke's and Brenton's secular view of dragons, subsequent popular Bible dictionaries and lexicons saw a shift in the 1870s and afterward (like Strong's, NAS Hebrew Lexicon, the Hebrew and Aramaic Lexicon of the Old Testament, Brown-Driver-Briggs, the Theological Wordbook of the Old Testament, etc.) followed Brenton's and Clarke's view that dragons were a myth, and therefore reinterpreted the Hebrew word for dragon as being anything but a "real" dragon creature. These resources now deviated from previous scholarship for 2,000 years and essentially ended with the 1874 Wigram Hebrew Concordance.

Thus, dragons and dinosaurs were erroneously disconnected from the Bible in the minds of certain academic elites who had already deviated from the biblical age of the earth. If we're allowed to compromise in one area of Scripture, why not another? The door was now wide open to further erroneous reinterpretation and translation errors.

---

20. Samuel Davidson, *On a Fresh Revision of the English Old Testament* (London: Williams and Norgate Publisher, 1871), p. 51–52.
21. Ibid., p. 139–140.

Why Did Subsequent Scholars Settle on Jackals?

Brenton never considered to use "jackal" to replace dragon. So where did it come from? I suggest it was influenced from Clarke's view. At this point in history, certain academics didn't view dragons as real, so they needed something else. As previously discussed, Brenton didn't know what to put so he resorted to using all sorts of different things instead of *dragon*.

The next wave of scholars and translators needed something a bit more consistent. Thus, they actively looked for a replacement. Clarke was their answer, which then directed translational work toward "jackals" after Brenton.

However, this resulted in a major problem — there are other words in Hebrew that mean "jackal" or "jackals"! For instance, John Calvin, a leading Reformer, relates in a footnote in his commentary notes on Psalm 63:9–11:[22]

> Under the Hebrew word שׁוּעָל, *shual,* here rendered *fox,* was comprehended, in common language, *the jackal,* or *Vulpes aureus, golden wolf,* so called in Latin because its color is a bright yellow; and in this sense שׁוּעָל, *shual,* has been generally interpreted here, because the jackal is found in Palestine, and feeds on carrion. Both of these circumstances are, however, also applicable to the fox, and, moreover, Bochart has made it probable that the specific name of the jackal (the θώς of the Greeks) in Hebrew was אִי, *aye, the howler,* being so called from the howling cry which he makes particularly at night. The term occurs in **Isa 13:22, 34:14;** and **Jer 50:39;** where אִיִּים, *ayim,* is rendered, in our version, "the wild beasts of the islands," an appellation very vague and indeterminate. At the same time, it is highly probable that *shual* generally refers to the jackal. Several of the modern oriental names of this animal, as the Turkish *chical,* and the Persian *sciagal, sciachal,* or *schachal* — whence the English jackal — from their resemblance to the Hebrew word *shual,* favor this supposition; and Dr Shaw, and other travelers, inform us, that while jackals are very numerous in Palestine, the common fox is rarely to be met with. We shall, therefore, be more correct, under these circumstances, in admitting that the jackal of the East is the Hebrew *shual.*[23]

---

22. "But those who seek my life, to destroy it, Shall go into the lower parts of the earth. They shall fall by the sword; They shall be a portion for jackals [*shual*]. But the king shall rejoice in God; Everyone who swears by Him shall glory; But the mouth of those who speak lies shall be stopped" (Psalm 63:9–11; NKJV), denoted. KJV uses "foxes" because Tyndale used them as they are abundant in England whereas jackals are not.

23. John Calvin Commentary Notes for Psalm 63:9, footnote 437, https://www.sacred-texts.com/chr/calvin/cc09/cc09028.htm#fn_436.

Admittedly, that quote from Calvin is long and arduous! But the point is that there are other words for jackal which don't always get translated as jackal (sometimes as "fox" or "hyena," etc.), so pay close attention — they are not *tan, tannin, tannim, or its variations*. Nonetheless, translators were looking for a substitute for dragon, and jackal seemed to fit the bill. But why? Where did jackal come from? Adam Clarke said he got it from Newcome. But where did William Newcome get it from?

A Brief Comment by John Gill

Dr. John Gill (1697–1771) was an amazing English Baptist pastor, Bible commentator, theologian, and Hebrew scholar who largely rescued Hebrew from extinction. Most (if not all) Hebrew translators (unlike Brenton who was translating from the Greek LXX) are surely intimately acquainted with Dr. Gill's work.

There is much to learn from his immense amount of writing and research. Many Christians, including myself, have been blessed by much of his teaching, though with some caveats (there are certain things that I disagree with him on). Nonetheless, I have tremendous respect for him.

In a biographical sketch of Dr. Gill, it says, "To say that Dr. Gill influenced evangelical Christians in general and Baptists in particular is like saying the sun influences the daytime. He was the first Baptist to write a complete systematic theology and the first to write a verse-by-verse commentary of the entire Bible. Gill wrote so much that he was known as Dr. Voluminous."[24]

Gill's work in Christian academic circles, particularly regarding Hebrew, is still immensely influential to this day. The point is that Gill was well known to Hebrew translators and academics throughout the 1800s. Gill writes in his commentary notes on Malachi 1:3:[25]

> A learned Jew is of opinion, that not serpents, but jackals, are here meant, which are a sort of wild howling beasts, that live abroad in desolate places.

Jackals are basically dogs, whose cackling howls are well known. Coyotes are similar in their cackling howls and are sometimes known as American jackals.

Nevertheless, the Jewish scholar in reference was a poet who lived near Spain, named Tanchum ha-Yerushalmi, and died around A.D. 1300. This

---

24. "Biography of John Gill," *The Baptist Page*, January 5, 2014, https://comingintheclouds.org/about-protestant/teachers-preachers/biography-of-john-gill/.

25. "And I hated Esau, and laid his mountains and his heritage waste for the dragons of the wilderness" (Malachi 1:3; KJV).

reference is known because of Richard Pococke (sometimes spelled Pocock), from whom Gill garnered this information (Micah 1:8[26]). Pococke was known for his travels in Europe and his diaries. Pococke briefly mentions Tanchum's suggestion that these are jackals and thought this suggestion was reasonable. Gill did not necessarily agree (Gill often discussed dragons as real creatures) but rather was merely relaying the information from Pockocke along to his readers.

Hebrew translators researching dragons, including Clarke, were undoubtedly familiar with Gill's reference. So, is this possibly where Clarke, in a round-about way, and more specifically Archbishop Newcome got the idea for jackals to replace land dragons?

Gill (d. 1771) was an elder contemporary of Newcome (d. 1800) so I believe there is little doubt that Newcome, who was a translator of Old Testament Hebrew, was acquainted with Gill's Hebrew works. How could he not? Dr. John Gill was the very man who revived, if not rescued, Hebrew from near extinction! That is, it was Gill that made Hebrew translation possible again. Newcome was translating Old Testament Hebrew texts just a few years later for Clarke to read and comment on, so his familiarity with Gill's works should be blatantly obvious.

But pause for a moment. This idea of using jackal(s) came from an unbeliever, who was completely unfamiliar and disconnected from the biblical settings thousands of years before. And this idea wasn't even entertained as a legitimate possibility until increased secular influence held sway over some church leaders to relegate dragons to a myth, which disconnected dinosaurs from dragons.

And because of this compromise in the church, most modern translations, along with scholarly works, since Brenton's LXX and Clarke's commentary have implemented the idea of using "jackals" (or a few other creatures) in place of dragons. Merril Unger who penned Unger's Bible Dictionary in the mid-1900s wrote:

> (Hebrew *tannin*) This word is used in the Authorized Version with several meanings: (1) In connection with desert animals (Isa. 13:22; 34:13, 14, etc.), it is best translated by *wolf*, and not by *jackal* as in the Revised Version. The feminine form of the Hebrew *tannah* is found in Mal. 1:3. (2) *Sea monsters* (Psa. 74:13; 148:7; Isa. 27:1). (3) *Serpents*, even the smaller sorts (Deut. 32:33; Psa.

---

26. "Therefore I will wail and howl, I will go stripped and naked: I will make a wailing like the dragons, and mourning as the owls" (Micah 1:8; KJV).

91:13)....one of the Hebrew words, usually rendered dragon is in some places translated *serpents* (Exodus 7:9, 10, 12).[27]

Unger was still debating against jackals in the mid-1900s for another creature — a wolf! Nevertheless, jackal seemed to win out among those denying the existence of dragons.

Micah 1:8[28] mentions the wailing, mourning, and lamentation sound of a dragon (*tannim*). And so, to better justify the use of "jackals" in this verse, some modern translations have chosen to switch to the word "howl" (instead of wail or lament). Consequently, one reinterpretation has now led to another in some instances.[29] For instance, the Christian Standard Bible (CSB) reads:

> "Because of this I will lament and wail; I will walk barefoot and naked. I will howl like the jackals and mourn like ostriches."

Overall, this is the inevitable result of Christians adopting a secular worldview, regarding dinosaurs and long ages that cause the false relegation of dragons to the realm of myth. Hopefully you can now see the influence that a secular worldview has on Bible translation, which has allowed the use of jackals to become the norm in modern translations.

Lastly, this should serve as a reminder that we must not allow the latest (man-made) "religion of the day" to compromise our Christianity — especially in the area of Bible translation.

---

27. Merril Unger, *Unger's Bible Dictionary* (Chicago, IL: Moody Press, 1957), entry for Animal Kingdom, sub Dragon, p. 58.
28. "Therefore I will wail and howl, I will go stripped and naked: I will make a wailing like the dragons, and mourning as the owls" (Micah 1:8; KJV).
29. There are other mental gymnastics that must also be overcome such as instances where *tan* and *tannim* don't fit the context for jackals (e.g., being sea creatures, etc.) so the appeal is to state these are copyist mistakes to remedy but without textual justification.

21

Does the Bible Mention Dinosaurs?

When bringing up the topic of dinosaurs and the Bible in conversation, people will normally pose the question, "Does the Bible even mention dinosaurs?" Of course, we have already pointed out in previous chapters that all dinosaurs are dragons, which are referenced several times in Scripture. But, as a reminder, not all dragons are specifically dinosaurs.

Specifically Specific

The specific question is whether certain dragon accounts in the Bible are describing dinosaurs (i.e., certain land dragons) and not sea-dwelling or flying dragons. For instance, when the Bible discusses land dragons, such as in Psalm 91:13[1] or Jeremiah 49:33,[2] it's possible the Bible is actually referencing dinosaurs.

It's important that we don't overlook the fact that *some* of these land dragons may well have been dinosaurs. However, the Bible simply doesn't give us enough information about these specific reptiles to conclusively say whether they had a hip structure that allowed them to stand erect or not (the most basic aspect of the definition of dinosaurs).

In Genesis 1, we read about the "beasts of the earth" and the "beasts of the field" (a smaller subset of "beasts of the earth"). Beasts of the earth include dinosaurs. No doubt *some* of the beasts of the field were also dinosaurs. So,

---

1. "Thou shalt tread upon the lion and adder: the young lion and the dragon shalt thou trample under feet" (Psalm 91:13; KJV).
2. "And Hazor shall be a dwelling for dragons, and a desolation for ever: there shall no man abide there, nor any son of man dwell in it" (Jeremiah 49:33; KJV).

from a big picture, we can see hints of dinosaurs in the *categories* of dragons or the "beasts of the earth" in Scripture.

But are there any specific examples of a potential dinosaur? Yes, there is one *excellent* example that we can find in the Bible.

Behold Behemoth

Behold the behemoth, in Job 40, which is one of the most oft-mentioned creatures in the Bible, may well have been a dinosaur. Unlike the many other brief mentions of land dragons or beasts elsewhere in the Bible, the behemoth in Job 40 is discussed in great detail. It is a land creature of immense size that is described with features similar to a sauropod. Job 40:15–24 says,

> 15 "Look now at the behemoth, which I made along with you; He eats grass like an ox.
>
> 16 See now, his strength is in his hips, And his power is in his stomach muscles.
>
> 17 He moves his tail like a cedar; The sinews of his thighs are tightly knit.
>
> 18 His bones are like beams of bronze, His ribs like bars of iron.
>
> 19 He is the first of the ways of God; Only He who made him can bring near His sword.
>
> 20 Surely the mountains yield food for him, And all the beasts of the field play there.
>
> 21 He lies under the lotus trees, In a covert of reeds and marsh.
>
> 22 The lotus trees cover him with their shade; The willows by the brook surround him.
>
> 23 Indeed the river may rage, Yet he is not disturbed; He is confident, though the Jordan gushes into his mouth,
>
> 24 Though he takes it in his eyes, Or one pierces his nose with a snare."

This massive creature can go into the water (verse 23) — not just any water, but a flooding (raging) Jordan River, without fear.[3] It can wade among the

---

3. Bear in mind that the land of Israel today is far less lush than what it was in Moses' day. Thus, there is far less rainfall today (consider Deuteronomy 28:11–24). In lush years past, the Jordan River was likely much more imposing than what it is today and during flooding or raging, it would have been quite fearful, but not to behemoth.

marshes and lie at its edges in the reeds and willows where brooks enter the river (verse 21).

The Jordan River today isn't much of an imposing river (except when it is flooding). But what was it like in Job's day? The area surrounding the Jordan back then was considered good land that was much lusher compared to today. In the past, this area had much more rainfall, with enough water to sufficiently cover the fields (Job 5:10[4]), and was blessed by God (e.g., Deuteronomy 3:25[5]), thus it likely had a much more significant Jordan River.

But God warned the Israelites that He would withhold the rain, as a consequence of their disobedience, due to their sin (e.g., Deuteronomy 11:17[6]). The Holy Land website comments on the Jordan River today saying:

> Though an old song says the River Jordan is "deep and wide," the modern river is neither. In places it is more like a creek than a river — less than 10 metres across and 2 metres deep.[7]

It is indicative of its size today compared to it being more abundant in the past. In many places, the Jordan River plain shows its size in the past, and the modern river winds back and forth through the valley where it used to run more significantly.

Also, the Jordan River would have certainly *raged* (as described in Job 40:23[8]) during the flooding season — which may give us an indication on the time of year the Lord was speaking to Job. Being a more imposing river *and* during its flooding season, gives powerful hints to the creature that has no fear while standing in raging river allowing the water to gush into its mouth (verse 23).

The behemoth also goes among the field and can eat grass. And it finds food to eat among mountains, which is more shrubbery and with other types of vegetation. So, this creature migrates and survives great distances without a problem.

The behemoth is described as the "first" or the "chief" of the ways of God, clearly indicating it as a creature that stands out in a crowd in

---

4. "He gives rain on the earth, And sends waters on the fields" (Job 5:10).

5. "I pray, let me cross over and see the good land beyond the Jordan, those pleasant mountains, and Lebanon" (Deuteronomy 3:25).

6. "lest the LORD's anger be aroused against you, and He shut up the heavens so that there be no rain, and the land yield no produce, and you perish quickly from the good land which the LORD is giving you" (Deuteronomy 11:17).

7. "Jordan River," See The Holy Land.net, accessed August 23, 2022, https://www.seetheholyland.net/jordan-river/.

8. "Indeed the river may rage, Yet he is not disturbed; He is confident, though the Jordan gushes into his mouth" (Job 40:23).

comparison to other animals. When it lies down, Lotus trees give it shade (verses 21–22[9]). Note, Lotus trees were typically deciduous trees that grew up to 100 feet (30 m) high.[10] The Date Plum (*Diospyros lotus*), for example, is a specific type of lotus tree that reaches these heights, which is sometimes translated as "shady tree," based on the context of it *giving shade*.

Also note that the text says the behemoth *lies down* under trees. This means it is *not* a creature, like an alligator, crocodile, or komodo dragon, with legs protruding out to its side, which naturally lay on its belly. Instead, the behemoth must make an effort to lie down, suggesting that its legs are *underslung*, which gives further biblical evidence of it being dinosaur-like.

Interestingly, one may run across a Bible commentary that suggests this behemoth might be an elephant or a hippopotamus.[11] Job 40:15[12] says this creature eats grass like an ox. So, clearly, it isn't an ox. But this also means

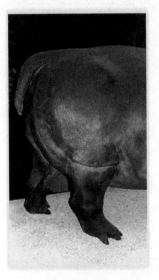

Hippo tail

that it clearly isn't an elephant! Have you ever seen the way an elephant eats grass? It uses its trunk to wrap around grass, pull it out, and lift it up to its mouth. Oxen do *not* do this! Rather, they wrap their mouth around the grass and use their teeth to pull the grass out. These two methods are not similar at all!

The hippopotamus does eat grass like an ox. However, Job 40:17[13] says the behemoth moves its tail like a *cedar*. The flap of a "tail" (if you can even call it that!) on a hippopotamus that wildly wiggles back and forth does not (in any way, shape, or form) resemble a *cedar* gracefully moving in the wind. Nor should that little flap even be compared to a tree!

Likewise, the tail on an elephant moves more like a weeping willow, basically whipping

---

9. "He lies under the lotus trees, In a covert of reeds and marsh. The lotus trees cover him with their shade; The willows by the brook surround him" (Job 40:21–22).

10. The Lotus trees of antiquity are not to be confused with the small (no more than about 7 feet) Lotus plants native to India that people use for their flower gardens today.

11. For example, the Zondervan NIV Study Bible, Grand Rapids, Michigan, (1985–2002 Fully revised Study Bible notes), p. 774, text note on Job 40:15 says, "Possibly the hippopotamus or the elephant." In a further end to justify this, they suggest the *tail* might be a "trunk" in Job 40:17 in a text note — yet the word for tail is זָנָב *zanab* and means *tails, end, or stump* so it is a far stretch to put it as a trunk on the opposite end of the animal.

12. "Look now at the behemoth, which I made along with you; He eats grass like an ox" (Job 40:15).

13. "He moves his tail like a cedar; The sinews of his thighs are tightly knit" (Job 40:17).

about to knock flies and other insects off its back. So, clearly, the hippopotamus and the elephant do not fit the description of the behemoth.

Cedar trees in Scripture, such as the famous cedars of Lebanon, were tall and imposing trees. These trees were considered rigid in their size and powerful in their beauty (e.g., 2 Kings 19:23,[14] Isaiah 2:13[15]). So to compare the swaying motions of such majestic trees to an elephant or hippo tail is completely unwarranted!

Elephant tail

Rather, it makes more sense (biblically and logically) that this tail was more like an imposing sauropod tail. It's much easier to imagine this type of tail "moving like a cedar."

So, was the behemoth a dinosaur? Most likely, yes! (This massive beast fits the context anyway.)

Sauropod tail

---

14. "By your messengers you have reproached the Lord, And said: 'By the multitude of my chariots I have come up to the height of the mountains, To the limits of Lebanon; I will cut down its tall cedars And its choice cypress trees; I will enter the extremity of its borders, To its fruitful forest'" (2 Kings 19:23).

15. "Upon all the cedars of Lebanon that are high and lifted up, And upon all the oaks of Bashan" (Isaiah 2:13).

22

Ancient Dragons in History, Art, and Petroglyphs

Dragons have been the subject of discussion by ancient historians, anatomists and scientists, literature writers, and classic commentators for ages. One can easily find vast numbers of ancient scholars and historians, who discussed and/or made images of dragons — as if they were any other animal.

In the past, dragons were largely believed to be real creatures and commonly associated with other animals. However, as dragon and dinosaurian creatures faded to extinction, comments about them naturally faded. In fact, only over the past 200 years have dragons been relegated to the realm of myth.

This chapter is by no means exhaustive when it comes to references (there are obviously too many to list!). But let's at least examine some examples of dragons that can easily be verified from the pages of history, starting with these:

1. "But according to accounts from Phrygia there are Drakones (Dragon-Serpents] in Phrygia too, and these grow to a length of sixty feet."[1]

2. "Africa produces elephants....But it is India that produces the largest, as well as the dragon."[2]

---

1. Aelian (ca. A.D. 220), *De Natura Animalium*, https://www.theoi.com/Thaumasios/Dra-konesPhrygioi.html.
2. Pliny (ca. A.D. 70) Natural History, Book 8, Chapter 11, https://annonetheelephant. com/2012/05/01/pliny-on-elephants-and-dragons/. See also another older translation here: https://archive.org/details/plinysnaturalhis00plinrich/page/16/mode/2up .

3. "Even the Egyptians, whom we laugh at, deified animals solely on the score of some utility which they derived from them; for instance, the ibis, being a tall bird with stiff legs and a long horny beak, destroys a great quantity of snakes: it protects Egypt from plague, by killing and eating the flying serpents that are brought from the Libyan desert by the south west wind, and so preventing them from harming the natives by their bite while alive and their stench when dead."[3]

4. "Among Egyptian birds, the variety of which is countless, the ibis is sacred, harmless, and beloved for the reason that by carrying the eggs of serpents to its nestlings for food it destroys and makes fewer of those destructive pests. These same birds meet winged armies of snakes which issue from the marches of Arabia, producing deadly poisons, before they leave their own lands."[4]

5. Gilgamesh, hero of an ancient Babylonian epic, killed a huge dragon named Khumbaba/Humbaba in a cedar forest.[5]

6. "The dragon, when it eats fruit, swallows endive-juice; it has been seen in the act."[6]

These references are just some examples of ancient historians and writers clearly describing dragons as real creatures. In these types of first-hand accounts, dragons are normally described in the context of other types of animals that still live today. Some historians even describe the fiery flying serpents as real creatures in regions that are referenced in the Old Testament (e.g., Numbers 21:6–8[7]; Deuteronomy 8:15[8]; Isaiah

---

3. Marcus Tullius Cicero (ca. 45 B.C.), *De Natura Deorum*, I, 36, https://penelope.uchicago. edu/Thayer/E/Roman/Texts/Cicero/de_Natura_Deorum/1B*.html.
4. Ammianus Marcellius (ca. A.D. 380), *Res Gestae*, 22, 15:25–26a, http://penelope.uchicago. edu/Thayer/E/Roman/Texts/Ammian/22*.html.
5. The Epic of Gilgamesh, http://www.ancienttexts.org/library/mesopotamian/gilgamesh/.
6. Aristotle, *Historia Animalium*, http://etext.virginia.edu/etcbin/toccer-new2?id=AriHian. xml&images=images/modeng&data=/texts/english/modeng/parsed&tag=public&part=9&- division=div2 (accessed June 14, 2013).
7. "So the LORD sent fiery serpents among the people, and they bit the people; and many of the people of Israel died. Therefore the people came to Moses, and said, 'We have sinned, for we have spoken against the LORD and against you; pray to the LORD that He take away the serpents from us.' So Moses prayed for the people. Then the LORD said to Moses, 'Make a fiery serpent, and set it on a pole; and it shall be that everyone who is bitten, when he looks at it, shall live'" (Numbers 21:6–8).
8. "who led you through that great and terrible wilderness, in which were fiery serpents and scorpions and thirsty land where there was no water; who brought water for you out of the flinty rock" (Deuteronomy 8:15).

14:29,[9] 30:6[10]) and point out the *winged* nature of these flying serpents. These historical accounts are a great confirmation of the biblical text.

Moreover, classic Bible commentators often spoke of dragons as real creatures. Here's just a small sample of their writings on the subject:

1. Dr. John Gill wrote, "Of these creatures, both land and sea dragons (see Gill on Micah 1:8; see Gill on Malachi 1:3); Pliny says the dragon has no poison in it; yet, as Dalechamp, in his notes on that writer observes, he in many places prescribes remedies against the bite of the dragon; but Heliodorus expressly speaks of some archers, whose arrows were infected with the poison of dragons; and Leo Africanus says, the Atlantic dragons are exceeding poisonous: and yet other writers besides Pliny have asserted that they are free from poison. It seems the dragons of Greece are without, but not those of Africa and Arabia; and to these Moses has respect, as being well known to him."[11]

2. John Calvin stated, "Then he says, he has swallowed me like a dragon. It is a comparison different from the former, but yet very suitable; for dragons are those who devour a whole animal; and this is what the Prophet means. Though these comparisons do not in everything agree, yet as to the main thing they are most appropriate, even to show that God suffered his people to be devoured, as though they had been exposed to the teeth of a lion or a bear, or as though they had been a prey to a dragon. "[12]

Even the artwork for John Calvin's commentary for Genesis (when translated from Latin to English in A.D. 1578) included images of dragons on the upper right of the cover artwork such as the one on the following page.

3. Charles Spurgeon, when speaking of London, said, "We are not sure that Nineveh and Babylon were as great as this metropolis, but they certainly might have rivaled it, and yet there is nothing left of it, and

---

9. "Do not rejoice, all you of Philistia, Because the rod that struck you is broken; For out of the serpent's roots will come forth a viper, And its offspring will be a fiery flying serpent" (Isaiah 14:29).

10. "The burden against the beasts of the South. Through a land of trouble and anguish, From which came the lioness and lion, The viper and fiery flying serpent, They will carry their riches on the backs of young donkeys, And their treasures on the humps of camels, To a people who shall not profit" (Isaiah 30:6).

11. John Gill, Commentary notes Deuteronomy 32:33, https://www.biblestudytools.com/commentaries/gills-exposition-of-the-bible/deuteronomy-32-33.html.

12. John Calvin, Commentary notes Jeremiah 51:34; https://www.bibliaplus.org/en/commentaries/3/john-calvins-bible-commentary/jeremiah/51/34.

the dragon and the owl dwell in what was the very center of commerce and civilization."[13]

4. John Trapp stated, "Anger is a short madness; it is a leprosy breaking out of a burning, and renders a man unfit for civil society; for his unruly passions cause the climate where he lives to be like the torrid zone, too hot for any to live near him. The dog days continue with him all the year long; he rageth, and eateth firebrands, so that every man that will provide for his own safety must flee from him, as from a nettling, dangerous and unsociable creature, fit to live alone as dragons and wild beasts, or to be looked on only through a grate, as they; where, if they will do mischief, they may do it to themselves only."[14]

5. Church fathers, on Philip killing a dragon in Hierapolis, stated, "And as Philip was thus speaking, behold, also John entered into the city like one of their fellow-citizens; and moving about in the street, he asked: Who are these men, and why are they punished? And they say to him: It cannot be that thou art of our city, and askest about these men, who have wronged many: for they have shut up our gods, and by their magic have cut off both the serpents and the dragons."[15]

There are a host of other quotations from leading church leaders who often spoke of dragons as real creatures, not questioning their reality. But the point is already made: people of the past repeatedly believed dragons were real, just like any other animal.

In fact, there are examples from all over the world on virtually every continent — except Antarctica (for obvious reasons!). Here are just some examples.

---

13. C.H. Spurgeon, "A Basket of Summer Fruit" (sermon, Exeter Hall, London, England, October 28, 1860).

14. John Trapp, *Complete Commentary*, s.v. Proverbs 22:24, http://www.studylight.org/com/jtc/view.cgi?bk=19&ch=22 (accessed June 14, 2013).

15. The Acts of Philip, *Of the Journeyings of Philip the Apostle: From the Fifteenth Acts Until the End, and Among Them the Martyrdom,* http://archive.org/stream/apocryphalgospel00edin/apocryphalgospel00edin_djvu.txt (accessed June 14, 2013).

Australia

In the far north of Queensland, Australia, Aborigines from the Kuku Yalanji tribe described and painted a sea and lake monster that looked surprisingly like a plesiosaur.[16]

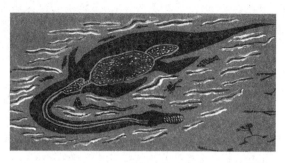

Babylon, Middle East/Asia

Babylon is the heart of early civilization after the Flood. A famous entrance called the Ishtar Gate was built by Nebuchadnezzar II (a powerful ruler during the Israelites' Babylonian exile). This gate displays a reptilian creature with four legs, standing upright on its hips like a dinosaur.

China, Asia

Chinese dragons, well-known throughout the world, even appear on China's twelve-year calendar cycle. Eleven of these animals are common today (dog, rat, monkey, etc.), so why assume that the twelfth (a dragon) was mythological? *The Travels of Marco Polo* describes some of these long and lanky "serpents," which included short legs and claws. He claimed the Chinese would use special methods to kill these dragons. Some of the dragons' body parts were used for medicinal purposes, and others were eaten as a delicacy.[17]

Egypt, Africa/Middle East

Herodotus, an ancient Greek writer, records in *The Histories*, "There is a place in Arabia [modern Egypt], situated very near the city of Buto, to which I went, on hearing of some winged serpents; and when I arrived there, I saw bones and spines of serpents, in such quantities as it would be impossible to

---

16. Rebecca Driver, Answers in Genesis, December 1, 1998, https://answersingenesis.org/dinosaurs/humans/australias-aborigines-did-they-see-dinosaurs/.
17. Marco Polo, (ca. A.D. 1300th Century) *The Travels of Marco Polo, XLVII* — The Province of Karazan and its great Serpents, p. 160, for example, https://ia902704.us.archive.org/26/items/travelsofmarcopo00polo/travelsofmarcopo00polo.pdf.

describe. The form of the serpent is like that of the water snake; but he has wings without feathers, and as like as possible to the wings of a bat."[18]

North Africa, Africa

The Roman historian Cassius Dio recounted how a Roman army once killed a dragon. The original fragment from Book 11 of his *Roman History*, now lost, was repeated by John of Damascus (A.D. ~676–749), in his book *On Dragons and Ghosts*: "One day, when Regulus, a Roman consul, was fighting against Carthage, a dragon suddenly crept up and settled behind the wall of the Roman army. The Romans killed it by order of Regulus, skinned it and sent the hide to the Roman senate. When the dragon's hide, as Dio says, was measured by order of the senate, it happened to be, amazingly, one hundred and twenty feet long, and the thickness was fitting to the length."[19]

Sweden/Denmark, Europe

The epic Anglo-Saxon historical poem *Beowulf* (ca. A.D. 495–583) tells how the title character of Scandinavia killed a dragon named Grendel and its supposed mother, as well as a fiery flying serpent.

A depiction of baryonyx
creativecommons.org/licenses/by-sa/3.0/. Wikipedia. 2022.

Interestingly, in the ancient Anglo-Saxon account, the dragon called Grendel was known to have a heavy claw on its finger, yet had a fairly small arm.[20] (Beowulf was famous for ripping the arm off of this dragon.) Correspondingly, we have a dinosaur with smaller arms (whose remains are found in Europe) called *baryonyx*, which literally means "heavy claw!" Its arms are

18. Niki Gamm, "The Great Birds of Middle Eastern Legend: Myths or Reality?" *Huttiyet Daily News*, https://www.hurriyetdailynews.com/the-great-birds-of-middle-eastern-legend-myths-or-reality-25445.

19. "St. John of Damascus on Dragons," Classical Christianity, https://classicalchristianity.com/2011/12/31/st-john-of-damascus-on-dragons/.

20. Beowulf, https://www.gutenberg.org/files/16328/16328-h/16328-h.htm.

actually smaller too! The common descriptions of Grendel and baryonyx are strikingly similar.

The Anglo-Saxon epic poem *Beowulf* describes three encounters Beowulf, king of the Geats (Gothenburg, Sweden, today), has with three creatures. The last one, encountered in Sweden, is a fiery flying serpent that lived underground and came out only at certain times. The injuries from this battle led to Beowulf's death.

England, Europe

Bishop Bell, who died in 1496, is buried in the foundation of the famous Carlisle Cathedral. The ornate brass engravings around the grave show several animals, some of which appear to be dinosaurs, like a longneck sauropod and a horned ceratopsian.

Brass engraving from Bell's grave

Wissington/Wiston Dragon

Bishop Bell's grave

The Wissington/Wiston Dragon was painted inside of St. Mary's Church in the A.D. 1300s. Apparently, the painting was of a dragon killed not far from the building in the neighboring creek. This author had a chance to visit the church and see the actual image on the wall. You couldn't miss it — it was huge!

Peru, South America

Peru is known for dragon and dinosaur-like creatures in their pottery and other artifacts. For example, the Museum of the Nation displays a dragon-like dinosaur on a piece of pottery attributed to the Moche culture (A.D. 400–1100).

Utah, North America

Several petroglyphs (etchings in stone) resemble air or land dragons, such as one in San Rafael Swell, which looks similar to a *Pteranodon* or *Pterodactyl,* and one in Natural Bridges National Monument, which looks similar to a sauropod.

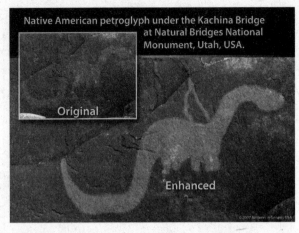
Native American petroglyph under the Kachina Bridge at Natural Bridges National Monument, Utah, USA.
Original
Enhanced

Though these images stir up controversy on the secular side, they are still great resources.[21]

There were numerous dragon *slayers* in history as well. To not belabor the point, here's a short table that lists just some of their names, dates, and locations:

Table 1: Short Table of Dragon Slayers and Capturers[22]

	Slayer/Capturer	Approximate Date	Place
1	Martha of Tarascon	A.D. 48–70	Tarasque
2	Apostles Philip and Barnabas	Before A.D. 70	Hierapolis
3	St. George	A.D. 250-300	North Africa
4	St. Sylvester I	A.D. 300	Italy
5	Sigurd	Likely before A.D. 400–500[23]	Northern Europe
6	Beowulf	A.D. 400–500	Denmark, Sweden
7	Tristan	Possibly A.D. 700	British Isles

And here's a (relatively) short table that lists just some of the past dragon occurrences, dates, and locations (in no specific order):

21. For example see: Ishmael Abrahams, Kachina Bridge Dinosaur Petroglyph, Answers in Genesis, March 8, 2011, https://answersingenesis.org/dinosaurs/humans/kachina-bridge-dinosaur-petroglyph/.

22. Bibliography for this table includes *The Golden Legend,* various texts of the church fathers, *Encyclopædia Britannica, Beowulf, Volsunga Saga,* and several others.

23. Although the more complete account of Sigurd and the dragon is discussed in the 13th century document called *Volsunga Saga,* Sigurd is mentioned in the Beowulf account, so it must have preceded it.

Table 2: Short Table of Dragon References

	Approximate Date	Event (Who/What)	Reference
1	Late A.D. 1800s	Tombstone Epitaph	Found in the Desert, *The Tombstone Epitaph*, April 1890, Tombstone, Arizona
2	A.D. 400–500s	Beowulf and Grendel, Grendel's mother, and a flying serpent	Beowulf[24]
3	A.D. 250–300s	Saint George slays a dragon	*Legenda Aurea* by Jacobus de Voragine[25]
4	A.D. 1800s	Leicestershire Museum and Art Gallery dragon	Flooring at the entrance[26]
5	A.D. 1600s	Athanasius Kircher's dragon	Mundus Subterraneus
6	400s B.C.	Herodotus's fiery winged serpents	Histories[27]
7	A.D. Mid 700s	John of Damascus on dragons (on Lucius Cassius Dio's dragon from the A.D. 200s)	The Works of St. John Damascus
8	A.D. 1200s	Marco Polo's dragons	The Travels of Marco Polo
9	A.D. 800[28]	Welch Red Dragon	Historia Brittonium
10	Early A.D. 1900s	Sea serpents	Encyclopedia Britannia, entry under sea serpents, 1902[29]

24. https://www.gutenberg.org/files/16328/16328-h/16328-h.htm.
25. https://sourcebooks.fordham.edu/basis/goldenlegend/GL-vol3-george.asp.
26. This happens to be the museum of Alfred Russell Wallace who competed with Darwin to publish an evolutionary worldview. Darwin's popularity far surpassed Wallace, though Wallace was a famous evolutionist in his and Darwin's day.
27. https://www.gutenberg.org/files/2707/2707-h/2707-h.htm.
28. The flag of Wales is an ancient flag and symbol of the Welsh people. The flag was officially recognized in 1959 as the national symbol. The Red Dragon of Wales has been a long part of their history stretching at least 1,000 years. Records depict it as far back as A.D. 600. The dragon represented a strong leader, reflecting the strength of a dragon, hence its use in flags and coats of arms throughout the region.
29. Although they acknowledged them as real in the past, the encyclopedia writers were attempting to explain modern circumstantial claims away.

11	A.D. 1000s	Bayeux Tapestry	Bayeux Tapestry
12	Intertestamental	Bel, Daniel, and the Dragon	Apocryphal piece *Bel and the Dragon*
13	A.D. 1100–1300s	Dragon Petroglyph	Wupatki National Park, Arizona; Lacey and Hodge[30]
14	A.D. 900–1299	Carved Dragon Petroglyph	Embden, Maine; Lacey and Hodge[31]
15	A.D. 400–1100	Moche Culture Dragon	Museo de la Nación, Lima, Peru[32]
16	Pre A.D. 1500s	Legitimate Ica Stones[33]	Swift[34]
17	Pre-Colombian	Black Dragon Canyon Pterosaur	San Raphael Swell, Utah; Johnson[35]
18	A.D. 800–1400s	Cambodian Muzzled Stegosaurs	Cole[36] and Woetzel[37]
19	Late A.D. 1400s	Carlisle Cathedral brass dinosaur etchings	Tomb of Bishop Bell, Carlisle, England

30. Troy Lacey and Bodie Hodge, "Humans with Dinosaurs Evidence," *Answers in Depth*, October 23, 2020, https://answersingenesis.org/dinosaurs/humans/humans-with-dinosaurs-evidence/.

31. Troy Lacey and Bodie Hodge, "Humans with Dinosaurs Evidence," *Answers in Depth*, October 23, 2020, https://answersingenesis.org/dinosaurs/humans/humans-with-dinosaurs-evidence/.

32. Bodie Hodge, "The Dragons of Peru," *Answers Magazine*, October-December Issue, 2010, pp. 36-37, https://answersingenesis.org/dinosaurs/dragon-legends/the-dragons-of-peru/.

33. Ica Stones has stirred up controversy since the 1970s when a local began making stones to sell to unsuspecting buyers. These fraudulent stones are not to be confused with the good ones. Older ones from graves and those documented long before this in the Ica Museum are legitimate. It was usually easy to spot the differences. Old Ica Stones were oxidized and had desert varnish due to age weather sitting, where new ones were obviously newly etched and could easily be seen. New ones also contained a few faulty images of dinosaurs due the misconceptions due to artistic views that were popularized in that era of time (e.g., the T-rex standing almost straight up dragging its tail, etc.).

34. Dennis Swift, *Secrets of the Ica Stones and Nazca Lines*, Dennis Swift Publishing, ASIN: B000QCQ1RS, 2006.

35. Bill Johnson, "Thunderbirds," *Creation*, Vol. 24, No. 2 (March 2002): 28-32, https://answersingenesis.org/dinosaurs/dragon-legends/thunderbirds/.

36. Kenneth Cole, "Evidence of Dinosaurs at Angkor," *Answers in Genesis*, January 15, 2007, https://answersingenesis.org/dinosaurs/humans/evidence-of-dinosaurs-at-angkor/.

37. David Woetzel, "The Stegosaur Engravings at Ta Prohm," *Answers Research Journal*, 10(2017): 213–220, September 13, 2017, https://answersresearchjournal.org/stegosaur-engravings-at-ta-prohm/.

20	A.D. 1900s	*Dragon* Entry: New Century Dictionary	*The New Century Dictionary* (New York, NY: P.F. Collier & Son Corporation, New York, 1946), p. 45
22	Prior to A.D. 1600	Kachina Bridge	Utah's Testimony to Catastrophe[38]
23	Varies	Hosts of Dragons in the Anglo-Saxon records	Bill Cooper, The Early History of Man — Part 4. Living Dinosaurs from Anglo-Saxon and Other Early Records, *CEN Technical Journal*, Vol. 6(1), 1992, p. 49–66.
24	1300s	Wissington/Wiston Dragon	St. Mary Church, Wissington, Suffolk
25	Pre A.D. 1600s	Piasa (original) scaly flying monster that attacked the Illini tribe and lived in a cave	Journal of Father Jacques Marquette, 1673
27	A.D. 800–1000s	Mayan Hadrosaur	Vance Nelson (VN) p. 34–37
28	A.D. 800–1000s	Mayan Deinonychus Mural	Ibid. p 38–39
29	A.D. 500–1000s	Wari Protoceratops Vessel	Ibid. p. 44–45
30	A.D. 1200–1400s	Chancay Figurines	Ibid. p. 46–49
31	A.D. 1500s	Leonardo Da Vinci's Dragon	Lacey and Hodge[39]
32	From A.D. 600s	Gloucester Cathedral dragons	Still accessible today

38. Professor Andy McIntosh, "Utah's Testimony to Catastrophe," Answers in Genesis, May 8, 2007, https://answersingenesis.org/geology/natural-features/utahs-testimony-to-catastrophe/; see also: Ishmael Abrahams, "Kachina Bridge Dinosaur Petroglyph," Answers in Genesis, March 8, 2011, https://answersingenesis.org/dinosaurs/humans/kachina-bridge-dinosaur-petroglyph/.

39. Troy Lacey and Bodie Hodge, "Humans with Dinosaurs Evidence," *Answers in Depth*, October 23, 2020, https://answersingenesis.org/dinosaurs/humans/humans-with-dinosaurs-evidence/.

33	From A.D. 1100s	Bath Cathedral dragons	Still accessible today
34	From A.D. 1000s	Leicester Cathedral dragons	Still accessible today
35	From A.D. 1200s	Nigersaurus in St. David's Cathedral, Wales	Brian Thomas[40]
36	Medieval	Nothosaurus in the Saint George Tapestry, Barcelona, Spain	Brian Thomas[41]
37	A.D. 1550	Tapestries of Sigismund II Augustus Dragons	Philip Robinson[42]
38	A.D. 1100–1300	Metropolitan Museum of Art Dragons (1) Valve of a Mirror Case; (2) Chalice Brother Bertinus, (3) Bowl of a Drinking Cup	The Metropolitan Museum of Art[43]

Historically, there is little doubt that people viewed dragons as real creatures. So the belief that dragons are a myth is a modern idea, which only came about after dragons had largely gone extinct.

Imagine if we had not enacted the Endangered Species Act in 1973. Animals like elephants, rhinoceros, tigers, condors, lions, cheetahs, wolves, bears, hippos, owls, eagles, and hosts of other creatures could also be extinct. If that happened, people would probably question the real existence of these creatures as well.

Here's the main takeaway: just because we don't find certain creatures anymore doesn't automatically mean they are a myth. Rather, because this is a sin-cursed world (due to the curse in Genesis 3), real animals, including dragons, sometimes go extinct.

If you like this type of research (and I hope you do!) there are others who are spearheading much of this research, and I want to encourage them

40. Brian Thomas, "Dragon Art Defies Millions of Years," *Acts & Facts,* 51(2) March–April, 2022, p. 14–17.

41. Ibid.

42. Philip Robinson, "Dragons on Noah's Ark," *Creation* 39(1):14–15, January 2017.

43. "Valve of a Mirror Case," https://www.metmuseum.org/art/collection/search/471283; "Chalice," Brother Bertinus, https://www.metmuseum.org/toah/artist/brother-bertinus/; "Bowl of a Drinking Cup," https://www.metmuseum.org/art/collection/search/471268.

in their pursuits. Although I do not agree with all their interpretations, I still suggest you check out at least some of their work, starting with these researchers and initiatives:

- Vance Nelson loves this type of research and a sampling of his work can be found in his book *Dire Dragons*[44] in which he has tracked down hosts of accounts, figurines, and petroglyphs (think of etchings, drawings, and painting).

- Dave Woetzel, who runs *Genesis Park*,[45] is also on the prowl for such evidence that confirms Scripture regarding dinosaurs and dragons.

- Brian Thomas, a friend from the Institute for Creation Research, enjoys looking into and publishing on these types of evidences.

- *Historical Dinosaurs*[46] is a book by Russel Tingley researching many of these dinosaur-like accounts and putting them into one volume.

- Lastly, I recommend the Creation Research Society's iDINO and iDINO II research initiatives.[47]

---

44. Vance Nelson, *Dire Dragons* (Canada: Untold Secrets of Planet Earth Publishing Company, 2018).

45. https://www.genesispark.com/.

46. Russel Tingley, *Historic Dinosaurs* (San Jose, CA: Terrordactyl Studios, 2015).

47. https://www.creationresearch.org/idino-investigation-of-dinosaur-intact-natural-osteo-tissue/.

23

Are There Any Human and Dinosaur Fossils Buried Together?

This question is intriguing (in case you didn't notice). Why? Because this question has huge implications on the evolutionary (humanistic) narrative, which says humans and dinosaurs (supposedly) never existed together. That is, finding human and dinosaur fossils buried together in the same rock layer would provide a devastating piece of evidence that could logically be used to argue against the secular worldview and destroy their religious narrative.

But note that the lack of finding humans and dinosaurs buried together doesn't actually affect either the biblical or secular worldview. It's important to understand that biblical creation is true, regardless of such a find. Humans and crocodiles, for instance, have never been found buried together in the same rock layer. Based on this evidence, do evolutionary ("long age") believers argue that humans and crocodiles never lived together? Of course not!

Biblical creationists, trusting in God's infallible Word as their starting point, know that humans and dinosaurs lived together in the past, because God, the perfect eyewitness to history, said that He created man and land animals, which includes dinosaurs, on Day 6 (Genesis 1:24–31) and that settles the issue.

But those who reject the plain reading of the Bible, such as many non-Christians and biblical compromisers (those who try to mix Christianity with the secular view of origins), believe the bulk of rock and fossil layers were laid down slowly over many eons of time (based on uniformitarian assumptions), thus representing millions/billions of years of earth history.

Ultimately, these beliefs fall in line with the secular humanistic religious belief that humans and dinosaurs are separated by millions of years.

Do Fossil Rock Layers Represent Many Eons of Time?

No — most of the layers are largely a result of the global Flood, as described by God in Genesis 6–8, which occurred over the course of about a year.

This belief that rock layers were gradually laid down over millions of years doesn't come *from* the Bible but actually from sources *outside* the Bible — man's ideas (supposed secular history). Rock layers that contain dinosaur fossils are generally lower (deeper) than the layers with human fossils.[1] Therefore, long-age believers interpret this observation as dinosaurs dying out millions of years before humans "appeared" in history.

Old-earth proponents (those who believe in the "millions of years" story) persistently say that if humans and dinosaurs lived together, then their fossils should be found in the same layers. But, logically speaking, this is actually a very odd (and fallacious) claim. Think about it, what are the odds of humans being buried with every single thing that co-existed with them at any given point in history? As a simple (hypothetical) test, if there was a global flood today (which is impossible to happen by God's decree in Genesis 9:11[2]), what are the odds you and a Saola (a rare mammal) would be buried together? Probably very low!

Since no one has found definitive evidence of humans and dinosaurs in the same rock layers (Cretaceous, Jurassic, and Triassic),[3] old-earth proponents, in

---

1. Note that any layer could be exposed at the surface in various places around the world. But when layers are together, certain ones tend to be on top of certain other layers. This is where the general stacking comes from. Cretaceous rock layer, for example, is higher than Permian rock layer, which is higher than Cambrian rock layer, when found together. Yet that doesn't mean all layers have to be represented in an area either — there are often missing layers in various places, and inversions, and so on.

2. "Thus I establish My covenant with you: Never again shall all flesh be cut off by the waters of the flood; never again shall there be a flood to destroy the earth" (Genesis 9:11).

3. Note that if a dinosaur is found in a rock layer that isn't "supposed to have dinosaurs," then that rock layer (only in that local area) normally gets *redefined* to be a rock layer corresponding to that dinosaur. For example, if a dinosaur typically seen in Cretaceous rock is found in Permian rock, then that Permian rock layer (only in that local area) is redefined to be Cretaceous rock.

general, say that humans and dinosaurs are separated by millions of years of time and, therefore, didn't live together. But *why don't we find human fossils with dinosaur fossils if they lived together?*

The fact is that just because certain creatures lived at the same time doesn't necessarily mean they will be buried together, especially if they are living in different parts of the world. We tend to find human fossils, and their remains, in layers that most creationists largely consider post-Flood. Most of these finds are probably from burial or other means of disarticulation (single bones for example) due to post-Flood catastrophes *since* the Flood, along with the scattering of humans from Babel (Genesis 11).

It is true that human and dinosaur fossils have yet to be found in the same layers. But does that mean long-age believers are correct in stating that dinosaurs died out *millions of years* before humans "came into existence"? Not at all. Let's investigate this question further.

Were All the Human Pre-Flood Remains Completely Obliterated so That No Evidence Will Be Left?

This common argument is derived from biblical passages, such as Genesis 6:7,[4] 7:4,[5] and 7:23,[6] where God says He will "blot out" man and every living thing from the face of the earth, using the global Flood. After a lengthy study, Fouts and Wise present a strong case that the Hebrew word māhâ (machah), translated as "blot out" or "destroy," does not mean to completely obliterate something, leaving no evidence behind. They say:

> Although māhâ is properly translated "blot out," "wipe," or even "destroy," it is not to be understood to refer to the complete obliteration of something without evidence remaining. In every Biblical use of māhâ where it is possible to determine the fate of the blotted, wiped, or destroyed, the continued existence of something is terminated, but evidence may indeed remain of the previous existence and/or the blotting event itself. Even the theological

---

4. "So the LORD said, 'I will destroy man whom I have created from the face of the earth, both man and beast, creeping thing and birds of the air, for I am sorry that I have made them'" (Genesis 6:7).

5. "For after seven more days I will cause it to rain on the earth forty days and forty nights, and I will destroy from the face of the earth all living things that I have made" (Genesis 7:4).

6. "So He destroyed all living things which were on the face of the ground: both man and cattle, creeping thing and bird of the air. They were destroyed from the earth. Only Noah and those who were with him in the ark remained alive" (Genesis 7:23).

consideration of the "blotting out" of sin suggests that evidence
usually remains (e.g., consequences, scars, sin nature, etc.).[7]

Bear in mind that God didn't just say that He would blot out man, but also
animals. And yet, we find innumerable animals fossilized in Flood sediment.

So, in light of this, it is highly possible that human fossils from the
Flood do still exist but simply haven't been found yet. To answer this further,
we need to consider the following points: the estimated number of humans
before the Flood, the likelihood of their remains being preserved and fossilized, their distribution, and the amount of Flood sediment.

Pre-Flood Population

Genesis doesn't give extensive family size and growth information prior to
the Flood, so any estimates for the pre-Flood human population are based
on very little information. We know that Noah was in the tenth generation
of his line, when the Flood occurred about 1,650 years after creation. Genesis also indicates that in Noah's lineage, children were being born when their
fathers were between the ages of 65 (Enoch to Methuselah) to well over 500
(when Noah began to have his three sons).

We know Adam's descendants, from Adam to Noah, normally lived for
about 900 years.[8] But we can't be certain everyone in this line lived for that
many years. Nor can we be certain the frequency and number of children
that were born nor their death rates.

Yet, despite this lack of information, some estimates have still been
done. For instance, Tom Pickett gives a range of about 5 to 17 billion people.[9] This is based on various modern population growth rates and assuming
16–22 generations existed prior to the Flood. But recall that Noah was in
the tenth generation, so this estimate is likely well beyond the higher end of
the population maximum. Henry Morris had more conservative estimates
as low as 235 million pre-Flood people. Using modern population growth
rates, he calculated about 3 billion pre-Flood people.[10]

---

7. David Fouts and Kurt Wise, "Blotting Out and Breaking Up: Miscellaneous Hebrew
   Studies in Geocatastrophism," Proceedings of the Fourth International Conference on
   Creationism, Creation Science Fellowship, Pittsburgh, PA, 1998, p. 219.

8. Ken Ham and Bodie Hodge, gen. eds., *New Answers Book 2* (Green Forest, AR: Master
   Books, Chapter 13, "Ancient Biblical Lifespans: Did Adam Live Over 900 Years?" by Drs.
   Georgia Purdom and David Menton, https://answersingenesis.org/bible-timeline/genealo-
   gy/did-adam-and-noah-really-live-over-900-years/.

9. Tom Pickett, "Population of the PreFlood World," *Lambert Dolphin's Library*, April 8,
   1998, http://www.ldolphin.org/pickett.html.

10. Henry Morris, *Biblical Cosmology and Modern Science* (Grand Rapids, MI: Baker Book
    House, 1970), p. 77–78.

John Morris reports similar ranged estimates of about 350 million pre-Flood people.[11] So, based on these estimates, pre-Flood populations ranged from hundreds of millions to 17 billion people. However, note that these estimates are based on modern trends, where we tend to only have children within the typical child-bearing age window for a woman, which is normally just a few decades (not when she is 80 years old, for example).

But obviously, this limitation wasn't a consideration prior to the Flood when people lived much longer ages (upwards of 900 years old). That is, one didn't need to rush to have children because time was short. Thus, let's remember to exercise caution when applying modern population growth rates to the pre-Flood era.

This author believes these estimates are actually far too high. Let's compare these 10 generations, from Adam to Noah, to the 10 generations of Israelites from their time in Egypt to the time Joshua brought them into the Promised Land. When the Israelites were in Egypt, God gave them explosive population growth just as He promised (Genesis 13:16,[12] 22:17,[13] 26:4;[14] Exodus 1:7,[15] 12,[16] 20[17] with Deuteronomy 1:10,[18] Deuteronomy 10:22,[19] and Nehemiah 9:23[20]).

In only four generations in Egypt, they were living contemporaneously with the tenth generation and beyond. For example, Moses, who was part of the fourth generation in Egypt on his father's side (third generation by his

---

11. John Morris, *The Young Earth* (Green Forest, AR: Master Books, Eleventh Printing, May 2002), p. 71.
12. "And I will make your descendants as the dust of the earth; so that if a man could number the dust of the earth, then your descendants also could be numbered" (Genesis 13:16).
13. "Blessing I will bless you, and multiplying I will multiply your descendants as the stars of the heaven and as the sand which is on the seashore; and your descendants shall possess the gate of their enemies" (Genesis 22:17).
14. "And I will make your descendants multiply as the stars of heaven; I will give to your descendants all these lands; and in your seed all the nations of the earth shall be blessed" (Genesis 26:4).
15. "But the children of Israel were fruitful and increased abundantly, multiplied and grew exceedingly mighty; and the land was filled with them" (Exodus 1:7).
16. "But the more they afflicted them, the more they multiplied and grew. And they were in dread of the children of Israel" (Exodus 1:12).
17. "Therefore God dealt well with the midwives, and the people multiplied and grew very mighty" (Exodus 1:20).
18. "The LORD your God has multiplied you, and here you are today, as the stars of heaven in multitude" (Deuteronomy 1:10).
19. "Your fathers went down to Egypt with seventy persons, and now the LORD your God has made you as the stars of heaven in multitude" (Deuteronomy 10:22).
20. "You also multiplied their children as the stars of heaven, and brought them into the land which You had told their fathers to go in and possess" (Nehemiah 9:23).

mother Jochebed's side, per Exodus 6:20[21] and Numbers 26:59[22]) lived alongside Joshua, who was part of the tenth generation (1 Chronicles 7:22–27)!

The point is that God gave the Israelites several generations more than normal during this initial period. This was clearly a blessing from God. By the time the Israelites entered the Promised Land, the population had grown to more than 1.2 million people (if you presume there were about the same number of females as males over the age of 20, in Numbers 1 and 2:32[23]). With children and elderly, this number could have been as high as 1.5-2 million.

Of course, we are given no indication that the 10 generations between Adam and Noah were given explosive growth by God though the timeframe is much longer — the key is number of *generations*. In parallel to the line from Adam to Noah, we are also given the pre-Flood lineage from Adam to Namaah through Cain's line of only 8 generations (Genesis 4:17–22).[24] These two lineage standards in Scripture imply slower growth before the Flood.

With that in mind, using the 10 generations from Egypt to Joshua, we can set a maximum number of about 1.5–2 million people before the Flood. But other factors need to also be employed. Like, for instance, we know from Scripture that people, for 120 years prior to the Flood, were continually evil, wicked, violent, and worthy of judgment (e.g., Genesis 6:5–7[25]).

As history notes in evil cultures, sadly, the children usually get the brunt of said evil with atrocities like child sacrifice, abortion, physical abuse (even to the point of death), castrated/sterilized, and so on. So how many children were there for *that last 120 years* leading up to the Flood? If rampant child sacrifice was occurring, how many were still alive? The Bible says there were "men of renown" per Genesis 6:4,[26] which means making a name for

---

21. "Now Amram took for himself Jochebed, his father's sister, as wife; and she bore him Aaron and Moses. And the years of the life of Amram were one hundred and thirty-seven" (Exodus 6:20).

22. "The name of Amram's wife was Jochebed the daughter of Levi, who was born to Levi in Egypt; and to Amram she bore Aaron and Moses and their sister Miriam" (Numbers 26:59).

23. "These are the ones who were numbered of the children of Israel by their fathers' houses. All who were numbered according to their armies of the forces were six hundred and three thousand five hundred and fifty" (Numbers 2:32).

24. Some believe that Namaah was Noah's wife and hence her lineage is given next to Noah's, but the Bible doesn't explicitly say this so we cannot be certain.

25. "Then the LORD saw that the wickedness of man was great in the earth, and that every intent of the thoughts of his heart was only evil continually. And the LORD was sorry that He had made man on the earth, and He was grieved in His heart. So the LORD said, 'I will destroy man whom I have created from the face of the earth, both man and beast, creeping thing and birds of the air, for I am sorry that I have made them'" (Genesis 6:5–7).

26. "The Nephilim were on the earth in those days, and also afterward, when the sons of God came in to the daughters of man and they bore children to them. These were the mighty men who were of old, the men of renown" (Genesis 6:4; ESV).

themselves infamously. Clearly, they had no intention of making a name for their children. They were also considered "mighty men," which has a negative connotation in the context. Again, children likely bore the brunt of this evil.

Since people were exceedingly wicked and violent prior to the Flood, murder was certainly commonplace back then. And with every thought being evil all the time (Genesis 6:5[27]), the murder rate was likely very high.

Consider that the entire world back then may well have been filled with murderers (outside of Noah and his family). If so, this means, on any given day, the entire world's population could be continually cut in half. After 120 years of this mentality, what would have been the resulting population? I suggest the pre-Flood population may have been in serious decline — even from that potential 2 million people.

The bottom line is, prior to the Flood, there may not have been too many people around.

Were All Humans Evenly Distributed in the Flood Sediment?

We know humans tend to live in groups like in towns, villages, or cities. For instance, huge portions of the population today live within 100 miles of the coastline.

Hence, people were probably not evenly distributed before the Flood (this can also be implied from Genesis 4:17[28]). So, if people weren't evenly distributed across the pre-Flood world, then the likelihood of humans being evenly distributed in Flood sediment becomes extremely remote.

How Much Flood Sediment Is There?

John Woodmorappe's studies indicate that there are about 700 million cubic kilometers of Flood sediment, which translates to about 168 million cubic miles of the same.[29] This number actually comes from International Geology Review 24(11), A.B. Ronov, "The Earth's Sedimentary Shell," 1982, pages 1321–1339.

John Morris states that there are about 350 million cubic miles of Flood sediment.[30] However, this number may be high since the total volume of

---

27. "Then the LORD saw that the wickedness of man was great in the earth, and that every intent of the thoughts of his heart was only evil continually" (Genesis 6:5).
28. "And Cain knew his wife, and she conceived and bore Enoch. And he built a city, and called the name of the city after the name of his son — Enoch" (Genesis 4:17).
29. John Woodmorappe, *Studies in Flood Geology* (El Cajon, CA: Institute for Creation Research, 1999), p. 59.
30. J. Morris, *The Young Earth* (Green Forest, AR: Master Books, 2002), 71.

water on the earth is estimated at about 332.5 million cubic miles, according to the U.S. Geological Survey.[31]

Either way, there is a lot of Flood sediment, ranging somewhere between 168–350 million cubic miles. Combine this factor with the smaller percentage of actual pre-Flood humans (being less than 2 million) and it's easy to see why very few humans were candidates for fossilization.

Furthermore, many animals likely started with more than two within their respective kinds. So after about 1,650 years, they were likely in great abundance, thus having a higher likelihood of being fossilized. This is unlike man and woman (Adam and Eve), who started with only two people and reproduced for about 8–10 generations.

What Do We Find in the Fossil Layers?

Since the Flood was a marine (water-based) catastrophe that overtook the land, we would expect marine fossils to be dominant in the fossil record, which is exactly what we find:

- ~95% of all fossils are marine organisms
- ~95% of the remaining 5% are algae, plants/trees
- ~95% of the remaining 0.25% consists of invertebrates, including insects

The remaining 0.0125% are vertebrates, consisting of mostly fish (95% of land vertebrates consist of less than 1 bone, and 95% of mammals fossils are from the *Ice Age* after the Flood).[32]

Also, vertebrates (animals with a backbone) are not as common as other types of life forms. Therefore, we wouldn't expect to find as many in the fossil record. This helps to make sense of these percentages and understand why vertebrates are poorly represented, and even overwhelmed, by marine organisms in the fossil record.

Why Aren't Dinosaurs Intermixed in All the Sediments?

There is a general order, regarding creatures, buried in the fossil layers.[33] Let's think about this logically. Marine creatures, which sat at the bottom of the

---

31. National Ocean Service, "Where Is All of the Earth's Water?" National Oceanic and Atmospheric Administration, 2/26/2021, https://oceanservice.noaa.gov/facts/wherewater.html#:~:text=The%20ocean%20holds%20about%2097%20percent%20of%20the,about%2097%20percent%20is%20found%20in%20the%20ocean.

32. Andrew Snelling, "Where Are All the Human Fossils?" *Creation Magazine* 14(1):28–33, December, 1991; John Morris, *The Young Earth* (Green Forest, AR: Master Books, Eleventh Printing, May 2002), p. 70.

33. The secular world often misinterprets this ordering as an evolutionary onward and upward trend of complexity on their evolutionary tree. Yet extreme complexity is seen at all levels in the fossil layers.

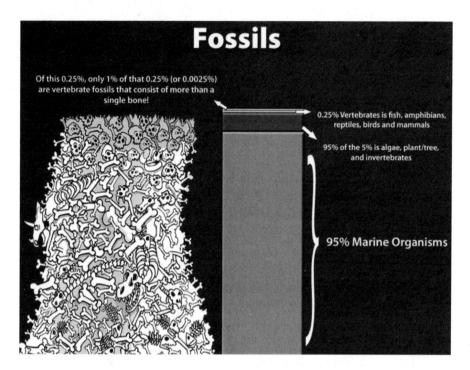

Fossils

Of this 0.25%, only 1% of that 0.25% (or 0.0025%) are vertebrate fossils that consist of more than a single bone!

0.25% Vertebrates is fish, amphibians, reptiles, birds and mammals

95% of the 5% is algae, plant/tree, and invertebrates

95% Marine Organisms

sea when the Flood occurred, had nowhere to go and were likely caught up in the initial sediments from the churning water. Thus, they were among the first things to be covered, buried, and fossilized in sediment.

Here's another aspect to consider, which relates more specifically to the burial order in the fossil record: why are some animals typically buried lower than other animals in the fossil layers if they are all from the same flood?

There are several models that explain why certain animals are buried deeper. Naturally, the things at the lowest level will be buried first at the onset of the Flood, including the things that can't flee or float like shells, bottom dwellers, and marine plants. From here, two of the more popular models (which may also work in conjunction) are the *ecological zonation model* and the *natural sorting power of water model.*

Don't let the names frighten you! *Ecological zonation* basically means that creatures living at different elevations and locations are going to be buried at those respective levels during certain phases within the Flood. At the initial part of the Flood, some animals can naturally flee greater distances (i.e., higher and higher) than other animals — a horse can flee much farther than a mouse, for example.

Simply put, without the technical jargon, things that live at a lower elevation will be buried first and things at a higher elevation will be buried last. For instance, creatures like crocodiles, which live around sea level, will be buried before horses, which normally dwell higher. So, in a general sense, we should expect the burial order to be first bottom-dwelling sea creatures, followed by shallow sea creatures, then coastal creatures, then land creatures, and then finally high hills/mountain creatures. Of course, since the Flood is a water catastrophe, we'd still expect some marine organisms to get mixed into all of it.

With the *natural sorting power of water model,* other scientific laws come into play. Have you ever walked along a beach and noticed that the sand in one spot is initially very fine, and then starts to become more course the farther out into the water you go, which then becomes pebbles, larger rocks, and shells? This is an example of the sorting power of water.

As water moves, it separates things out. This is an amazing property of water (the conjunction of water adhesion to surface-to-weight ratios of things). When water stops moving, things suspended in it begin to settle out of the water as a result of gravity. Even materials, like limestone, were dissolved and precipitated out of the water at certain stages of the Flood (based on the specific temperatures and gasses trapped in the water, like CO_2). This model helps explain why different rock layers have different things that make them up (e.g., sandstone, limestone, etc.), which obviously depended upon the conditions and actions of the water during the Flood and its early aftermath.

Another aspect of this model includes a property of water called buoyancy. In simple terms, how "floatable" is something? Different creatures and plants, depending on its composition, will sink or float at certain rates, or possibly get waterlogged and then sink. Reptiles and amphibians, for instance, tend to sink when they die — they are heavier than water when dead.

Crocodiles, for instance, keep air in their lungs to stay afloat. And after death, as the air starts to come out of their lungs, they begin naturally sinking in the water.

Birds and mammals generally tend to float and are naturally lighter than water. And so, we'd expect them to be higher in any fossil record. Remember how things fossilize? Recall that the primary key is rapid burial with chemical rich watery sediment. So, unlike creatures that sink to the bottom, the ones that float are *far less likely* to become prime candidates for fossilization! Hence, we expect to find more reptiles and amphibians in the rock layers than birds and mammals — and at different levels — even from the same Flood!

God made humans with a physiology similar to mammals. Therefore, we tend to float upon death. So, in contrast to the rapidly buried dinosaurs, which had sunk, most humans likely ended up rotting and decaying (thus, not fossilizing) after death.

And to further reduce the chances of humans getting fossilized, keep in mind that people are resourceful, so it's possible many had grabbed hold of floating things (like debris) and simply affixed themselves to these things, thus allowing them to stay afloat for a period of time. But, of course, this was still a futile attempt to strive against God's judgment, which ultimately caught up to everyone outside the Ark.

There are exceptions, of course, like several marine birds buried in dinosaur rock layers. And, to a lesser extent, there could have also been instances of disarticulation (where certain body parts had become dislodged and sunk). Nonetheless, these are the exceptions, not the general rule for lighter-than-water creatures.

At the same time, these models could both be in play (along with other possible models too). Overall, having dinosaurs living in an area where man isn't (such as at different elevations, for instance) and the sorting power of water, gives good reasons why we shouldn't expect to find humans and dinosaurs buried together.

Let's Think About the Question

Often, people believe that if human bones aren't found with dinosaur bones, then they didn't live together. But as previously noted, this is a clearly fallacious conclusion. Let's instead think properly about this: if human bones aren't found buried with dinosaur bones, it simply means they weren't buried together (at least based on what is found and reported).

As a great example, Coelacanth fossils are found in and below dinosaur rock layers.[34] Yet the evolutionary narrative says the Coelacanth went extinct about 70 million years ago because their fossils are not found after this "time" (based on secular humanistic interpretations of the rock layers).

However, in 1938, living populations were found in the Indian Ocean![35] This example shows that the fossil record is obviously not complete. That is, it is not truly representative of living populations. Remember, we don't find human bones buried with coelacanths either, but we still live together today. And people are even enjoying them for dinner in some parts of the world! This is but one of the many living fossils that illustrates this concept.

If human and dinosaur bones are ever found in the same geologic layers, it would be consistent with the biblical view. But it would be a

---

34. Lynn Dicks, "The Creatures Time Forgot," *New Scientist*, October 23, 1999; 164: (2209), p. 36–39.

35. Rebecca Driver, "Sea Monsters…More Than a Legend?" *Creation Magazine* 19(4):38–42, September 1997, found online here: http://www.answersingenesis.org/creation/v19/i4/sea-monsters.asp.

huge problem for those who accept the secular interpretation of the geologic layers as evidence for millions of years. Because, in the old-earth view, humans aren't supposed to be that "old" or dinosaurs that "young."

Again, as biblical creationists, we don't *require* that human and dinosaur fossils must be found buried together. As previously stated, the biblical view is not affected whether they are found together or not. It's possible that the evidence left behind for humans before the Flood simply has not been found yet, not reported, or misinterpreted. After all, very little Flood evidence has actually been sifted through.

24

What Is Going on with the "Human and Dinosaur Footprints" (Ichnites) Debate?

The subject of human and dinosaur footprints being found together is a "hot button" debate. Why? Because, from a secular perspective, if human and dinosaur footprints are found together, the timeline of the secular "long-age" worldview would be disrupted. Humans and dinosaurs are supposed to be separated by millions of years (unless one views birds as dinosaurs!) in that religion.

From the Christian viewpoint, finding human and dinosaur footprints together is *not* necessary for the truthfulness of the biblical worldview, but it would be another *confirmation* of the timeline of biblical events. Nevertheless, there are people on both sides of this debate who have a strong vested interest in this topic due to their worldview.

Fossil Footprints from the Flood

The word *Ichnite*, or *Ichnolite*, comes from the Latinized form (*ikhnos*) of the Greek word that means track or footprint. When *ichn-* is combined with *–ite*, it means mineralized or fossilized. Thus, *ichnology* is the *study of fossil footprints*.

We find hosts of fossil footprints throughout the rock record, laid down by the Flood. By the 150th day of the Flood, however, there were no new footprints and trackways from land-dwelling, air-breathing animals as the Bible says:

> And all flesh died that moved on the earth: birds and cattle and beasts and every creeping thing that creeps on the earth, and every man. All in whose nostrils was the breath of the spirit of life, all

that was on the dry land, died. So He destroyed all living things which were on the face of the ground: both man and cattle, creeping thing and bird of the air. They were destroyed from the earth. Only Noah and those who were with him in the ark remained alive. And the waters prevailed on the earth one hundred and fifty days (Genesis 7:21–24).

Since all land-dwelling creatures died by the 150th day, there were no new footprints or trackways at this point — until after the Flood. Some initial erosion, after the 150th day of the Flood, when the waters were retreating from the land, washed away some of the top layers of sediment that had been deposited at the end stages of the inundation of the Flood. This exposed the layers below that have footprints, thus allowing them to be found near the surface in many parts of the world.

This runoff of water and sediment washed away some of the sediments in the uppermost layers (post-Day 150 layers) that were devoid of footprints. Though some recessional rock layers were formed during this phase of the Flood, there was also a mixture of some being eroded and some being formed. This was the transitional stage of the Flood as mountains rose and valleys sank (e.g., Psalm 104:8–9,[1] coupled with Genesis 9:11–16). Some of the sediment from those layers that washed away were deposited on top of other layers at a lower elevation (i.e., valleys).

Out-Of-Place Footprints

Virtually everyone agrees that there are human footprints found in rock layers where there are "supposed to be *none*." Yes, even the secular side agrees, even though it is a challenge to their worldview, specifically the long-age timeline.

In the paganized secular view, these trackways of human prints are *close enough* in their timeline to be reinterpreted as "ape-like" ancestors of humans, "aliens" (yes, strangely, some actually believe these were alien creatures), or some other alleged creatures, all of which supposedly with feet and stride similar to humans. In this chapter, we'll evaluate some of the popular footprints, such as the Laetoli Footprints and the Cretan Footprints, before we dive into the alleged human and dinosaur ichnites.

Laetoli Footprints

In 1978, a team led by Mary Leakey (an evolutionist) discovered a trail of human footprints in the Laetoli site in Tanzania, Africa, which consists of about 70 human ichnites for about 88 feet (~27 meters). The tracks are

---

1. "The mountains rose, the valleys sank down to the place that you appointed for them. You set a boundary that they may not pass, so that they might not again cover the earth."

preserved in volcanic ash, along with other critter footprints.

Why the big deal? In the secular story, this ash bed is supposedly *3.6 million* years old. Whereas, from a biblical viewpoint, these tracks were made post-Flood, post-Babel (likely descendants of Noah's grandson Cush, who inhabited much of that area[2]). During this time, people were migrating around the world, and many were caught in the ash of post-Flood volcanic activity.

In the secular religion, though, humans hadn't evolved yet. According to the evolutionary (religion) story, early variations of humans supposedly evolved in Africa about 2 million years ago.[3] And modern

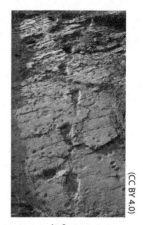

Laetoli footprints

humans didn't arrive until supposedly *200,000 to 100,000* years ago (of course, this story tends to vary from year to year).

Yet the Laetoli prints are undoubtedly *human*.[4] So how did evolutionists respond? They began proposing reinterpretations as *rescuing devices* for their worldview. Perhaps the most common interpretation is that these human prints were left by some sort of human ancestor or "ancient cousin," such as *Australopithecus (Au.) Afarensis* — which is an ancient extinct variation of a chimpanzee (think of the famous extinct ape called "Lucy").

Chimps and *Au. Afarensis* have feet that are *very* different from human feet… so what gives?! The (arbitrary) assumption is that these *Au. Afarensis* feet had already evolved "human feet," regardless of the fossil evidence! The Smithsonian, an evolutionary organization, writes:

> The shape of the feet, along with the length and configuration of the toes, show that the Laetoli Footprints were made by an early human, and the only known early human in the region at that time was *Au. afarensis*. In fact, fossils of *Au. afarensis* were found nearby to the footprints and in the same sediment layer, telling scientists that *Au. afarensis* was in the area at the same time the footprints were left.[5]

2. Bodie Hodge, *Tower of Babel* (Green Forest, AR: Master Books, 2013), p. 124–127.

3. Becky Little, "How Did Humans Evolve?" History.com, March 5, 2020, https://www.history.com/news/humans-evolution-neanderthals-denisovans.

4. Ian Anderson, "Who Made the Laetoli Footprints?" *New Scientist,* vol. 98, May 12, 1983, p. 373.

5. "Laetoli Footprint Trail," Smithsonian Institution, December 17, 2020, https://humanorigins.si.edu/evidence/behavior/footprints/laetoli-footprint-trails.

At first glance, this statement sounds logical, from their worldview, until you realize that the *Au. Afarensis* fossils have feet and hips similar to apes ("knuckle walkers"), not humans.[6] If the Laetoli prints were from an *Au. afarensis*, then the footprints would be very different and the stride would not match a human at all. This is still a major problem for the Laetoli trackway.

Ileret Footprints

In 2009, several human footprints were found in Kenya, located in pathways vertically separated by about 16 feet (5 meters).[7] Like the Laetoli prints, these human footprints were found with animal footprints as well. In the secular story, these footprints are supposed to be about *1.5 million* years old.

These footprints appear just like modern human footprints in size, stride, and sometimes even with similar toe marks to modern humans. Again, the problem is that modern humans weren't supposed to be fully evolved until *200,000 to 100,000* years ago. So, again, how did evolutionists respond? In the same way they did with the Laetoli prints — by coming up with another arbitrary *rescuing device!*

They (again) claim that an alleged early human ancestor (of which we have no evidence!) had already evolved human feet and stride. This arbitrary interpretation is just that — *arbitrary*. Again, when looking at the finer points of this discussion, the Ileret trackway is yet another major problem for the secular story.

Ciampate del Diavolo (Devil's Trails Footprints)

In 2001, archaeologists discovered 81 human footprints in Italy that are supposedly *325,000 to 385,000* years old (as reckoned by the secular story).[8]

---

6. Michael Oard, "Did Lucy Walk Upright?" *Journal of Creation* 15(2), August 2001, p. 9–10, https://answersingenesis.org/human-evolution/lucy/did-lucy-walk-upright/; Elizabeth Mitchell, "Lucy Makeover Shouts a Dangerously Deceptive Message about Our Supposed Ancestors," *Answers in Depth*, October 5, 2013, https://answersingenesis.org/human-evolution/lucy/lucy-makeover-shouts-a-dangerously-deceptive-message-about-our-supposed-ancestors/; Dave Menton and Elizabeth Mitchell, "Lucy, the Knuckle-Walking 'Abomination'?" *Answers in Depth*, October 24, 2012, https://answersingenesis.org/human-evolution/lucy/lucy-the-knuckle-walking-abomination/.

7. Robin Crompton and Todd Pataky, "Stepping Out," *Science* 323, February 27, 2009, p. 1174–1175.; Matthew Bennett et al, "Early Hominin Foot Morphology Based on 1.5-Million-Year-Old Footprints from Ileret, Kenya," *Science* 323, February 27, 2009, p. 1197–1201.

8. Katy Pallister, "New Footprints Found on the 'Devil's Trail' Suggest Neanderthals Climbed Up a Recently Erupted Volcano," *IFL Science*, January 22, 2020, https://www.iflscience.com/plants-and-animals/new-footprints-found-on-the-devils-trail-suggest-neanderthals-climbed-up-a-recently-erupted-volcano/; Adolfo Panarello et al, "On the Devil's Tracks: Unexpected News from the Foresta Ichnosite (Roccamonfina Volcano, Central Italy)," *Journal of Quaternary Science*, January 9, 2020, https://doi.org/10.1002/jqs.3186.

The tracks were made in pyroclastic (hot, fast-moving) mudflows from the Roccamonfina volcano that had cooled enough to walk on, and yet, still soft enough to leave impressions, which then hardened into rock.

According to the evolutionary story, since modern humans were not supposed to be, these footprints need to be reinterpreted. The current explanation is that Neanderthals made the tracks, which again is utterly arbitrary.

This yet again brings up a major issue for the secular story. First, Neanderthals are human. Second, fossils of Neanderthals are supposedly at least *130,000* years old — by the secularists' own dating methods. Their claims of Neanderthals going back *350,000+* years in their story is (again) just another *rescuing device* — an arbitrary story.

Neanderthals are post-Babel people (all the features of Neanderthals are within the human population today) that had migrated and settled in various places around the world, such as Asia, Europe, and the Middle East.

But notice that the secularists are actually agreeing the footprints in question were indeed human by agreeing they were Neanderthal!

Happisburgh, Norfolk Footprints

In May 2013, along the beaches of the British coast, several sets of human footprints became exposed. And within that same year, they had eroded away.[9] But all was not lost. Researchers successfully made casts of them, between tides, before they disappeared.

The trackway was likely made by five different individuals. Secular dating put them at *850,000 to 950,000* years ago. These footprints have heels, arch, and sometimes toe prints that are nearly identical to modern humans. The secular explanation, of course, is some sort of alleged "human-like" ancestor must have made these prints — again, another arbitrary speculation.

Crete Footprints

In 2002, Polish paleontologist Gerhard Gierlinski (while on vacation near the town of Trachilos) discovered a trail of human ichnites on the Greek Island of Crete[10] (where some of the descendants of Javan/Greece settled

---

9. Maev Kennedy, "850,000-year-old Human Footprints Found in Norfolk," *The Guardian*, February 7, 2014, https://www.theguardian.com/science/2014/feb/07/oldest-human-footprints-happisburgh-norfolk.

10. Patricia Claus, "Hominid Footprints on Crete Could Change Evolutionary Theory for Good," *Greek Reporter*, July 10, 2020, https://greece.greekreporter.com/2020/07/10/hominid-footprints-on-crete-could-change-evolutionary-theory-for-good/; Gerard Gierliński et al, "Possible Hominin Footprints from the Late Miocene (c. 5.7 Ma) of Crete?" *Proceedings of the Geologists' Association*, Volume 128, Issues 5–6, October 2017, p. 697–710 .

after displacing the Caphtorim who descended from Mizraim/Egypt after Babel[11]). He later worked with a team of experts to verify this claim.

The footprints are in late Miocene rock, which evolutionists believe are *5.3 million* years old (according to the secular story). By humanistic reckoning, these are far older than the Laetoli human prints. Nevertheless, this is long before humans supposedly evolved in the secular evolutionary story.

The secular interpretation is immediately an appeal to their worldview. Like Laetoli, the secular claim is that the Cretan footprints must be from a "human-like" ape ancestor, whose feet and stride had already evolved to be "human-like." But again, this is merely an arbitrary conjecture.

To summarize, per the evolutionary (religious) worldview, footprints of humans are not supposed to be in these rock layers. So, in response, they offer arbitrary conjectures (i.e., *rescuing devices*) as an explanation for these findings, in order to still hold to their religious worldview. On the other hand, from the *biblical worldview*, finding human footprints in rock layers is not a problem but actually a confirmation of what we expect to find — humans have been leaving footprints since Day 6 of Creation Week. However, any footprints left *prior to* the Flood were likely destroyed in the Flood. During the Flood, just like animals, human tracks are a possibility up until the 150th day.

Take note that in each instance so far, the prints are clearly in line with modern human footprints, stride, and even features like toes in some instances. The only reason the secular community does not accept them as human, and instead propose some other explanation, is due to their religious worldview (rejecting God's Word and thus the global Flood). And, on top of that, they offer these (arbitrary) explanations without any justification of fossil evidence. You need to realize that these arbitrary explanations are not a refutation of these tracks being human. I hope you realize the subtlety of these claims.

Preliminary Comments on the Next Section

Notice that the secularists interpret each of these previous sets of human footprints and trails as *real*, yet still reinterpret *the alleged maker* of those prints as some sort of hypothetical creature (between a modern human and an animal). Did you notice this was the tact of secular researchers in each instance?

In the next sections, we'll embark on investigating sets of footprints that are "much older" than the previous sets (by secular reckoning). With

---

11. Bodie Hodge, *Tower of Babel* (Green Forest, AR: Master Books, 2013), p 165–169. See also John Gill, Commentary notes on Amos 9:7, https://www.biblestudytools.com/commentaries/gills-exposition-of-the-bible/amos-9-7.html.

these "older" sets, you should notice right away that secular researchers do not always take the same tact. In these cases, they appeal to several different possible explanations that fit within their religious worldview, arbitrarily claiming the prints are either:

[1] Fake (etched, manipulated, chiseled, etc.)

[2] Made by a creature that happened to have "human-like" feet (and if on a trail, had a human-like stride too) but were not human nor a "close-human" ancestor

[3] Aliens

[4] Misinterpreted animal prints or a mere geological formation

[5] The date must be wrong

Hence, these "older" prints obviously stir up controversy too. The assessment is mixed, especially on certain ones, *even* by creationists. And rightly so. In following God's Word, Christians should always strive to have an honest assessment of the fossil tracks (e.g., Proverbs 12:17,[12] 22[13]; 2 Corinthians 8:21[14]). In some cases, many creationists actually agree with some of the assessments of evolutionists. Nevertheless, we'll attempt to examine these controversial fossils and tracks in a balanced and honest way, based on the research available.

British Columbia/Wolverine Creek and Tumbler Ridge

This first site is located in Canada, in the Dunvegan Formation, classed as Upper Cretaceous rock, which is Flood rock by biblical reckoning (i.e., Noah was floating on the surface of the Flood when the Cretaceous rock was being formed). By secular humanistic dating, it is placed as over *65 million* years old. It should be obvious that these are starkly different approaches, depending on religious view.

There are a number of theropod dinosaur footprints found in this area. After some flooding in Flatbed Creek (Tumbler Ridge), some local boys found some dinosaur footprints in the summer of A.D. 2000. After further study and research, more dinosaur tracks and bones were found in this area. At Tumbler Ridge, the prints are not human but animal in their origins.

---

12. "He who speaks truth declares righteousness, but a false witness, deceit" (Proverbs 12:17).
13. "Lying lips are an abomination to the LORD, but those who deal truthfully are His delight" (Proverbs 12:22).
14. "providing honorable things, not only in the sight of the Lord, but also in the sight of men" (2 Corinthians 8:21).

Some dinosaur footprints also turned up in a nearby creek called Wolverine Creek, and upstream of these initial finds at Wolverine Creek yielded some human-like prints. The discoverers (Fred and Ruth Walkley with Bruce and Joan Zimmerman) contacted a professional geologist, Emil Silvestru, to further research this finding, who then assessed the site and published his research in a peer-reviewed journal.

The assessment was inconclusive. In one set of footprints, an arch was present, thus indicating a possible human footprint. However, none of these prints yielded any toe prints, so it's not certain that these were made by humans. And the prints were larger than any *normal* human footprint (though human feet do have tremendous range in size). Nevertheless, from the 2 tracks (out of 7 total) that had enough quality to study properly (specifically, track 2 and track 6), Silvestru concluded:

> Personally, I lean towards interpreting WOC 02 and 06 as metatarsal dinosaurian footprints, too, although I would not completely rule out the possibility of them being human. However, without a sequence of at least three consecutive prints, I would not even consider trying to build such a case.[15]

Regarding human footprint trails, notice that at least three consecutive prints are necessary in his assessment. Why? Because it gives an indication of stride. Humans are unique in the way we walk, compared to apes or other extant animals. Silvestru gives further useful advice for finding and searching for potential human footprints (this is why I wanted to cover this case first):

1. Check the parallelism of any track's bottom plane with the local dip of the host layers. If they are not parallel, discard the item.

2. Look for trackways (minimum of two consecutive left-right or right-left footprints). Isolated prints will never suffice to build a case.

3. Try to rule out any alternative explanation (like mud collapse, slumping, eroded metatarsal print of a tridactyl animal, etc.).

These suggestions are helpful to keep in mind when assessing potential human tracks/trackways. Although a trackway is a great starting point in assessing the legitimacy of an actual potential human print, it isn't necessarily conclusive evidence. Rather, it may just become more difficult to ascertain the truth. In addition, it's important to work with a respectable and

---

15. Emil Silvestru, Human and dinosaur fossil footprints in the Upper Cretaceous of North America, *Technical Journal*, 18(2), 2004, pp. 114-120, https://creation.com/images/pdfs/tj/j18_2/j18_2_114-120.pdf.

professional geologist, anatomist, archaeologist, and/or paleontologist to help document any alleged finds in the peer-review process.

Again, bear in mind that secularists, *prior* to looking at any evidence, have a (usually very strong) religious bias that the prints found in these "old" rock layers cannot be human. On the other hand, reputable creationists hold to the view that any alleged prints may or may not be human, which means they will likely give a better (honest) assessment, without the strong bias.

Nevertheless, the final assessment is still based on the bits of found evidence, and still up for debate whether these are human prints or not.

Meister Sandal Print

In 1968, William Meister discovered the Meister Print, which was later assessed by Geologists Clifford Burdick and Melvin Cook to verify the claim. They later sent the collected data on the specimen to scientists in Australia. Clifford Burdick said in 1987:

> Most notable was the information from my work at Antelope Springs in northern Utah. I went up there in August 1968 with William Meister. A couple of months before, he had found a human sandal print with several trilobites right inside the human print in shale. I found a couple of child's footprints at the same location. The finds were corroborated by other geologists, including Dr. Melvin Cook of the University of Utah.
>
> The Australian scientists who received this data said they jumped for glee because of the importance of the finds. You see, the human prints were found with trilobites in a so-called "Cambrian" trilobite bed. This showed that trilobites and human prints were fossilized together, but humans were not supposed to be contemporaneous with trilobites. The Cambrian is dated at about 500 million years by evolutionists, and humans are supposed to have evolved only in the last four million years or so.[16]

However, that particular print was not part of a trackway. Furthermore, that area has natural geologic phenomena that yield shapes similar to this flat sandal-like shape. Due to these ambiguities, many creationists and evolutionists have been hesitant to affirm this print as solid evidence for humans walking in the Cambrian. And rightly so.

Even from a Flood geology perspective, this would be an odd find. The primary reason being that Cambrian rock is from the *bottom* of the Pre-Flood

---

16. Gerald Heyes, "Pioneer of Creationism, an Interview with Geologist Clifford Burdick," *Creation* 9(3):9–12, June 1987.

seas. During the Flood of Noah's day, when the "Springs of the Great Deep" burst forth (Genesis 7:11[17]), and the water, dirt, sediment, rock fragments, and so forth initially began burying things, the bottom-dwelling sea creatures at the *lowest level* were buried first. These sea creatures were the first to be subdued by the sedimentary layers to form fossils (by sealing out the oxygen to prevent decay and thus make them candidates for fossilization).

The point is that we would obviously not expect humans to be walking around at the bottom of the ocean (called the "great deep" or "seas" before the Deluge) at the initial stages of the Flood! Again, if this finding had been introduced into the peer-reviewed process, much of this detail could have come to light sooner. Nonetheless, for this case, most creationists and evolutionists agree the Meister Print is not a human print.

Paluxy River Sites in Texas

Arguably the most controversial trails of footprints have come from the Paluxy River near Glen Rose, Texas — which is about an hour drive from the Fort Worth/Dallas area. Located here are multiple sites with produced trackways that have stirred up continual controversy for more than half of a century. Among these sites are the Shelf Site and the famous Taylor Trail (named for Stan Taylor).

I went to the Taylor Trail in 1998. I only saw dinosaur tracks, but that's because this trip was just a brief visit (merely passing through), and not a trip for in-depth research or study.

The history of the Paluxy River site is rich in details, extending back to the time of the depression, in the late 1920s, through the 1930s. The published (and even unpublished) accounts of the intermixed human and dinosaur tracks drew much attention. However, many of these tracks are not able to be studied. Most tracks have been eroded, while some tracks have been removed to prevent potential damage from construction in the area.

Furthermore, during the depression, some of the better prints were reported to be cut out of the river bed and sold to help certain locals survive the long-lasting economic downturn.[18] In particular, there were local claims of two old timers, named George Adams and Jim Ryals, that supposedly carved out footprints and sold them for money.

Even so, from the 1960s to the 1980s, various teams could still see the remnant holes where the footprints were cut out and sold (or at least the

---

17. "In the six hundredth year of Noah's life, in the second month, the seventeenth day of the month, on that day all the fountains of the great deep were broken up, and the windows of heaven were opened" (Genesis 7:11).

18. John Morris, "The Paluxy River Mystery," *Acts & Facts*, January 1, 1986, https://www.icr.org/article/255.

depressions that were cut out and potentially modified).[19] One such print was the Burdick Print, which was removed, due to construction, by Al Berry in 1938. It still exists to this day — although not without controversy. Was it forged or not?

George Adam's nephew claimed that slabs were removed and carved out under a shade tree, where, prior to construction, the Burdick print was separately cut out by another man.[20]

In 1968, Stan Taylor and his film crew decided to go to the site and take a look. In 1973, he published a film, called *Footprints in Stone* for Films for Christ, Inc., and wrote a subsequent book in 1980 called *Tracking Those Incredible Dinosaurs and the People Who Knew Them.*

Naturally, this stirred up controversy. But sometimes controversy can be a good thing since it tends to force people to analyze things more closely.

Interestingly, many of the trails at Paluxy have prints that appear similar, but not exact, to human trackways. For instance, one similarity was that the tracks have an alternating pattern. And these trails are intermixed with dinosaurian 3-toed trackways as well.

For years, many creationists hailed these prints as solid evidence that humans and dinosaurs lived together. If this evidence is valid, then it only confirms what we already know to be true from the Bible, which has revealed to us that God created man and land creatures (including dinosaurs) on the same day of creation (Day 6). Thus, from a biblical standpoint, we'd expect to find evidence of humans and dinosaurs living together.

Besides the Taylor Trail, some of the other controversial trackways of ichnites at Paluxy are the Giant Trail, Turnage Trail, and Ryals Trail. However, after about 15 years of observations, something unexpected happened. These alleged human footprints continued to erode, but *not* as expected. They began to erode into *3-toed footprints.*[21]

Why is this significant? Because what appeared to be human footprints were actually dinosaur footprints. This was actually a print of the upper part of its foot and leg (think of its ankles and just above) where it stepped into the mud. It's likely that as the dinosaur lifted its 3-toed foot out of the mud, its 3 toes retracted together as it lifted up. As a result, this left an impression of the upper part of its leg, still intact, with some of the mud infilling the track, specifically the dinosaur toes. So, this mud collapse just happened to superficially resemble a human footprint that hardened into stone.

---

19. Ibid.
20. John Morris, *Tracking Those Incredible Dinosaurs* (San Diego, CA: Creation-Life Publishers, 1980), p. 240.
21. Ibid.

Other problems, which should have been initial red flags, are the footprints being larger than modern human feet, along with the stride/pace being much larger too.[22] So, even though the trackways are indeed similar, the *differences* are still significant. Had proper documentation of these facts existed early on, better conclusions might have been drawn.

John Morris, son of the famed Henry Morris (a well-respected creationist), published on these footprints at the Taylor Trail, affirming the possibility that these tracks were made by humans.[23] But by 1986, Morris backed off this position and publicly affirmed the following:

> In view of these developments, none of the four trails at the Taylor
> site can today be regarded as unquestionably of human origin.
> The Taylor Trail appears, obviously, dinosaurian, as do two prints
> thought to be in the Turnage Trail. The Giant Trail has what
> appears to be dinosaur prints leading toward it, and some of the
> Ryals tracks seem to be developing claw features, also.[24]

Professor A.E. Wilder-Smith also initially thought these tracks might be good evidence of human and dinosaur footprints together, but then later pointed out the problems when he updated his book.[25] He commented:

> Taylor had not paid sufficient attention to the details of the tracks.
> He apparently did not realize the absolute importance of the presence of five toes, an instep and a heel to make a sure diagnosis of a
> human track…. Glen Rose has thus been so totally ridiculed, that
> it is almost impossible to publish on any work in this area in any
> respectable journal.[26]
>
> To sum them up shortly, it may be fairly stated that the majority
> of these works come to the conclusion that the Stanley Taylor
> trail is not a human trail at all, such as certain creationists had
> thought it to be. Some saurian allegedly walking on its metatarsals made the elongated footprints which Stanley Taylor had
> mistaken for human tracks. On top of all this, in place of the

22. Emil Silvestru, "Human and Dinosaur Fossil Footprints in the Upper Cretaceous of North America?" *Technical Journal,* 18(2):114–120, August, 2004.
23. John Morris, "The Paluxy River Tracks," *Acts & Facts,* May, 1976, https://www.icr.org/articles/print/81/.
24. John Morris, "The Paluxy River Mystery," *Acts & Facts,* January 1, 1986, https://www.icr.org/article/255.
25. A.E. Wilder-Smith, *Man's Origin Man's Destiny* (Wheaton, Illinois: Harold Shaw Publishers, 1968, updated in 1993).
26. Ibid, p. 117.

five toes seen in some of the tracks and apparently mistakenly seen in the Taylor trail, in some specimens three horns resembling those of three toed dinosaur tracks had now apparently appeared, slowly over the years with little sign of the expected five human toes.[27]

So why did it take so long to come to this conclusion? And why so much controversy? (Which, by the way, still rages today!) I suggest it was because of the lack of peer review done by both creationists and evolutionists, coupled with the possibility that it just took a while for researchers to realize their long-held (erroneous) conclusion was indeed false.

So, after this realization, did everyone just pack up and leave Paluxy, satisfied with this conclusion? Not at all. In fact, it has instead drawn more people and even more finds since this time. Since then, a number of oddities have been found — one which we'll discuss next.

Alvis Delk Print

In July of 2000, amateur archaeologist Alvis Delk, along with his friend James Bishop, found a dinosaur footprint track inlayed with sediment near the McFall I and II Sites (near the Paluxy River in Texas), which they removed and took with them.

This track sat in the possession of Delk for years until he finally decided to clean it, clearing off the debris and sediment, which then revealed an alleged human (size 11) right footprint being stepped on by a three-toed dinosaur print (specifically with its front left two toes).

As expected, his finding quickly sparked interest, with both creationists and evolutionists lining up on both sides (though wisely keeping their distance for the time being).

Evolutionist Glen Kuban (whose religious worldview does not allow the possibility of dinosaurs and humans living together) argued that this piece was simply forged or misinterpreted, whereas creationist Ian Juby, the director of the Creation Science Museum of Canada (who holds to a different religious worldview than that of Kuban), leans in the direction of this fossil being legitimate. Kuban responds to Juby, saying:

> Here he neglects the fact that humans can make footprints with tools as well as their feet. He also doesn't mention that some creatures (including certain dinosaurs) are known to have sometimes left superficially human-like tracks, and that in some cases such

---

27. Ibid, p. 118.

tracks were selectively enhanced and/or misinterpreted as human footprints.[28]

Note that Kuban makes two different arguments in this statement. First, he argues that the prints were enhanced and modified with tools (i.e., a fake). Second, he argues that the human-looking print was merely misinterpreted. (Also, note that these two excuses were the most common often used by his predecessors.) So, in his (weak) conclusion, Kuban essentially argues that it was either carved or heavily altered, with no convincing evidence presented as proof for either position.

Kuban goes on to say:

> In the 1970s, Glen Rose resident Wayland "Slim" Adams, explained to a group of creationists how his uncle George Adams, who carved human tracks on loose blocks and sold them to tourists during the Great Depression, usually did start with existing (but not human) depressions. George's granddaughter recently confirmed this, as well as her grandfather's use of acid to blur chisel marks.[29]

Kuban further concludes by saying:

> The Alvis Delk Print is not a convincing human footprint in ancient rock. Its advocates have failed to present the necessary data and details to adequately support their assertions.[30]

This conclusion is obviously very odd. Science is designed to *disprove*, not to prove. Nothing is ever proved "by science" since it is always subject to further information and analysis, which is the nature of scientific methodology. (This is basic science 101!) One can always collect additional research data to deny a hypothesis but it can never actually prove anything.

Even so, the specimen *is* the data to be analyzed. But the real oddity is that the argument sets up a *guilty until proven innocent* scenario when he states: *"...present the necessary data and details to adequately support their assertions."* Science doesn't work this way but rather vice versa. Worldview interpretations aside, data and evidence are usually taken as legitimate, unless concrete proof is offered to object. Kuban continues in his conclusion saying:

28. http://www.paleo.cc/paluxy/delk.htm
29. http://www.paleo.cc/paluxy/delk.htm.
30. http://www.paleo.cc/paluxy/delk.htm.

...the collective weight of several lines of evidence, including the uncertain circumstances of the discovery, lack of *in situ* documentation, the knowledge that similar tracks have been carved in the Glen Rose area, the serious morphological abnormalities in the prints, and the considerations about potentially misleading scanning artifacts such as beam hardening, point to the strong likelihood that both the "human footprint" and dinosaur track on this loose slab were carved or heavily altered from less distinct depressions.[31]

At first glance, this conclusion may sound convincing. But let's evaluate it from a logical perspective:

1. **"Uncertain circumstances of the discovery"**: This is circumstantial and not evidence against. In fact, it happens all the time in the secular research arena.
2. **"Lack of *in situ* documentation"**: Again, this is circumstantial and not evidence against. It would it be nice, yes; but massive numbers of significant finds have not been rejected because they were not properly documented *in situ* by secular researchers.[32] Nevertheless, finding it *in situ,* and more specifically, within a trackway would have bolstered it.
3. **"The knowledge that similar tracks have been carved in the Glen Rose area"**: This is irrelevant to the specimen at hand (technically, it is a "part-to-whole" fallacy); furthermore, this is predicated on a story about someone referring to someone else in the 1930s that has not been observed firsthand by researchers nor duplicated by researchers.
4. **"The serious morphological abnormalities in the prints"**: Footprints in mud have abnormalities. This is actually expected but is not evidence against. Even recognized footprints, like the Laetoli, have certain prints in the trail that have serious morphological abnormalities too.
5. **"Considerations about potentially misleading scanning artifacts such as beam hardening"**: *Potentially* isn't proof against.

6. [These five evidences listed above]..."**Point to the strong likelihood that both the "human footprint" and dinosaur track on this loose**

---

31. http://www.paleo.cc/paluxy/delk.htm.

32. For example, an amber fossil with feathers was not found *in situ* and was not rejected. Emily Chung, "Dinosaur Feathers Found in Alberta Amber," CBC News, September 15, 2011, https://www.cbc.ca/news/technology/dinosaur-feathers-found-in-alberta-amber-1.1086765.

slab were carved or heavily altered from less distinct depressions":
Evidence doesn't point to anything, but rather evidence is subject to interpretation. Researchers, based on their worldview, point to things. Nevertheless, none of these five pieces of evidence "prove" that this specimen was faked. Rather, this actually presents Kuban's case as a weak inductive argument. So, all in all, his final conclusion failed to disprove the case for authenticity.

But please note that I'm *not* making a case that the Alvis Delk find is truly legitimate/real or that it is faked/manipulated. I'm simply saying more research is required to make a better assessment rather than jumping to conclusions *without* warrant. Furthermore, this debate needs to take place in a proper peer-reviewed journal (this is where it should be).

Nonetheless, whether this finding is real or faked is irrelevant to those who hold to a biblical worldview. If this finding is legitimate (a dinosaur really did step on a human print in the mud, prior to fossilization), then it would be *consistent* with the biblical account of history, which says humans and dinosaurs lived at the same time (both created on Day 6 of Creation Week), and representatives of both fled and died in the global Flood of Noah's day.

If this finding is truly faked, then this leaves open several unanswered questions. Was it an oldtimer just fiddling around years ago, simply to make some money to survive the depression? Why leave it in the river then and not sell it? Did the alleged carver forget about it? Why didn't the carver remove the print from the river and take it under a tree to carve it like the old-time story relates? Why didn't it erode away since the 1930s like hosts of other dinosaur prints at the river that have come and gone? Where are all the other fakes from these carvers in the 1930s? Why take the time to carve out a dinosaur overlaying a human track when it would have been easier to carve a human track stepping on one of the many dinosaur tracks (dinosaur tracks are readily available all over the area).

Or, even worse, were the two prints (dinosaur and human) overlaying each other done deliberately to deceive? If so, then it simply confirms the condition of the heart of man that we read from the Bible — that it's deceitful, sinful, and wicked (e.g., Genesis 8:21,[33] Jeremiah 17:9,[34] Romans

---

33. "And the Lord smelled a soothing aroma. Then the Lord said in His heart, 'I will never again curse the ground for man's sake, although the imagination of man's heart is evil from his youth; nor will I again destroy every living thing as I have done'" (Genesis 8:21).

34. "The heart is deceitful above all things, and desperately wicked; who can know it?" (Jeremiah 17:9).

3:23[35]). This is why we, as *sinners*, need to repent and put our faith in Jesus Christ, who bled and died on that Cross and rose from the grave to save us from our sins.

So, either way (manipulated or real), the actual outcome won't affect those of us who hold a biblical worldview. But as Christians, we should desire to *know the truth* rather than settle for a bunch of mere opinions on the subject — specifically from those who merely state their religious conviction and expect people to just follow that religious viewpoint on the issue.

As mentioned previously, the point is that we need to have an *honest* assessment of evidence. Again, evolutionists have an open bias based on their religious worldview regarding human and dinosaur footprints — and I'll admit that so do many creationists. Some creationists hastily interpret these fossils, basically at "face value," without a great deal of assessment and review, while other creationists step back and err on the side of caution, thus quickly agreeing with the evolutionary interpretation, and that's it. But is either of these options an honest assessment? Not really.

There is nothing wrong with being cautious. But, at the same time, it's wise to always do more research before reaching conclusions. With the Alvis Delk print, I suggest more research be done, along with better peer-reviewed documentation, on *both* sides of the debate.

But as it stands, the secular side has not actually disproved the legitimacy of this fossil — they've merely put forth their religious views (like normal) and expect people to simply trust their (again, arbitrary) assertions.

Amanniyazov Track

In the former communist Soviet Union (USSR), in early (January) 1995, Alexander Bushev reported that he found *in situ* human tracks in the same rock layers with dinosaur tracks in Jurassic sediment, supposedly *200 million* years old (by secular reckoning). Apparently, these tracks were originally reported back in 1983.[36] In case you're unaware, the USSR was a strictly evolutionary country, essentially where the religion of evolutionism was the imposed standard at every level — even though Christianity, Islam, and few other religions battled to remain pure in certain parts.

In the region of the Turkmenian plateau, specifically the Kughitang-Tau Plateau (now Turkmenistan), a Russian state newspaper (*Komsomolskaya Pravda*) reported that the Russian scientist and Professor Kurban Amanniyazov

---

35. "for all have sinned and fall short of the glory of God" (Romans 3:23).
36. Rubstsov, "Tracking Dinosaurs," *Moscow News*, 1983, No. 24, p. 10, English version.

had found human footprints where they shouldn't be (again, by the secular standard). Professor Amanniyazov said:

> We've imprints resembling human footprints, but to date have failed to determine, with any scientific veracity, whom they belong to, after all.[37]

Recall that in the evolutionary worldview, humans and dinosaurs are not supposed to be living at the same time, which means identifying these prints as human would be a major problem in the secular religion. Nevertheless, the article goes on to presume that they couldn't be human prints. Bushev argued:

> He suggested that, because "we know" that humans appeared much later than dinosaurs, there was an extraterrestrial "who walked in his swimming suit along the sea-side."[38]

So the human-like footprints were not questioned by the Russians. But their interpretation was that *aliens* came to earth and made the prints or perhaps, as he said in other publications, a "human-like animal" made the prints (if you recall, this was a similar assessment given to the Laetoli, Crete, and other footprints higher in the sediment).

Professor Amanniyazov says elsewhere that if these prints really are human then it would be a "revelation in the science of man," having man "at least *150 million* years old." But he really leans towards them being a "human-like animal."[39] In other words, he really believes that something other than humans left the prints (even though they look human), hence the possible science-fiction explanation of aliens with human-like feet. And presumably, these aliens are wearing their swimming suits (like humans have since Adam and Eve sinned)! Since the timespan is *unquestionable,* in the secular religion, this explanation was plainly accepted.

You might think, "Wow... their *rescuing device* is aliens... really?" But in fact, other human-like prints have also been commonly linked to aliens (usually without second thought!). For instance, Joe Taylor wrote about an encounter with a retired secular engineer, who was an amateur paleontologist, regarding some specific alleged human prints in Texas:

---

37. Sergei Golovin, "Human and Dinosaur Footprints in Turkmenistan?" *Creation*, 18(4), September 1996, p. 52.
38. Ibid.
39. Kurban Amanniyazov, "Old Friends Dinosaurs," *Science in the USSR,* T 986, No. 1, p. 101–107.

As we were working I began relating what the former curator of the Dallas Museum of Natural History had told as an explanation of the human tracks at Glen Rose. "Yeah," I began, "I hear one of your friends said that the human tracks at Glen Rose were made by aliens, who were following the dinosaurs around taking pictures of them, and that's how someday we'll know what dinosaurs looked like." I was chuckling as I finished. My retired engineer friend looked at me and in an offended voice said "So…?" No smiles — no laughs. I was frankly speechless. You heard it. Aliens.[40]

Aliens, of whom there is absolutely *zero* evidence, making "human-like" footprints is a more common explanation than you might expect. Technically, this puts the secular view as borderline science fiction (if we want to be precise about it).

Returning to the Turkmenistan Prints, precious few have been made available for study.[41] Few, if any, pictures exist for proper analysis or even the exact site to locate these prints.

Right now, as people banter back and forth, it is merely a debate over Professor Amanniyazov's exact meaning of his writings. Obviously, the correct solution is simply a better, more proper documentation, and an in-depth analysis in the peer-review process.

In doing so, there also needs to be answers to questions regarding trackway and print analysis with further *in situ* documentation if possible. And the erosional and potential in-filling, as well as the contour features of these presumed prints, need to be evaluated, while also having these data be publicly debated. Until then, nothing conclusive can be truly said on the verdict of these prints.

Berean/Kentucky Prints

Unlike the Meister prints (discussed previously), which were found in sediment essentially at the bottom of the pre-Flood ocean, these alleged tracks were found in Flood sediments (where land creatures were buried and fossilized from the Flood). The prints were found in Carboniferous rock, which includes the Mississippian and Pennsylvanian rock layers (many fossils in these rock layers are of land plants).

In other words, the burial of this sediment is where we could have a reasonable possibility of finding a human track (similar to Jurassic and

---

40. Joe Taylor, *Fossil Facts & Fantasies* (Crosbyton, TX: Mt. Blanco Publishing Co., 1999), p. 73.
41. Note that a couple of pictures have been thrown out without much sourcing, so we can't even be certain that Professor Amanniyazov actually studied these.

Cretaceous, which are also inclusive of land creatures) because the rock layers are transitioning from sea to land sediments. Although, from a Flood geology perspective, we'd still expect to find many sea creatures buried in among these layers (since the Flood completely overtook the land).

In 1885, the Berean tracks were first discovered about 12 miles from Berea, Kentucky, in sandstone. These tracks were examined by Professor J.F. Brown of Berea College, Kentucky, as reported in the *American Antiquarian*.[42] The report indicated that there were two well-preserved human prints, with proper-sized feet and toes visibly spread.

Later, in 1930–31, Professor of Geology and founder of the Geology Department, Wilbur Burroughs of Berea College, and William Finnell (the tracks were on the Finnell farm) investigated these *in situ* footprints. There were altogether 12 prints that ranged upwards from size 4.5 (though most were at 9.5 inches). A *Science News Letter,* from October 29, 1938, writes:

> Practically everyone who sees them thinks at first they were made by human feet and it is almost impossible to persuade people that they were not.[43]

And rightly so. These prints are described with having five toes, a ball, heel, and a normal stride akin to humans. Having two prints, standing side-by-side, also allowed a standing measurement, which was the same as the typical human. Displaced mud surrounding the heel was also evident. On May 24, 1953, Dr. Burroughs wrote, in the *Louisville Courier-Journal,* stating:

> Of these, two pairs show the left foot advanced relative to the right. The position of the feet is the same as that of a person. The distance from heel to heel is 18 inches. One pair shows the feet parallel to each other, the distance between the feet being the same as that of a normal human being.

Note, if this trackway of at least 12 prints was found in a (post-Flood) layer near the top of the rock record, where humans are now (such as the Pleistocene), no one would question the veracity of the trackway being made by humans. But…they weren't.

Dr. Burroughs couldn't believe that human footprints could even potentially be found in *300 million*-year-old sediment (by humanistic evolutionary reckoning). So, based on his religious assumptions, he believed the prints

---

42. E.A. Allen, "Footmarks in Kentucky," *American Antiquarian,* Volume 7:39, 1885.
43. Dave Tabler, "Human-Like Tracks in Stone are Riddle to Scientists," *Appalachian History,* March 7, 2016, https://www.appalachianhistory.net/2016/03/human-like-tracks-in-stone-are-riddle.html.

must've been made by an animal that had human-like feet and walked in a stride like humans.

The problem is that there are no animals that have feet like humans and strides like a human. So, as an arbitrary speculation, he proposed that an unknown giant bipedal ("walked on two-feet") amphibian made the prints. Yet there were no tail prints or four-legged indications (common for many amphibians) in the rock record in the area, which, of course, means this was nothing more than just an arbitrary *rescuing device* for his religious views.

One of the long-time editors of *The Scientific American* (Albert Ingalls) wrote a paper on it, basically stating that he agrees the prints "look human" but cannot be human (of course, because of his religious secular conviction that humans cannot be around in that era of the evolutionary story).[44] The bulk of the short (one-page) article is essentially reiterating this religious belief and offering two possible explanations:

1. They were faked by carving by Native Americans [per David Bushnell of the *Smithsonian Institute*]. However, none of the firsthand researchers like Professors Brown or Burroughs entertained the idea these were carved or etched but instead documented that the tracks were real.

2. They were made by an unknown extinct animal that walked and had feet like a human (i.e., the walking amphibian hypothesis).

These two explanations match the most common arguments (*rescuing devices*) that secularists prefer to use whenever they find an alleged human print(s) in rock layers where they are not supposed to find human remnants (again, based on their humanistic religious beliefs). Interestingly, the *Scientific American* paper included four photographs of carved Native American prints (part of their writing/communication system) with chalk outlines — but did not show any images of the Berean tracks or trackway being discussed, even though they had access to photos of the actual site.

Yet the Native American carvings are *not* even remotely close to the prints of the Berean trackway. Everyone agrees that the Native American carvings are carvings, which obviously don't even look like a human footprint in sandstone but looks more like a child's awkward depiction of feet. This tactic was very deceptive — including these carvings with no photos of the actual prints. In fact, once the *Scientific American* article was released,

---

44. Albert Ingalls, "The Carboniferous Mystery," *Scientific American*, Volume 162, Number 1, January, 1940.

refusing to use actual images of the site, even Burroughs lamented their deliberate deception (per the Berean College Archives documentation).[45]

Sadly, the people who did not read the paper carefully probably also erroneously believed these (obviously false) chalk-surrounded, carved prints were the Berean footprints and trackway. These carvings in the *Scientific American* are shown here:

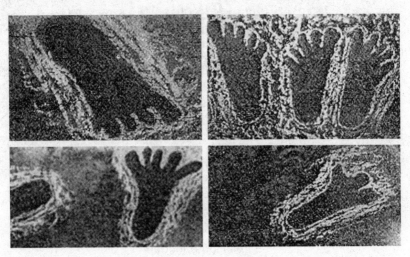

One site, *Talk Origins*, repeats these four images and cites the *Scientific American* paper with a simple statement that reads:

> These prints found in Carboniferous rock are claimed by creationists to be out-of-order human footprints. They do not, however, look particularly human.[46]

However, these prints are *not* the Berean footprints. And these prints are *not* a possible set of out-of-order human footprints, as supposedly claimed by some creationists. Rather, these images are clearly *Native American carvings!*

Though the actual prints have since been cut out of the Finnell Farm site, fortunately (by God's providence) pictures still survive. The actual Berean footprint trail looks like that on the following page.[47]

---

45. Ian Juby, "Special Report #1: The Strange Fossil Footprints of Berea, Kentucky," *Creation Science Newsletter,* February, 18, 2012, https://ianjuby.org/feb-18-2012-crevo-news-with-ian-juby-and-core-ottawa/.

46. "Berea, Kentucky Carboniferous 'Footprints,'" accessed February, 23, 2021, http://www.talkorigins.org/faqs/berea/.

47. Wilbur G. Burroughs papers (https://bereaarchives.libraryhost.com/repositories/2/resources/129), box 11, folder 5, Site: Loman Hill, Site Number: 15RK49, County: Rockcastle, Topographic Map: Johnetta, Date: August, 1970, Recorded by Fred E. Coy, Jr.

Berean footprint trail
Wilbur G. Burroughs papers, Berea College Special Collections and Archives, taken
in 1970, used by permission.

Secularists view these prints and state their evolutionary religious viewpoints via conjecture, while not providing any actual evidence or argumentation that disproves them as human prints. The fact that the *Scientific American* deliberately hid the prints from publication exposes their heart of hearts — that they know these tracks may well be *real* human tracks but chose to withhold the evidence out of *fear* that people won't believe their religious story.

Of all the trackways, these ichnites appropriately fit the necessities outlined by Dr. Emil Silvestru. Nevertheless, I would still like to see more documentation before making a definitive assessment.

Smithsonian Simian, Bear, and Bird Footprints in Permian Rock

In 1987, in the Robledo Mountains in southern New Mexico, secular amateur paleontologist (at the time) and sociologist Jerry Paul MacDonald excavated a treasure trove of Permian fossils — particularly footprints and trackways. Some of these fossils were exquisite and highly praised for their excellent preservation. His fieldwork was funded by several prominent sources.

By 1992, some of MacDonald's Permian fossils were on display in *Smithsonian's Museum of Natural History.* The site, which is clearly mapped as Permian rock, has produced an immense amount of expected Permian tracks. However, there were a few finds in this Permian rock that were not anticipated in the secular view.

The *Smithsonian* magazine, in their July 1992 issue, says:

> The fossil tracks that MacDonald has collected include a number of what paleontologists like to call "problematica." On one trackway, for example, a three-toed creature apparently took a few steps, then disappeared — as though it took off and flew. "We don't know of any three-toed animals in the Permian," MacDonald pointed out. "And there aren't supposed to be any birds." He's got several tracks where creatures appear to be walking on their hind legs, **others that look almost simian.** On one pair of siltstone tablets, I notice some unusually large, deep and scary-looking footprints, each with five arched toe marks, like nails. I comment that they look just like bear tracks. "Yeah," MacDonald says reluctantly, "they sure do." Mammals evolved long after the Permian period, scientists agree, yet these tracks are clearly Permian[48] (**emphasis added**).

Let's discuss this for a moment. Permian rock is *lower* than the three rock layers with dinosaurs in them (Cretaceous, Jurassic, Triassic). By secular reckoning, it is supposedly around *280 million* years old. So, in the secular story, there should be *no birds* (since dinosaurs had not "evolved into birds" yet), *no three-toed dinosaurs* (since dinosaurs hadn't evolved yet either), and *no mammals* (since mammals hadn't evolved yet either).

The Smithsonian paper included a picture of the fossilized bear track, and it really does look like a bear print. So, finding tracks that look identical to bears and three-toed birds are a huge problem (or *"problematica")* in the secular story.

You may not be familiar with the term *"simian"* (which I emphasized). *Simian* means the track was similar to monkeys, apes, or humans (many on the secular side try to also lump man as a primate). Reading the paper, you may have glossed over it, not realizing its significance. Since no image was provided for these simian prints (plural as denoted by MacDonald) it was tough to ascertain what was really found.

Since this time, others have also made their way to sites nearby, where at least one print was discovered and photographed, which naturally stirred

48. Doug Stewart, "Petrified Footprints: A Puzzling Parade of Permian Beasts," *The Smithsonian*, Vol. 23, No. 4, July, 1992, p.70–79.

up controversy and the natural *rescuing devices* too (like it being a faked carving). See image on this page.

Apparently, this shallow print is difficult to see unless it is wet. Of course, it'd be great if these prints by Mac-Donald were published and shown so as to be discussed — with both pros and cons — more properly and battled out in peer-reviewed journals.

According to my (best effort) research, the prints commented on by MacDonald as *"simian"* in the *Smithsonian* magazine have never been shown to the public.

Nevertheless, what was the response by MacDonald? The *Smithsonian* magazine writes:

> MacDonald feels there must be a plausible explanation. These may be creatures whose gaits are unknown; or an animal's back feet may have obliterated its front footprints; or a funning five-toed animals may have grazed the mud with only its middle three digits, then gobbled up on the hoof as it were.[49]

So, in this instance, rather than admit the more obvious answer (the tracks were made by an animal normally recognized with that type of footprints), the *rescuing device* used here is that the tracks were made by some other unexpected animal. The sad thing is people began attacking MacDonald as though he were "exaggerating his finds...even that he'd carved all the tracks himself."[50] So, even *secularists* were attacking *him* for simply trying to be honest with the evidence! Though I do not agree with MacDonald's worldview, I do appreciate his honesty in commenting on the finds. I was hoping to find more discussion on this in his book *Earth's First Steps*, but there was virtually nothing. Here is what I could find:

> When Glen Kuban, an expert on, among other things, "odd" tracks, saw this section of canyon, he noted that the limestone pits preserved better looking pseudo "man tracks" than the world-famous (or infamous) "man tracks" he studied in the

---

49. Ibid.
50. Ibid.

Paluxy River of Texas. Glen used up a whole roll of film photographing them all.[51]

Beyond that, photographs and scientific analysis were missing in the book regarding the alleged Robledo simian tracks, just a lengthy discussion of the Paluxy River tracks and why they were dinosaurian!

If these ichnites had been found in upper rock layers (where evolutionists have no problem with man, birds, and bears existing), few would even question the veracity of the finds. But being in Permian, it becomes a huge problem for the long-age believer. Hence, there was essentially neglect on the finds. Take notice that the legitimacy of fossil tracks found in the same rock fossil bed *that was expected* in the Permian is largely not questioned. *They only question the finds that are considered "problematica"* and then leave them alone. Even so, my conclusion is that we still need more research here.

This brings up a serious question though. If evolutionists honestly think that a human-looking print or even bears, birds, or other creatures that shouldn't be in a particular rock layer due to their beliefs, why not publish it with an analysis and let scientists debate the subject? Is an evolutionary worldview so weak that its adherents cannot defend its propositions?

Concluding Remarks on Human and Dinosaur Ichnites

Of course, there are many more tracks and trackways, both historical and modern cases, that could be discussed at length. And, again, I suggest we need more proper documentation to proceed in the peer-review process to at least open up more discussion on each of these cases briefly mentioned.

Specifically, I would love to see more documentation in professional journals on the Nicaraguan Prints,[52] Hadley — Massachusetts Impressions,[53] El Salvadorian Footprints,[54] Dakota Footprints,[55] Carson Footprints,[56] the

51. Jerry MacDonald, *Earth's First Steps* (Boulder, CO: Johnson Printing, 1994), p. 266.
52. Earl Flint, *American Antiquarian*, 6:112–113, 1884; William Corliss, "Strange Artifacts," Volume M-1 (Glen Arm, MD: *The Sourcebook Project*, 1974), p. 13–23; Alan Bryan, "New Light on Ancient Nicaraguan Footprints," *Archaeology*, 26:146–147, 1973.
53. Charles Hitchcock, "Impressions (chiefly Tracks) on Alluvial Clay, in Hadley, Mass.," *The American Journal of Science and Arts*, May, 1855, p. 391–396.
54. Wolfgang Haberland and Willi-Herbert Grebe, "Prehistoric Footprints from El Salvador," *American Antiquity*, 22:282–285, 1957; William Corliss, "Ancient Man" (Glen Arm, MD: *The Sourcebook Project*, 1978), p. 643–644.
55. Herbert Hubbell, "Human Footprints in Stratified Rock," *Popular Science Monthly*, 22:262, 1882.
56. Joseph Le Conte, *Nature*, 28:101–102, May 31, 1883; William Corliss, "Strange Artifacts," Volume M-1 (Glen Arm, MD: *The Sourcebook Project*, 1974), p. 12–13.

Tennessean Tracks,[57] and the St. Louis Tracks.[58] I also encourage more documented research in journals on recent Texas discoveries/rediscoveries, such as the Sir George Tracks, O.W. Willet Print, Feminine Print, Texas Hand Print, and the Japanese Print.[59]

Though some of these cases are not the most impressive from the outset, nonetheless, I still encourage thorough research on the specimens utilizing modern scientific observations and techniques.

The Dinosaur (Not the Elephant!) in the Room

If an evolutionist found a *100%* true human footprint trail *with* dinosaur tracks running through it, how would that evolutionist respond? This is a "thought experiment."

Before you answer, consider some of the responses from the cases we previously examined. Recall that the *Scientific American* refused to show images in the case of the Berean prints. And to date, the *Smithsonian* still has not offered any images of the "simian" prints.

Naturally, we would expect an evolutionist to hold to their religiously held beliefs (via their worldview) and come up with (arbitrary) rescuing devices like "aliens," "other proposed animals," "misinterpreted data," and so on — basically anything but *humans,* which could then be used to argue for humans co-existing with dinosaurs.

But let me ask another question regarding the moral character of evolutionists who flatly deny the Bible in places like Genesis. Would we expect them to follow biblical teachings like honesty, truth, or any sort of integrity? Not necessarily! That is, if evolutionists are *consistent* with their professed naturalistic religion, where there is no God (i.e., no lawgiver, so no ultimate standard for right and a wrong).

At this point, it's necessary to point out that those who reject the Bible have *no ultimate basis to be honest* with the evidence.[60] That doesn't mean they won't, but it means they would have to give up their professed worldview and borrow from a biblical worldview in order to do so.

Don't get me wrong, I believe there are many secular researchers who put forth their best efforts to be truthful and honest in their work — and,

---

57. Editors, "Alleged Human Footprints in Tennessee Rocks," *Scientific American*, 47:388, 1882, p. 644–645.
58. Henry Schoolcraft, "Remarks of the Prints of Human Feet, Observed in the Secondary Limestone of the Mississippi Valley," *American Journal of Science*, 1:5:223–230, 1822.
59. Joe Taylor, *Fossil Facts and Fantasies* (Crosbyton, TX: Mt. Blanco Publishing Company, 1999), p. 70–72. The print was found in Texas with a Japanese film crew present, hence the name "Japanese" print.
60. Jason Lisle, "Evolution and the Challenge of Morality," *Answers in Genesis*, April 14, 2008, https://answersingenesis.org/morality/evolution-and-the-challenge-of-morality/.

of course, that should be commended. But being truthful and honest when doing research is a *Christian principle*, not one that comes from secular religions (atheism, naturalism, materialism, etc.).

So, this brings me to the *"dinosaur in the room."* Would some evolutionists just *ignore* the evidence? Would some evolutionists go so far as to *destroy* the evidence? I wish the answer was "Never!" But, in reality, we are all living in a sin-cursed and broken world where, sadly, many people refuse to tell the truth, thus not always being honest — especially if research dollars are on the line or their job could be eliminated, or they may be accused of being a fraudster. If the secular world is so confident in their worldview, then why not present the evidence? Science thrives on controversy.

This is not a full sweeping rant against my fellow colleagues who happen to be evolutionists! Please don't get me wrong. I have several friends and associates who are evolutionists. At the same time, if I can be equally blunt, some creationists are not perfect either!

That being said, the bottom line is I would like to see more researchers properly documenting alleged human ichnites and giving honest assessments regardless of which religious side you stand on when you view the evidence.

25

Short Answers to Other Common Dinosaur Questions

There are so many pointed questions that entire chapters could be dedicated to them. However, I do want to give short answers to some of the common questions that arise regarding dinosaurs. Ready, set, *GO!*

What About Christians Who Believe the Evolutionary Story of Dinosaurs?

Christians who buy into the origins account from another religion like secular humanism (e.g., naturalism, materialism, atheism, evolutionism, etc.) are essentially mixing their religion with another religion. To be more precise, they are mixing it with a *false* religion (e.g., Exodus 32; Nehemiah 13:26[1]). This is commonly called *syncretism* or (in laymen's terms) *compromise*.

Syncretism is the attempted process of syncretizing two (or more) religions together. However, this attempt foolishly *elevates* man's (fallible) ideas to supersede the (infallible) Word of God. As a result, God and His Word, which is the absolute authority on all matters, gets demoted, deleted, reinterpreted, or thrown out (simply because an individual "feels" like it). Simply put, it is a faulty appeal to authority fallacy.

Yet another major problem occurs. If one takes the secular view of origins (like believing the rock layers represent "millions of years" instead of being Flood sediment) and attempts to insert this view into the Bible before Adam and sin, then we have a gigantic theological problem — *"death before sin."*

---

1. "Did not Solomon king of Israel sin by these things? Yet among many nations there was no king like him, who was beloved of his God; and God made him king over all Israel. Nevertheless pagan women caused even him to sin" (Nehemiah 13:26).

The Bible makes it abundantly clear that death/suffering is the result of man's *sin*. Both man and animals were affected by Adam's sin in Genesis 3. The first recorded death of anything was in Genesis 3:21,[2] having coats or tunics of *skins* to cover Adam and Eve's sin. Hence the direct relationship between human sin and animal death was instituted — animal sacrifice for sin.

But in the secular (religious) long-age scenario, they have millions/billions of years of death, pain, struggle, suffering cancer, tuberculosis, animals eating other animals *prior* to sin (as seen in the fossil record). This scenario utterly attacks the character of God by making a mockery of Him, who is the God of Life and *is* the Life (John 14:6[3]). Deuteronomy 32:4[4] says every work of God is *perfect*. So we expect the work of creation to be *perfect* — a world full of life, not death. Genesis 1:31[5] says everything that God had made was *very good*. And God would not call millions of years of death and suffering very good.

Genesis 1:29–30[6] states that all animals and man were originally vegetarian.[7] It wasn't until *after the Flood* that God first permitted man to eat meat (Genesis 9:3).

But it's critically important to notice that if *death* was around prior to sin, then it undermines the *Gospel of Jesus Christ*, who came to save us from sin and *death* and to put an end to the sacrificial system (which had been set up in some form since Genesis 3). Christ's death was sufficient once for all time (Hebrews 7:27,[8] 9:12,[9] 10:10[10]).

---

2. "Also for Adam and his wife the Lord God made tunics of skin, and clothed them" (Genesis 3:21).
3. "Jesus said to him, 'I am the way, the truth, and the life. No one comes to the Father except through Me'" (John 14:6).
4. "He is the Rock, His work is perfect; for all His ways are justice, a God of truth and without injustice; righteous and upright is He" (Deuteronomy 32:4).
5. "Then God saw everything that He had made, and indeed it was very good. So the evening and the morning were the sixth day" (Genesis 1:31).
6. "And God said, 'See, I have given you every herb that yields seed which is on the face of all the earth, and every tree whose fruit yields seed; to you it shall be for food. Also, to every beast of the earth, to every bird of the air, and to everything that creeps on the earth, in which there is life, I have given every green herb for food'; and it was so" (Genesis 1:29–30).
7. Note, in a biblical sense, plants were given as food, and thus aren't actually "living" (even though we define them as "living" in a biological sense).
8. "who does not need daily, as those high priests, to offer up sacrifices, first for His own sins and then for the people's, for this He did once for all when He offered up Himself" (Hebrews 7:27).
9. "Not with the blood of goats and calves, but with His own blood He entered the Most Holy Place once for all, having obtained eternal redemption" (Hebrews 9:12).
10. "By that will we have been sanctified through the offering of the body of Jesus Christ once for all" (Hebrews 10:10).

God the Son (Jesus Christ) took the infinite punishment from the infinite Father (the full wrath of God on our behalf) when He died on the Cross, and provided the way for salvation through His death, burial, and Resurrection. So having *death before sin* causes massive theological problems! Especially if death and suffering are seen as *good* things — why did Jesus come to save us from death?

What Do Evolutionists Believe Happened to Dinosaurs?

The most popular view, in general today, is that some dinosaurs eventually "turned into birds" over time.[11] This idea originally became popular in the 1860s when a man named Thomas Huxley, an early follower of Charles Darwin, first promoted the idea that small theropod dinosaurs evolved into birds (i.e., the "Dino-to-Bird Hypothesis"). However, not all evolutionists believe dinosaurs turned into birds.

Impactor

The second most popular view is an asteroid, comet, large meteorite, or other "impactor" struck the earth about 65–66 million years ago and caused the extinction of the dinosaurs. They claim there are two possible locations for this impact. The primary (and most popular) site is said to be located off the coast of the Yucatán Peninsula in Mexico (called the Chicxulub crater). The second (and lesser known) site is said to be located off the coast of Guinea in West Africa (called the Nadir crater).[12]

This belief is primarily based on the evolutionists' interpretation of the fine layering of iridium, which is often found in *meteorites*, imbedded in sedimentary layers at the K/T boundary,[13] between the Cretaceous and the lowest layer of the Tertiary sediment, called the Paleocene.

However, that's *not* the only explanation. Iridium can also be produced from significant volcanic action. One secularist writes,

> On the other hand, if there were a large number of volcanoes active at this time their dust could have produced the iridium layer from material below the earth's crust.[14]

---

11. Yes, they essentially believe you're eating "fried dinosaur" when eating lunch at Chick-fil-A!
12. Jamie Carter, "What Killed the Dinosaurs? New Discovery in Africa Hints at Multiple Asteroid Strikes, Say Scientists," *Forbes Science*, August 18, 2022, https://www.forbes.com/sites/jamiecartereurope/2022/08/18/what-killed-the-dinosaurs-new-discovery-in-africa-hints-at-multiple-asteroid-strikes-say-scientists/?sh=25e98f0329a7.
13. This abbreviation comes from the German words: Kreidezeit (Cretaceous) and Tertiär (Tertiary).
14. Doug Dixon, *The Illustrated Dinosaur Encyclopedia* (New York, NY: Gallery Books, 1988), p. 128–129.

From a Christian perspective, the volcanoes that erupted all over the earth during certain stages of the global Flood (Psalm 104:8–9[15]) could have easily produced the layer of iridium we find at the K/T boundary.

Impactor + Dino-to-Bird

Some evolutionists try to combine this "impactor hypothesis" with the idea that dinosaurs evolved into birds. In their story, they essentially argue that the impact event didn't kill off *all* the dinosaurs but (somehow) left a *few* alive — such as theropods — which then evolved into birds.

This idea seems like a fable or myth considering that there are several birds known to be living before this alleged impact strike even *by the evolutionary story*. They are:

- Microraptor Gui
- Confuciusornis
- Archaeopteryx
- Parrot[16]
- Turducken[17]

It's odd, even from an evolutionary perspective, to believe that birds didn't change into birds but insist on a theropod changing into birds.

Previous Reptile Hypothesis

Another hypothesis, formulated by Dr. Alan Feduccia and his colleagues, states that some reptile other than dinosaurs, which supposedly existed long before dinosaurs, evolved into birds. So, in this view, any extinction model is acceptable since dinosaurs did not give rise to birds.

Other Proposals

There are hosts of other (lesser known) supposed extinction models that state the dinosaurs died because of:

- An explosion of a nearby star that sent deadly cosmic radiation to earth

---

15. "The mountains rose, the valleys sank down to the place that you appointed for them. You set a boundary that they may not pass, so that they might not again cover the earth" (Psalm 104:8–9).

16. Thomas Stidham, "A Lower Jaw from a Cretaceous Parrot," *Nature* 396, 29–30 (1998). https://doi.org/10.1038/23841.

17. Katherine Wu, "At 67 Million Years Old, Oldest Modern Bird Ever Found Is Natural 'Turducken,'" *Smithsonian Magazine*, March 20, 2020, https://www.smithsonianmag.com/smart-news/67-million-years-old-oldest-modern-bird-ever-found-was-natural-turducken-180974460/.

- Diseases (like viruses or bacterial outbreaks)
- Starvation
- Climate change
- Acid rain
- Toxic foods
- Tsunamis or other local floods
- An ice age
- Parasites
- Rapid fungal outbreaks
- Egg disorders
- Magnetic field reversals
- Mammals ate too many of their eggs
- Volcanic eruptions
- Aliens that invaded and killed or took them (yes, there are people who believe this)

Notice that *man hunting them and destroying their habitats to the point of extinction* is not listed as a possible reason and not even considered an option by evolutionists (since humans and dinosaurs cannot live together in their secular story). And yet this was surely the case, after the Flood, up until dinosaurs went fully extinct. Though it's possible to blame some of these models as partial reasons for their extinction (diseases, parasites, etc.), the ultimate reason is *sin* (since Genesis 3) when death began to reign, which thus caused the extinction of hosts of different animals.

Where Did Dinosaurs Come from in the Secular Story?

We often hear a great deal of talk about alleged dinosaur demise stories, such as dinosaurs supposedly evolving into birds, but there is little on the *origin* of dinosaurs. In the fossil record, they suddenly appeared with hosts of variation within their kinds. From the biblical model, we expect to find hosts of variations within each dinosaur kind rapidly buried in Flood sediment.

But finding this variation in the fossil record is a huge problem in the secular model. This is a major reason why the secular world has been conspicuously vague on this topic. Thus, as an (arbitrary) excuse, secularists claim that dinosaurs came from previous reptiles called *"dinosauromorphs."* But what exactly are the dinosauromorphs?

In the secular story, the *Herrerasaurus* is claimed to be among the "earliest" dinosaurs that existed about 230 million years ago (which, of course, is just Flood sediment for those paying attention). However, even these alleged ancestors of dinosaurs are problematic for the secular story. One popular article sums it up well, saying:

There are a bunch of places in Argentina and Brazil that are vying for the crown of the birthplace of the earliest definite dinosaurs," says Paul. "But when they first appeared, they were already recognisably dinosaurs. This suggests that dinosaurs had to have a longer evolutionary history that we don't yet know about, and there is some debate as to how much of that evolutionary history is currently missing.[18]

In short, they have *no clue*.

What about the Loch Ness Monster?

Loch (Lake) Ness is a famous lake in Scotland that is part of the three major lakes in the Great Glen rift valley in the Scottish highlands (the other two being Lochy and Oich). For over a thousand years, people have frequently reported seeing strange reptile-like water creatures in the Loch Ness, with the first reported sighting going all the way back to the 6th Century A.D. Over time, this "monster" became known simply as "Nessie," which exploded into popularity, in 1933, after a London surgeon took a photograph of it (with the hopes of capturing it for a circus).

However, don't get too excited. No evidence has been offered that's definitively confirmed the identity of this water reptile (like a plesiosaur). Was/Is Nessie a water creature that has simply gone extinct? Perhaps. Was/Is Nessie a victim of modern hoaxers? Perhaps. Though I would leave open a slim possibility that some of these presumed extinct water reptiles may still exist in some remote parts of the world's waterways, I don't have my hopes set too high. The predominant view is that many of these reptiles have gone the way of the dodo — which is reasonable — so I wouldn't expect to find them today.

Even so, wide reporting of a plesiosaur-like creature washed up on a Georgia Beach (Georgia's Barrier Islands) in 2018 that still causes people to wonder what may still roam about in the ocean.[19] People suggest this creature, now dubbed "Alty" for Altamaha-ha, could be one of many things

---

18. Josh Davis, "Where Did Dinosaurs Come From?" *Natural History Museum London*, accessed September 8, 2022, https://www.nhm.ac.uk/discover/where-did-dinosaurs-come-from.html.

19. Josh Hafner, "Loch Ness Monster-like Creature Washes Up on Georgia Shore," *USA Today*, March 20, 2018.

(decomposing basking shark, frilled shark, or a sturgeon shark) or simply some unknown creature. But the video shown in the reporting is intriguing, nonetheless. Without a scientific good analysis, we may be left with more questions than answers.

As a point of note, in 1977 there was a creature dredged up that many mistakenly took as a dead plesiosaur. However after further analysis, this creature, *Zuiyo-maru*, snagged by a Japanese fishing trawler, was found to be the corpse of a basking shark.[20]

Dinosaur Soft Tissue — What Does It Mean?

Dr. Mary Schweitzer was a lead researcher in dinosaur soft tissue finds.[21] Her work continues to send shockwaves through the entire science world in both the evolution and creation communities! In short, she and her team amazingly found preserved soft tissue (like blood vessels and red blood cells) from a T-rex femur that is supposedly millions of years old. The soft tissue even gave off an odor and was stretchy! They continue to inspire other researchers to look for soft tissue in dinosaur bones as well, which has now turned into an entirely new field within paleontological studies.

Many creationists have also found soft tissue in dinosaur bones, such as Drs. Mark Armitage and Kevin Anderson who found soft tissue after they cracked open a fossilized triceratops horn.[22]

Buddy Davis, Dr. John Whitmore (Cedarville University), and Mike Liston found some bones in Alaska that were initially thought to be fresh (as a result of being frozen instead of fossilized).[23] So it was presumed that these fresh bones could have the same significance as other soft tissue in dinosaurs. However, after further study, they were found to be *permineralized* and hence *had fossilized,* and the researchers now advise not calling these bones "unfossilized."[24]

20. Tommy Mitchell, "Didn't a Fishing Boat Find a Dead Plesiosaur?" *Answers in Genesis,* September 7, 2010, https://answersingenesis.org/creationism/arguments-to-avoid/didnt-a-fishing-boat-find-a-dead-plesiosaur/.

21. Mary Schweitzer et al, "Heme Compounds in Dinosaur Trabecular Bone," *Proceedings of the National Academy of Science USA,* Vol. 94, p. 6291–6296, June 1997; Mary Schweitzer et al, "Soft-Tissue Vessels and Cellular Preservation in *Tyrannosaurus rex,*" *Science,* Vol. 307, March 25, 2005, 1952–1955.

22. M.H. Armitage. and K.L. Anderson, "Soft Sheets of Fibrillar Bone from a Fossil of the Supraorbital Horn of the Dinosaur Triceratops Horridus," *Acta Histochemica,* 2013, 115:603–608; M.H. Armitage and K.L. Anderson, "Light and Electron Microscope Study of Soft Bone Osteocytes from a Triceratops Horridus Supraorbitalhorn," *Microscopy & Microanalysis* (Hartford, CT), 2014.

23. B. Davis, M. Liston, and J. Whitmore, *The Great Alaskan Dinosaur Adventure* (Green Forest, AR: Master Books, 1998).

24. John Whitmore, "'Unfossilized' Alaskan Dinosaur Bones?" *Journal of Creation,* 19(3), 2005, p. 66.

Due to many more finds (e.g., Ichthyosaur,[25] etc.), Dr. Brian Thomas at the Institute for Creation Research has been keeping track of hosts of soft tissue finds and continually publishing these findings. I suggest checking out his book on the subject (*Ancient and Fossil Bone Collagen Remnants*). Also, the late Dr. Kevin Anderson also published on this subject in an excellent book called *Echoes of the Jurassic*.

From a big picture, finding soft tissue is an amazing confirmation that dinosaurs died much more recently than the supposed claim of 65–68 million years ago (as per the evolutionary story timeline). Rather, it makes a lot more sense that dinosaur bones are only thousands of years old being buried rapidly during the Flood resulting in the preservation of soft tissue.

Carbon-14 in Dinosaur Bones? (Semi-technical)

The carbon-14 (^{14}C) radiometric dating method is often associated with archaeological finds. However, its accuracy is…if I'm blunt…not very good. In short, this dating method critically depends on several key assumptions, such as:

- What was the initial amounts of ^{14}C?

- Did the amount of ^{14}C remain constant? (i.e., was any ^{14}C added or removed?)

- Has the rate of decay (^{14}C into ^{14}N), chemical environments, in water (marine reservoir effect), and temperature remained constant?

(And if any of these assumptions are incorrect, then the result is not accurate!) Also, contrary to popular belief, it's important to realize that the carbon-14 dating method *cannot* even give dates on the order of *millions or billions* of years! This is actually a common (and major) misconception in the general public today. Rather, this dating method can only give dates on the order of *thousands* of years (50,000–100,000 years is the *theoretical maximum*).

Thus, long-age believers instead prefer to use other radiometric dating methods, like rubidium-strontium, potassium-argon, or uranium decay, to defend their religious belief of "millions or billions of years." Yet each of these methods is fraught with the same (or similar) assumptions as carbon-14 dating that also causes serious problems for the final assumed calculation.

On top of that, if these methods are truly accurate, then we'd expect them to yield the same date over and over again across methods. *But this*

---

25. Philip Robinson, "Soft Tissue Preservation in a Jurassic Ichthyosaur," *Creation* 42(1):36–37, January 2020.

doesn't happen![26] Furthermore, the results from some radiometric dating methods completely undermine other radiometric methods (^{14}C dating is one such example).

How does ^{14}C dating work? Simply put, when an organism is alive, it constantly takes in ^{14}C and ^{12}C (stable carbon) from the atmosphere through breathing and diet; however, when it dies, the carbon intake stops. Since ^{14}C is radioactive (it decays over time into ^{14}N), the amount of ^{14}C in a dead organism gets less and less over time.

Thus, "carbon-14 dates" are determined by measuring the ratio of carbon-14 to carbon-12 (^{14}C/^{12}C) in once living or growing things (i.e., organic material, such as wood or bone) and compared with the ratio in living things today. However, note that ^{14}C has a derived half-life presumed to be 5,730 years (an estimate based on lab experiments), which means all the ^{14}C in any organic material that's supposedly 100,000+ years old should have completely decayed into nitrogen.[27]

But here's the really interesting part. Because of its supposed "short" half-life, ^{14}C dating frequently undermines other radiometric dating methods. For instance, we find ^{14}C in wood that's trapped and encased in lava flows, which is said to be *millions* of years old by other radiometric dating methods.[28] If these items truly are *millions* of years old, then we should *not* find any traces of ^{14}C. All the ^{14}C should have completely decayed into nitrogen by then.

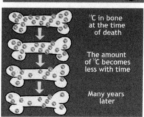

---

26. For a technical treatise on this subject, I suggest: Larry Vardiman, Andrew Snelling, and Eugene Chaffin, *Radioisotopes and the Age of the Earth*, Volume II, co-published by the Institute for Creation Research, El Cajon, CA, and the Creation Research Society, Chino Valley, AZ, 2005.

27. This does not mean that a ^{14}C date of 50,000 or 100,000 would be entirely trustworthy — it is a theoretical maximum which disproves any older date. I am only using this to highlight the mistaken assumptions behind uniformitarian dating methods.

28. Andrew Snelling, "Conflicting 'Ages' of Tertiary Basalt and Contained Fossilized Wood, Crinum, Central Queensland Australia," *Technical Journal* 14, no. 2 (2005): 99–122.

Even carbon-based materials — like coal and diamonds, which are normally found sandwiched between rock layers — are repeatedly said to be millions or billions of years old (based on the "age" of the rock layers that contain them). However, the ^{14}C ages on coal and diamonds have been shown to be on the order of only *tens of thousands* of years.[29] Obviously, coal and diamonds CANNOT be *millions/billions* of years old if they have any traces of ^{14}C still in them.

So then, which date (if any) is truly correct? Neither! Coal, for example, was made as a result of the Flood of Noah's day.

Also, diamonds can be made quickly both in nature (like in violent volcanic eruptions, such as Mt. St. Helens) and in labs.[30] And coal can be made easily in just a matter of weeks.[31] So the idea that coal and diamonds formed millions or billions of years ago is really a stretch.

Now, you might be wondering, is there any ^{14}C in dinosaur bones? Recall that we've found dinosaur bones with soft tissue (which means they have organic material, like *carbon*, still in them) and hence are eligible for ^{14}C dating. Guess what? Dinosaur bones *overwhelmingly* have ^{14}C in them![32] This is a great confirmation showing that dinosaurs bones are not *millions of years old*.

Scales or Feathers?

Did dinosaurs have scales or feathers? We find hosts of scaly skin imprints of dinosaurs, which is why anatomists, paleontologists, and other dinosaur experts, since the 1800s, have routinely classified them as reptiles. And rightly so! More specifically, dinosaurs have *scutes* (which are specialized types of scales). For example, according to the Smithsonian Institute, a skin imprint showed that T-rex was likely covered in scales, *not feathers*.[33] Also, duck-billed dinosaurs have dark,

Hadrosaur skin imprint (cast)

29. John Baumgardner, "^{14}C Evidence for a Recent Global Flood and a Young Earth," in *Radioisotopes and the Age of the Earth: Results of a Young-Earth Creationist Research Initiative,* ed. Vardiman et al (Santee, CA: Institute for Creation Research; Chino Valley, AZ: Creation Research Society), p.587–630, 2005.

30. Ken Ham and Bodie Hodge, *A Flood of Evidence* (Green Forest, AR: Master Books, 2016), p. 127–132.

31. Ibid., p. 117–122.

32. For example, see B. Thomas and V. Nelson, "Radiocarbon in Dinosaur and Other Fossils," *Creation Research Society Quarterly,* 2015. 51(4): 299–311; John Michael Fischer, "Carbon-14-dated Dinosaur Bones Are Less Than 40,000 Years Old," *New Geology,* accessed September 8, 2022, http://newgeology.us/presentation48.html.

33. Brigit Katz, "T. Rex Was Likely Covered in Scales, Not Feathers," *Smithsonian Magazine,* June 8, 2017, https://www.smithsonianmag.com/smart-news/t-rex-skin-was-not-covered-feathers-study-says-180963603/.

scaly skin imprints that have a basketball-like texture.[34]

In short, we do *not* find feathers on dinosaurs. *Period.* However, the secular world has convoluted this debate by trying to (arbitrarily) reclassify and redefine birds as dinosaurs (e.g., "avian dinosaurs"). So, when researchers find a bird in the fossil record, they call it a *"feathered dinosaur."* Simply put, birds are *birds* and dinosaurs are *dinosaurs.*

T. Rex skin imprint from Smithsonian.com

Some of this confusion is also from the fossilized collagen fibers (these are parts of rotting and decaying flesh that hold the tissues together) that are sometimes found in dinosaur fossils.[35] Some people have tried to justify these types of findings as "protofeathers" or the "beginning of feathers." But obviously, these are *not* feathers at all.

On top of that, some people have also misinterpreted muscle knobs (these are where muscles and other connective tissues connect to the bone) to be quill knobs for feathers.[36] This happens to be the case for the *Dakotaraptor* and *Velociraptor.*

Was the Serpent a Dinosaur?

Recall Satan's use of a *serpent* in the Garden of Eden that he used to deceive Eve, which led to the Fall (Genesis 3).[37]

34. Jennifer Nalewiski, "Rare Fossils Reveal Basketball-like Skin on Duck-billed Dinosaur," *Live Science*, September 6, 2022, https://www.livescience.com/hadrosaur-dinosaur-skin-bones-alberta-canada.

35. T. Lingham-Soliar, A. Feduccia, and X. Wang, "A New Chinese Specimen Indicates That 'Protofeathers' in the Early Cretaceous Theropod Dinosaur Sinosauropteryx Are Degraded Collagen Fibres," *Proceedings of the Royal Society*, published August 7, 2007, doi: 10.1098/rspb.2007.0352, Proc. R. Soc. B 7 August 2007 vol. 274 no. 1620 1823–1829, http://rspb.royalsocietypublishing.org/content/274/1620/1823.full.

36. Brian Thomas, "Do 'Quill Knobs' Show Dino-to-Bird Evolution?" *Institute for Creation Research*, December 3, 2015, https://www.icr.org/article/do-quill-knobs-show-dino-bird-evolution.

37. Some people argue that animals can't speak, but that is obviously not accurate since some animals today, like parrots, can speak phonetically very well. The cunning deception of Satan through this serpent is how the cleverness came through. The original serpent had the ability to phonetically speak in the beginning (e.g., Genesis 3:1–5) and perhaps lost it during the curse when it was made to be lower to the ground and to eat dust. Many theologians and scholars historically believed the serpent underwent a physical cursed design to be at a lower position). It is possible that that particular serpent has gone extinct as well.

Was this serpent involved in the deception a dinosaur? I doubt it. From Genesis 3:14, we read that the serpent would *crawl on its belly* because of the curse. Most people normally think of snakes (which obviously crawl on their belly). But any lizard that has legs extending out to the side (e.g., crocodiles, legless lizards, and monitor lizards) could also fit this description of "crawl on its belly."[38]

Dinosaurs had underslung legs to stand erect, so it's very unlikely Satan used a dinosaur. If the serpent was originally a dinosaur, it would have been cursed to no longer be a dinosaur like those recognized in the fossil record from the Flood.

Rather, biblically speaking, could the serpent be a type of viper? The Bible says the *seed* of the serpent would attack the *seed* of the woman (Genesis 3:15) and yet be crushed; Christ is that Seed (offspring) of the woman (Galatians 3:16). Consider the seed, brood, offspring of the serpent in these New Testament verses (emphasis added):

- But when he saw many of the Pharisees and Sadducees coming to his baptism, he said to them, "Brood of *vipers*! Who warned you to flee from the wrath to come?" (Matthew 3:7).

- "Brood of *vipers*! How can you, being evil, speak good things? For out of the abundance of the heart the mouth speaks" (Matthew 12:34).

- "*Serpents*, brood of *vipers*! How can you escape the condemnation of hell?" (Matthew 23:33).

- "Then he said to the multitudes that came out to be baptized by him, 'Brood of *vipers*! Who warned you to flee from the wrath to come?'" (Luke 3:7).

- You are of your *father the devil*, and the desires of *your father* you want to do. He was a murderer from the beginning, and does not stand in the truth, because there is no truth in him. When he speaks a lie, he speaks from his own resources, for he is a liar and the father of it (John 8:44).

How Could a Loving God Allow Dinosaurs to Go Extinct?

By and large, dinosaurs are likely extinct. But are dinosaurs *completely* extinct? This is a great question.... For me to say yes, I'd have to be able to look *everywhere* in the world at the exact same time. I'm not that powerful!

---

38. Also, the Bible describes Satan as the Great Dragon and the Ancient Serpent/Serpent of Old (Revelation 20:2), so it's very possible that he used some type of sprawling-legged lizard (since these types of lizards are usually categorized as dragons).

That is, I'd leave open the (rare) possibilities that some remaining dinosaurs could be living in remote places like in dense rainforests, underground, or even be semi-aquatic.

Extinctions and death occur because we all live in a sin-cursed world where animals die all the time. I've had many pets over the years, but I always had to remember that animals, unlike man, were not made in the image of God. Furthermore, I needed to remember that animals (e.g., Genesis 3:14[39]) and the entire world (Genesis 3:17[40]; Roman 8:21–22[41]) lay under the curse that God declared on all creation, after Adam and Eve sinned.

When man fell, the entire dominion that belongs to man also fell (Genesis 1:26[42]). Consequently, death reigned from Genesis 3 forward.

God is perfectly just and so He must punish sin perfectly. So, in each case, Adam (Genesis 3:17[43]), Eve (Genesis 3:16[44]),˙ the serpent (Genesis 3:14[45]), and Satan (Genesis 3:15), all received their due punishment. But in the middle of all these punishments is a promise — the seed of the woman — *Christ* (Galatians 3:16[46]).

In a world full of death, not only dinosaurs but many animal kinds have gone extinct. But in no way does that negate God's perfect love. Rather, this shows the effect of sin on our *relationship* to God. Due to sin, we have been given a taste of what life is like without God. Just imagine, for a moment, a world where God's blessings are fully removed!

---

39. "So the Lord God said to the serpent: 'Because you have done this, you are cursed more than all cattle, and more than every beast of the field; on your belly you shall go, and you shall eat dust all the days of your life'" (Genesis 3:14).
40. "Then to Adam He said, 'Because you have heeded the voice of your wife, and have eaten from the tree of which I commanded you, saying, "You shall not eat of it": 'Cursed is the ground for your sake; In toil you shall eat of it All the days of your life'" (Genesis 3:17).
41. "because the creation itself also will be delivered from the bondage of corruption into the glorious liberty of the children of God. For we know that the whole creation groans and labors with birth pangs together until now" (Romans 8:21–22).
42. "Then God said, 'Let Us make man in Our image, according to Our likeness; let them have dominion over the fish of the sea, over the birds of the air, and over the cattle, over all the earth and over every creeping thing that creeps on the earth'" (Genesis 1:26).
43. "Then to Adam He said, 'Because you have heeded the voice of your wife, and have eaten from the tree of which I commanded you, saying, "You shall not eat of it": 'Cursed is the ground for your sake; In toil you shall eat of it All the days of your life'" (Genesis 3:17).
44. "To the woman He said: 'I will greatly multiply your sorrow and your conception; In pain you shall bring forth children; Your desire [shall be] for your husband, And he shall rule over you'" (Genesis 3:16).
45. "So the Lord God said to the serpent: 'Because you have done this, you are cursed more than all cattle, and more than every beast of the field; on your belly you shall go, and you shall eat dust all the days of your life'" (Genesis 3:14).
46. "Now to Abraham and his Seed were the promises made. He does not say, 'And to seeds,' as of many, but as of one, 'And to your Seed,' who is Christ" (Galatians 3:16).

When Adam and Eve sinned against God, they committed *high treason* against God by disobeying Him and eating what they were told not to eat. Our life comes directly from Adam and Eve's life (consider Hebrews 7:9–10[47]). Hence, we too are made in the image of God, but we are also sinners inherently and by choice (Romans 3).

Because the world is cursed, God no longer upholds the world in a perfect state. Thus, the whole world is subject to death, disease, suffering, and extinctions, all because of sin. It is the punishment that should remind us of sin and give us a taste of what happens when we rebel against God. What we really need is a Savior to save us from sin and death.

The perfect punishment from God, who is infinite and eternal, is an infinite and eternal death, with the full wrath of an infinite God on us, in an eternal place called Hell (e.g., Revelation 21:8[48]). It is the perfect punishment we (as eternal beings made in the image of an eternal God) deserve. Hell is a place of eternal torment that was prepared for Satan and those who follow him (e.g., Matthew 25:41[49]) along with those who wage war against God (e.g., Daniel 12:2[50]; Matthew 25:46[51]; Revelation 20:14–15[52]).

In your sin, you war against God and there will be no peace unless you repent of your sin (wrongdoing and rebellion against God) and receive Jesus Christ as Lord and Savior. This is why Christians often remark on gravestones, to those in Christ, Rest in Peace (RIP) as there will be no rest for the wicked (consider Isaiah 57:20–21[53]; Revelation 14:11[54]). When you believe in Jesus — His death, burial, and Resurrection — you will receive the forgiveness He offers through His *grace alone* (apart from any "good" works).

---

47. "Even Levi, who receives tithes, paid tithes through Abraham, so to speak, for he was still in the loins of his father when Melchizedek met him" (Hebrews 7:9–10).
48 . "But the cowardly, unbelieving, abominable, murderers, sexually immoral, sorcerers, idolaters, and all liars shall have their part in the lake which burns with fire and brimstone, which is the second death" (Revelation 21:8).
49 . "Then He will also say to those on the left hand, 'Depart from Me, you cursed, into the everlasting fire prepared for the devil and his angels'" (Matthew 25:41).
50 . "And many of those who sleep in the dust of the earth shall awake, some to everlasting life, some to shame and everlasting contempt" (Daniel 12:2).
51 . "And these will go away into everlasting punishment, but the righteous into eternal life" (Matthew 25:46).
52 . "Then Death and Hades were cast into the lake of fire. This is the second death. And anyone not found written in the Book of Life was cast into the lake of fire" (Revelation 20:14–15).
53 . "But the wicked are like the troubled sea, when it cannot rest, whose waters cast up mire and dirt. 'There is no peace,' says my God, 'for the wicked'" (Isaiah 57:20–21).
54. "And the smoke of their torment ascends forever and ever; and they have no rest day or night, who worship the beast and his image, and whoever receives the mark of his name" (Revelation 14:11).

The infinite Son of God, Jesus Christ, became flesh (John 1:14[55]) and died the death we deserve on the Cross to take the infinite punishment and wrath from the infinite Father (e.g., Isaiah 53:4–11). Through His shed blood, we can have Christ's perfect righteousness transferred to us (imputed to us) to be seen as perfectly spotless (without blemish or sin) to be with God forever (Romans 4:23–24[56]), enjoying His blessing for eternity. This is what Heaven is — technically a new heaven and new earth — with the curse removed, enjoying God and His goodness for all eternity (e.g., Revelation 21:1,[57] 4[58]).

The power is in the Resurrection of Jesus Christ (Philippians 3:10[59]), having the power to lay down His life and take it up again (John 10:17[60]). Because of Christ's Resurrection, we too will be resurrected (1 Corinthians 15:12–22) — some to eternal life and others to eternal punishment. Dinosaurs may have come and gone, but your soul will go on forever.

I want to encourage you to have a better understanding of this gospel message from Scripture (God's revealed Word to all of us). Here are some great passages I want to encourage you to consider (Romans 10:17[61]).

The Genesis-Romans Road

- Genesis 1:1 — In the beginning God created the heavens and the earth.

- Genesis 1:31 — Then God saw everything that He had made, and indeed it was very good. So the evening and the morning were the sixth day.

- Genesis 3:17–19 — Then to Adam He said, "Because you have heeded the voice of your wife, and have eaten from the tree of which

---

55 . "And the Word became flesh and dwelt among us, and we beheld His glory, the glory as of the only begotten of the Father, full of grace and truth" (John 1:14).

56 . "Now it was not written for his sake alone that it was imputed to him, but also for us. It shall be imputed to us who believe in Him who raised up Jesus our Lord from the dead" (Romans 4:23–24).

57 . "Now I saw a new heaven and a new earth, for the first heaven and the first earth had passed away. Also there was no more sea" (Revelation 21:1).

58 . "And God will wipe away every tear from their eyes; there shall be no more death, nor sorrow, nor crying. There shall be no more pain, for the former things have passed away" (Revelation 21:4).

59 . "that I may know Him and the power of His resurrection, and the fellowship of His sufferings, being conformed to His death" (Philippians 3:10).

60 . "Therefore My Father loves Me, because I lay down My life that I may take it again" (John 10:17).

61 . "So then faith comes by hearing, and hearing by the word of God" (Romans 10:17).

I commanded you, saying, 'You shall not eat of it': "Cursed is the ground for your sake; in toil you shall eat of it all the days of your life. Both thorns and thistles it shall bring forth for you, and you shall eat the herb of the field. In the sweat of your face you shall eat bread till you return to the ground, for out of it you were taken; for dust you are, and to dust you shall return."

- Romans 5:12 — Therefore, just as through one man sin entered the world, and death through sin, and thus death spread to all men, because all sinned.

- Romans 3:23 — For all have sinned and fall short of the glory of God.

- Romans 6:23 — For the wages of sin is death, but the gift of God is eternal life in Christ Jesus our Lord.

- Romans 10:9 — That if you confess with your mouth the Lord Jesus and believe in your heart that God has raised Him from the dead, you will be saved. (See also John 3:16 and Acts 16:30-31.)

- Romans 5:1 — Therefore, having been justified by faith, we have peace with God through our Lord Jesus Christ.

Here are a few other passages worth noting about repentance and salvation (and many could be given, but I hope these speak to you):

- 2 Corinthians 7:10 — For godly sorrow produces repentance leading to salvation, not to be regretted; but the sorrow of the world produces death.

- 2 Peter 3:9 — The Lord is not slack concerning His promise, as some count slackness, but is longsuffering toward us, not willing that any should perish but that all should come to repentance.

- Acts 16:30–31 — And he brought them out and said, "Sirs, what must I do to be saved?" So they said, "Believe on the Lord Jesus, and you will be saved, you and your household."

- Ephesians 2:8–9 — For by grace you have been saved through faith, and that not of yourselves; it is the gift of God, not of works, lest anyone should boast.

My hope is that you truly give your life to Christ. I am up front about the fact that I want to see people saved from this sin-cursed, death-ridden, and broken world. My reason for discussing dinosaurs isn't just to teach about dinosaurs. I want people to realize the Bible is true and that dinosaurs are a great confirmation of the truth of the Scriptures. Because the Bible is true, the message of the Gospel (good news about Jesus) is also true. The Bible says:

- Mark 8:36 — "For what will it profit a man if he gains the whole world, and loses his own soul?

You need Jesus Christ, the Son of God, who paid the infinite punishment that you (and all the rest of us) deserve on the Cross. Only God the Son, who is infinite, could take the infinite punishment from an infinite God the Father to make salvation possible. We, as mankind in Adam, messed up God's perfect world, and Christ, in His love, stepped in to save us (Romans 5:8). That is truly a loving God.

- John 1:12 — But as many as received Him, to them He gave the right to become children of God, to those who believe in His name.

Final Remarks

I want to thank you for taking the time to read this book. My goal was to help you get started down a path to understand dinosaurs and dragons from a biblical viewpoint — using God's Word as the absolute basis to look at dinosaurs.

Though there is so much more I wanted to put into this book, it merely becomes a point of discernment as what to include and what to leave out. I want to encourage you to continue your studies of dinosaurs from a biblical viewpoint. God's Word is always right but we, as fallible people, can make errors from time to time and I ask for a little grace as I am not perfect either.

With this in mind, some of you may like more hefty science and more technical details. If you are in this camp, I suggest getting started with books and research projects like:

- *Dinosaurs — Marvels of God's Design* by Dr. Tim Clarey
- *Dinosaur Challenges and Mysteries* by Mike Oard
- *Echoes of the Jurassic* by Dr. Kevin Anderson
- iDino I and iDino II projects by the Creation Research Society

For those interested in laymen resources I suggest:

- *The Great Dinosaur Mystery Solved* by Ken Ham
- *Dinosaurs and Creation* by Dr. Don DeYoung

For great family resources, I suggest:

- *Dragons — Legends and Lore of Dinosaurs* by Bodie Hodge
- *Dinosaurs of Eden* by Ken Ham
- *Dinosaurs for Kids* by Ken Ham

For little kids:

- *D Is for Dinosaur* by Ken Ham

From here, there are so many more you can dive into. God bless you on your journey.

Bodie Hodge

Appendix 1

<hr>

Did Dinosaurs Evolve into Birds?
(abridged)

<hr>

Dr. David Menton

What Do Evolutionists Claim about the Origin of Birds?

Evolutionists have long speculated that birds evolved from reptiles. At one time or another, virtually every living and extinct class of reptiles has been proposed as the ancestor of birds. The famous Darwinian apologist Thomas Huxley was the first to speculate (in the mid 1800s) that birds evolved from dinosaurs.

While this notion has gone in and out of favor over the years, it is currently a popular view among evolutionists. Indeed, the origin of birds from dinosaurs is touted as irrefutable dogma in our schools, biology textbooks, and in the popular media.

While evolutionists now agree that birds are related in some way to dinosaurs, they are divided over whether birds evolved from some early shared ancestor of the dinosaurs within the archosauria (which includes alligators, pterosaurs, plesiosaurs, ichthyosaurs, and thecodonts) or directly from advanced theropod dinosaurs (bipedal meat eating dinosaurs such as the well known *Tyrannosaurus rex*). The latter view has gained in popularity since 1970 when John Ostrom discovered a rather "bird-like" early Cretaceous theropod dinosaur called *Deinonychus*.

An adult *Deinonychus* measured about 12 feet long, weighed over 150 pounds, and was about 5 feet tall standing on its two hind legs. Like other theropods (which means "beast foot"), *Deinonychus* had forelimbs much smaller than its hind limbs with hands bearing three fingers and feet bearing three toes. The most distinctive feature of *Deinonychus* (which means "terrible claw") is a large curved talon on its middle toe.

One of the main reasons that *Deinonychus* and other similar theropod dinosaurs (called dromaeosaurs) seemed to be plausible ancestors to birds is that, like birds, these creatures walk solely on their hind legs and have only three digits on their hands. But, as we shall see, there are many problems with transforming any dinosaur, and particularly a theropod, into a bird.

Problems with Dinosaurs Evolving into Birds

Warm Blooded vs. Cold Blooded

Seemingly forgotten in all the claims that birds are essentially dinosaurs (or at least that they evolved from dinosaurs) is the fact that dinosaurs are reptiles. There are many differences between birds and reptiles, including the fact that (with precious few exceptions) living reptiles are "cold-blooded" creatures while birds and mammals are "warm-blooded." Indeed, even compared to most mammals, birds have exceptionally *high* body temperatures resulting from a high metabolic rate.

The difference between cold- and warm-blooded animals isn't simply in the relative temperature of the blood, but rather in their ability to maintain a constant body core temperature. Thus, "warm-blooded" animals such as birds and mammals have internal physiological mechanisms to maintain an essentially constant body temperature and are more properly called "endothermic." In contrast, reptiles have a varying body temperature influenced by their surrounding environment and are called "ectothermic." An ectothermic animal can adjust its body temperature behaviorally (e.g., moving between shade and sun), even achieving higher body temperature than a so-called "warm-blooded" animal, but this is done by outside factors.

In an effort to make the evolution of dinosaurs into birds seem more plausible, some evolutionists have argued that dinosaurs were also endothermic,[1] but there is no clear evidence for this.[2]

One of the lines of evidence for endothermic dinosaurs is based on the microscopic structure of dinosaur bones. Fossil dinosaur bones have been

---

1. R.T. Bakker, "Dinosaur Renaissance," *Scientific American,* 1975, 232:58–78.
2. A. Feduccia, "Dinosaurs as Reptiles," *Evolution,* 1973, 27:166–169; A. Feduccia, "The Origin and Evolution of Birds," 2nd ed. (New Haven, CT: Yale University Press, 1999).

found containing special microscopic structures called osteons (or Haversian systems). Osteons are complex concentric layers of bone surrounding blood vessels in areas where the bone is dense. This arrangement is assumed by some to be unique to endothermic animals and thus evidence that dinosaurs are endothermic, but such is not the case. Larger vertebrates (whether reptiles, birds, or mammals) may also have this type of bone. Even tuna fish have osteonal bone in their vertebral arches.

Another argument for endothermy in dinosaurs is based on the eggs and assumed brood behavior of dinosaurs, but this speculation too has been challenged.[3] There is, in fact, no theropod brooding behavior not known to occur in crocodiles and other cold-blooded living reptiles.

Alan Feduccia, an expert on birds and their evolution, has concluded that "there has never been, nor is there now, any evidence that dinosaurs were endothermic."[4] Feduccia says that despite the lack of evidence "many authors have tried to make specimens conform to the hot-blooded theropod dogma."

"Bird-Hipped" vs. "Lizard-Hipped" Dinosaurs

All dinosaurs are divided into two major groups based on the structure of their hips (pelvic bones) — the lizard-hipped dinosaurs (saurischians) and the bird-hipped dinosaurs (ornithiscians). The main difference between the two hip structures is that the pubic bone of the bird-hipped dinosaurs is directed toward the rear (as it is in birds) rather than entirely to the front (as it is in mammals and reptiles).

But in most other respects, the bird-hipped dinosaurs, including such huge quadrupedal sauropods as Brachiosaurus and Diplodocus, are even less bird-like than the lizard-hipped, bipedal dinosaurs such as the theropods. This point is rarely emphasized in popular accounts of dinosaur/bird evolution.

The Three-Fingered Hand

One of the main lines of evidence sighted by evolutionists for the evolution of birds from theropod dinosaurs is the three-fingered "hand" found in both birds and theropods. The problem is that studies have shown that there is a digital mismatch between birds and theropods.

Most terrestrial vertebrates have an embryological development based on the five-fingered hand. In the case of birds and theropod dinosaurs, two

---

3. N.R. Geist and T.D. Jones, "Juvenile Skeletal Structure and the Reproduction Habits of Dinosaurs," *Science,* 1996, 272:712–714

4. A. Feduccia, T. Lingham-Soliar, and J.R. Hinchliffe,"Do Feathered Dinosaurs Exist? Testing the Hypothesis on Neontological and Paleontological Evidence," *Journal of Morphology,* 2005, 266:125–166.

of the five fingers are lost (or greatly reduced), and three are retained during development of the embryo. If birds evolved from theropods, one would expect the same three fingers to be retained in both birds and theropod dinosaurs, but such is not the case. Evidence shows that the fingers retained in theropod dinosaurs are fingers 1, 2, and 3 (the "thumb" is finger 1), while the fingers retained in birds are 2, 3, and 4.[5]

Avian Vs. Reptilian Lung

One of the most distinctive features of birds is their lungs. Bird lungs are small in size and nearly rigid but are, nevertheless, highly efficient to meet the high metabolic needs of flight. Bird respiration involves a unique "flow-through ventilation" into a set of nine interconnecting flexible air sacs sandwiched between muscles and under the skin. The air sacs contain few blood vessels and do not take part in oxygen exchange, but rather function like bellows to move air through the lungs.

The air sacs permit a unidirectional flow of air through the lungs, resulting in higher oxygen content than is possible in the bidirectional air flow through the lungs of reptiles and mammals. The air flow moves through the same tubes at different times both into and out of the lungs of reptiles and mammals, and this results in a mixture of oxygen-rich air with oxygen-depleted air (air that has been in the lungs for a while). The unidirectional flow through bird lungs not only permits more oxygen to diffuse into the blood, but also keeps the volume of air in the lung nearly constant, a requirement for maintaining a level flight path.

If theropod dinosaurs are the ancestors of birds, one might expect to find evidence of an avian type lung in such dinosaurs. While fossils generally do not preserve soft tissue such as lungs, a well-preserved theropod dinosaur fossil (*Sinosauropteryx*) has been found in which the outline of the visceral cavity has been well-preserved. The evidence clearly indicates that this theropod had a lung and respiratory mechanics similar to that of a crocodile — not a bird.[6] Specifically, there was evidence of a diaphragm-like muscle separating the lung from the liver much as you see in modern crocodiles (birds lack a diaphragm). These observations suggest that this theropod was similar to an ectothermic reptile, not an endothermic bird.

---

5. A. Feduccia, T. Lingham-Soliar, and J.R. Hinchliffe, "Do Feathered Dinosaurs Exist? Testing the Hypothesis on Neontological and Paleontological Evidence," *Journal of Morphology*, 2005, 266:125–166.

6. J.A. Ruben, T.D. Jones, N.R. Geist, and W.J. Hillenius, "Lung Structure and Ventilation in Theropod Dinosaurs and Early Birds," *Science*, 1997, 278:1267–1270.

Origin of Feathers

Do Feathered Dinosaurs Exist?

Feathers have long been considered to be unique to birds. Certainly all living birds have feathers of some kind, while no living creature other than birds has been found to have a cutaneous appendage even remotely similar to a feather.

Since most evolutionists are certain that birds evolved from dinosaurs (or at least are closely related to them) there has been an intense effort to find dinosaur fossils that show some suggestion of feathers or "protofeathers." With such observer bias, one must be skeptical of recent widely publicized reports of "feathered" dinosaurs.

Dinosaurs are reptiles and so it is not surprising that fossil evidence has shown them to have a scaly skin typical of reptiles. For example, a well-preserved specimen of *Compsognathus* (a small theropod dinosaur of the type believed to be most closely related to birds) showed unmistakable evidence of scales but alas — no feathers.[7]

Still, there have been many claims of "feathered" dinosaurs, particularly from fossils found in Liaoning province in northeastern China.[8] The earliest "feathered dinosaur" from this source is the very un-bird-like dinosaur *Sinosauropteryx* which lacks any evidence of structures that could be shown to be feather-like.[9]

Structures described as "protofeathers" in the dinosaur fossils *Sinosauropteryx* and *Sinithosaurus* are filamentous and sometimes interlaced structures bearing no obvious resemblance to feathers. It now appears likely that these filaments (often referred to as "dino-fuzz") are actually connective tissue fibers (collagen) found in the deep dermal layer of the skin.[10] Feduccia laments that "the major and most worrying problem of the feathered dinosaur hypothesis is that the integumental structures have been homologized with avian

---

7. U.B. Gohlich and L.M. Chiappe, "A New Carnivorous Dinosaur from the Late Jurassic Solnhofen Archipelago," *Nature*, 2006, 440:329–332.
8. P.J. Chen, Z.M. Dong, and S.N. Zheng, "An Exceptionally Well-preserved Theropod Dinosaur from the Yixian Formation of China," *Nature*, 1998, 391:147–152; X. Xu, X. Wang, and X. Wu, "A Dromaeosaurid Dinosaur with a Filamentous Integument from the Yixian Formation of China," *Nature*, 1999, 401:262–266; P.J. Currie and P.J. Chen, "Anatomy of Sinosauropteryx Prima from Liaoning, Northeastern China," *Can. J. Earth Sci.*, 2001, 38:1705–1727.
9. A. Feduccia, T. Lingham-Soliar, and J.R. Hinchliffe, "Do Feathered Dinosaurs Exist? Testing the Hypothesis on Neontological and Paleontological Evidence," *Journal of Morphology*, 2005, 266:125–166.
10. Ibid.

feathers on the basis of anatomically and paleontologically unsound and misleading information."[11]

Complicating matters even further is that fact that true birds have been found among the Liaoning province fossils in the same layers as their presumed dinosaur ancestors! The obvious bird fossil *Confuciusornis sanctus*, for example, has long, slender tail feathers resembling those of a modern scissor-tail flycatcher. Two taxa (*Caudipteryx* and *Protarchaeopteryx*) that were thought to be dinosaurs with true feathers are now generally conceded to be flightless birds.[12]

Thus far, the only obvious dinosaur fossil with obvious feathers that was "found" is *Archaeoraptor liaoningensis*. This so-called definitive "feathered dinosaur" was reported with much fanfare in the November 1999 issue of *National Geographic* but has since been shown to be a fraud.

What would it prove if features common to one type of animal were found on another? Nothing. Simply put, God uses various designs with various creatures. Take the platypus, a mosaic, for example. It has several design features that are shared with other animals, and yet it is completely distinct! So if a feathered dinosaur (or mammal, etc.) is ever found with feathers, it would call into question our human criteria for classification, not biblical veracity. What's needed to support evolution is *not* an unusual mosaic of complete traits, but a trait in transition, such as a "scale-feather" — what creationist biologists would call a "sceather."

Feathers and Scales Are Dissimilar

If birds evolved from dinosaurs or any other reptile, then feathers must have evolved from reptilian scales. Evolutionists are so confident that feathers evolved from scales that they often claim that feathers are very similar to scales. The popular Encarta computerized encyclopedia (1997) describes feathers as a "horny outgrowth of skin peculiar to the bird but similar in structure and origin to the scales of fish and reptiles."

In actual fact, feathers are profoundly different from scales in both their structure and growth. Feathers grow individually from tube-like follicles similar to hair follicles. Reptilian scales on the other hand are not individual follicular structures but rather comprise a continuous sheet on the surface of the body. Thus, while feathers grow and are shed individually (actually in symmetrically matched pairs!), scales grow and are shed as an entire sheet of skin.

The feather vane is made up of hundreds of barbs, each bearing hundreds of barbules interlocked with tiny hinged hooklets. This incredibly complex

---

11. Ibid.
12. Ibid.

structure bears not the slightest resemblance to the relatively simple reptilian scale. Still, evolutionists continue to publish imaginative scenarios of how long-fringed reptile scales evolved by chance into feathers, but evidence of "sceathers" eludes them.

Archaeopteryx, a True Bird, Is Older than the "Feathered" Dinosaurs

One of the biggest dilemmas for those who want to believe that dinosaurs evolved into birds is that the so-called "feathered" dinosaurs found thus far are "dated" to be about 20 million years more recent than *Archaeopteryx*. This is a problem for evolution because *Archaeopteryx* is now generally recognized to be a true bird.[13] Some specimens of this bird are so perfectly fossilized that even the microscopic detail of its feathers is clearly visible! So having alleged missing links of dinosaurs changing into birds when birds already exist doesn't help the case for evolution.

For many years, *Archaeopteryx* has been touted in biology textbooks and museums as the perfect transitional fossil, presumably being precisely intermediate between reptiles and birds. Much has been made over the fact that *Archaeopteryx* had teeth, fingers on its wings, and a long tail — all supposedly proving its reptilian ancestry. While there are no living birds with teeth, other fossilized birds such as *Hesperornis* also had teeth. Some modern birds such as the ostrich have fingers on their wings, and the juvenile hoatzin (a South American bird) has well-developed fingers and toes with which it can climb trees.

Origin of Flight

One of the biggest problems for evolutionists is explaining the origin of flight. To make matters worse, evolutionists believe that the flying birds evolved before the non-flying birds such as penguins.

The theropod type of dinosaur that is believed to have evolved into flying birds is, to say the least, poorly designed for flight. These dinosaurs have small fore limbs that typically can't even reach their mouths. It is not clear what theropods such as the well-known *Tyrannosaurus rex* did with its tiny front limbs. It is obvious that they didn't walk, feed, or grasp prey with them, and they surely didn't fly with them!

Another problem is that this bipedal type of dinosaur had a long heavy tail to balance the weight of a long neck and large head. Decorating such a creature with feathers would hardly suffice to get it off the ground or be of much benefit in any other way.

---

13. P.J. Currie, E.B. Koppelhus, M.A. Shugar, and J.L. Wright (eds.), *Feathered Dragons: Studies on the Transition from Dinosaurs to Birds* (Bloomington, IN: Indiana University Press, 2004).

Conclusion

Having a true bird appear before *alleged* feathered dinosaurs, no mechanism to change scales into feathers, no mechanism to change a reptilian lung into an avian lung, no legitimate dinosaurs found with feathers, etc., is a good indication that dinosaurs didn't turn into birds. The evidence is consistent with what the Bible teaches about birds being unique and created after their kinds.

Genesis is clear that God didn't make birds from pre-existing dinosaurs. In fact, dinosaurs (land animals made on Day 6) came *after* birds for the most part (winged creatures made on Day 5) according to the Bible. Both biblically and scientifically, chicken eaters around the world can rest easy. They aren't eating mutant dinosaurs.

Appendix 2

Dinosaurs in Birds' Clothing?
(abridged and edited)

Dr. Gabriela Haynes

Evolutionary Assumptions

n the secular story, dinosaurs supposedly evolved into birds. In light of this, the evolutionists require a change from scaled/scuted creatures to feathered creatures for that story to make sense. As a result, there are a number of specimens where evolutionists wildly interpret certain features to be feathers, evidence for feathers, or something "on the way to becoming" feathers.

Surprisingly, several Christians have unwittingly trusted and uncritically accepted many of the evolutionary claims about feathered dinosaurs. This article will discuss and analyze how the evolutionary worldview is applied in this hypothesis and how the consequences of this can lead to wrong conclusions about the definitions of relationships between birds and dinosaurs and supposed feathered dinosaurs.

Early Dino-Bird Theories

Biologist and secular humanist Thomas Huxley first proposed the idea of a relationship between birds and dinosaurs in 1868. As an avid supporter of Charles Darwin, Huxley saw in the discovery of *Archaeopteryx* (once considered a transitional form between reptiles and birds) a solution to the challenge of the supposed missing links in the evolutionary model.

Paleontologist John Ostrom revived this idea 100 years later after studying *Deinonychus* (classified by many evolutionists as a theropod dinosaur).

He noted similarities between *Archaeopteryx* (which we now know is a bird) and coelurosaurs (a subgroup of theropod dinosaurs), and proposed that birds were descendants of theropod dinosaurs.

Thus evolutionists, based on their naturalistic evolutionary belief that reptiles evolved into birds, have been working hard to try to fit the evidence they find into this belief. This means creationists should at least be very suspicious about claims concerning feathered dinosaurs. Or at least understand these claims are *biased*, since we all have a worldview from which we interpret the facts. Evolutionists are not immune to that.

Of course, God can create animals in any way he wants (consider the "mosaics" in the animal world, such as the platypus). But because of the intense efforts by evolutionists to "prove" dinosaurs evolved into birds, we should be extra careful in our research about claims of dinosaurs with feathers.

In 1881, Othniel Charles Marsh created the *Theropoda* suborder (now "clade," a new grouping of organisms according to how they supposedly evolved and are related), grouping all known dinosaurs from the Triassic and the carnivorous dinosaurs from the Jurassic and Cretaceous. Jacques Gauthier described *theropod* in 1986 via cladistics (which, as a classification system, already assumes evolutionary ancestry and relationships) as a group of birds and all saurischians (dinosaurs).[1] The meaning of the words *Theropoda* and *theropod* were thus changed because of evolutionary influences.

Now Linnaeus (considered the father of classification) based his groupings on similarities in creatures. But Darwin's classification was based on their supposed ancestry.[2] The animals and data have stayed the same, but the lenses used to interpret them have changed because the classification system is now based on evolutionary assumptions. Thus, the evolutionary classification of cladistics resulted from a change in the classification system itself. This has great consequences for how data is currently interpreted in regard to birds and dinosaurs.

The Evolution of a System

This short history demonstrates that terms and definitions have been changed to fit the evolutionary story. Another pertinent example is the term *Aves*, derived from the word *birds* in Latin (*Avis*). In the past, Aves was synonymous with birds. But this term now has four to six different

1. David B. Weishampel, Peter Dodson, and Halszka Osmólska, editors, *The Dinosauria* (Berkeley, CA: University of California Press, 2004).
2. Dalton de Souza Amorim, *Fundamentos de Sistemática Filogenética* (Ribeirão Preto: Holos, 2002).

meanings because of evolutionary ideas.[3] So, Aves and birds are no longer synonymous.

One more example is the term *feather*, which has been applied both to what we would normally regard as a feather (a complete, complex, and functional structure) and "its close evolutionary predecessors."[4] A new theory was proposed for the origin of feathers and their development based on evolution. The author stated, "I propose a new theory for the *evolutionary origin* [my emphasis] and diversification of feathers that *hypothesizes* [my emphasis] a transition series from the simplest feather follicle to the modern feather follicle through a series of novelties in feather development."[5] (See also Figure 1.)

Once a researcher accepts the current evolutionary hypothesis for how feathers supposedly "evolved," what is considered a "feather" has to be redefined — and suddenly a creature has feathers, when in reality, it does not. Even creationists can be led astray in their conclusions about the evidence if they trust and accept evolutionists' ideas. It is thus necessary to say that the traditional meanings are intended when the words *feather, bird*, and *Aves* are used in this article, not the modern meanings influenced by evolutionary ideas. Biologist and anatomist Dr. David Menton shows feathers are complex structures.

What Is a Bird, and What Is a Dinosaur?

Defining terms is vital to any discussion, or people may end up talking past one another. What is a bird? Feathers have been an essential feature to classify an animal as a bird based on the classical, conventional, and traditional taxonomy developed by Linnaeus in the 18th century. In the animal groups alive today, feathers are only present in birds.[6]

---

3. Jacques Gauthier, "Saurischian Monophyly and the Origin of Bird," *Memoirs of the California Academy of Sciences* 8 (1986): 1–55, https://biostor.org/reference/110202; and Jacques Gauthier and Kevin de Queiroz, "Feathered Dinosaurs, Flying Dinosaurs, Crown Dinosaurs, and the Name Aves," in *New Perspectives on the Origin and Early Evolution of Birds: Proceedings of the International Symposium in Honor of John H. Ostrom*, Jacques Gauthier and Lawrence F. Gall, editors (New Haven, CT: Yale University Peabody Museum, 2001), 7–41.

4. Xing Xu and Yu Guo, "The Origin and Early Evolution of Feathers: Insights from Recent Paleontological and Neontological Data," *Vertebrata Palasiatica* 47, no. 4 (2009): 311–329, https://www.researchgate.net/publication/272171464.

5. Richard Prum, "Development and Evolutionary Origin of Feather," *The Journal of Experimental Zoology* 285, no. (December 15, 1999): 291–306.

6. Jacques Gauthier and Kevin de Queiroz, "Feathered Dinosaurs, Flying Dinosaurs, Crown Dinosaurs, and the Name Aves," *New Perspectives on the Origin and Early Evolution of Birds: Proceedings of the International Symposium in Honor of John H. Ostrom*, eds. Jacques Gauthier and Lawrence F. Gall (New Haven, CT: Yale University Peabody Museum, 2001), 7–41.

1. The first feather, a hollow cylinder

2. Tuft of unbranched barbs attached to a calamus

3A. Planar feather with unbranched barbs fused to a central rachis

3B. Feather with barbs and barbules attached at the base to a calamus

3A+B. Planar feather with branched barbs and open vane

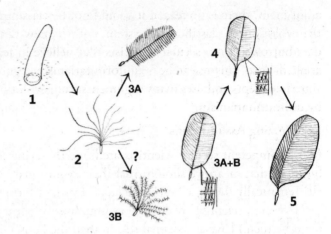

4. Closed pennaceous vane(hooklets on one barbule attach to grooves on barbules of adjacent barb)

5. Closed assymmetric vane (resembling modern flight feathers)

Figure 1. Supposed evolution-of-feathers diagram adapted from *Scientific American* (March 2003).[7]

One current creationist researcher, who is influenced by the secular view of feathered dinosaurs, argues that the presence of feathers on extant (living) birds should not be used as an argument for classifying a feathered animal as a bird because that implies uniformitarianism (that the present is the key to the past).[8] In other words, he is saying that it may be true today that all birds have feathers, but we should not make this assumption about the past, so some non-birds in the past (particularly dinosaurs) might have had feathers.

But this argument is fallacious. Many things today have been the same in the past (e.g., humans have always been humans), but some things have not been the same in the past (e.g., there's only been one global flood). So yes, biblical creationists do believe, based on God's Word, that some things have been much the same, but also some things have been very different.

There are reasonable explanations for using feathers to classify an animal as a bird that do not require uniformitarianism. Anatomical structures for flight (many uniquely avian features are required other than feathers) and feathers have always been related to birds.[9] So, if an animal possesses any or

7. Richard O. Prum and Alan H. Brush, "Which Came First, the Feather or the Bird?" *Scientific American* 288, no. 3 (2003): 84–93, http://www.jstor.org/stable/26060207.

8. Dr. Matthew McClain, *Thinking Biblically About Dinosaurs*, Video Series, 2021–2022, https://thinkbiblically.org/series/dinosaurs-in-the-bible/.

9. P.C. Sereno, "Definitions in Phylogenetic Taxonomy: Critique and Rationale," *Systematic Biology* 48 (1999): 329–351.

all of them, there is no reason it should not be classified as a bird — unless the evolutionary classification system, with its new terms, definitions, and data borrowed from secular scientists that believe in feathered dinosaurs is applied. Also, this researcher's uniformitarianism argument is inconsistent since he accepts and uses many arguments from evolutionists that are driven by uniformitarianism.

Recognizing Assumptions

Many competent secular scientists are honestly trying to do good research, but does that mean we should trust their evolutionary conclusions? Not at all. Technically that is a "respect fallacy," a variant form of genetic fallacy.

However, scientists' biases and assumptions (often unknown or unrecognized by them) have an essential role in their methods and the interpretations they draw. No one is truly neutral, and all that should be taken into consideration. Such an argument doesn't account for many other respected scientists (both evolutionary and creationary) who do not support the feathered dinosaur hypothesis. Shouldn't they also be trusted? How do we decide who to trust?

Furthermore, using the argument that the majority of scientists support the feathered-dinosaur hypothesis should not be used since it represents an appeal to majority fallacy. The majority of scientists also believe life arose by natural processes, so should we accept that and reject God as Creator? Of course not. History reveals the majority is not always correct!

Evolutionary ideas about dinosaurs and birds have now influenced the understanding and definition of a *dinosaur*.[10] In the new definition of dinosaurs, bird characteristics have actually been added. So now, the dinosaur group has been divided into what they call avian dinosaurs (birds) and non-avian dinosaurs (dinosaurs). So now a bird is considered to be a dinosaur!

What Is Archaeopteryx?

For those who don't know, *Archaeopteryx* is primarily a bird that evolutionists like to point to as a missing link between dinosaurs and birds. It seems unique among ancient birds because it has teeth and claws on its wings. So many evolutionists attach themselves to this bird and hail it as a missing link and claim that *Archaeopteryx* presents a mixture of bird and dinosaur traits. Once again, some creationists jump on board with this, such as Dr. Matthew McClain, who states, "Not every *Archaeopteryx*'s specimen preserves feathers, by the way." While this is technically true, of 12 specimens of *Archaeopteryx*, 11 do have preserved feathers that show complexity and

---

10. Jacques Gauthier, "Saurischian Monophyly and the Origin of Bird," *Memoirs of the California Academy of Sciences* 8 (1986): 1–55, https://biostor.org/reference/110202.

functionality, looking like the ones we see in living birds. Only the last specimen found does not have preserved feathers, and that is due to the poor preservation of the whole fossil specimen.

Dr. McLain then presents the following features of *Archaeopteryx* as dinosaur characteristics:

1. Long bony tail
2. Three-clawed digits on the hand
3. Teeth in jaws

But are they really dinosaur characteristics?

Claim 1: Long Bony Tail

The question here is this: How long is long enough? *Archaeopteryx* (clearly a bird) has around 23–21 caudal vertebrae, and dinosaurs have 50–30 (Figure 2).[11] Some extinct birds, such as *Jeholornis* from the Cretaceous, have the same "long" bony tail as *Archaeopteryx*.[12] The following figure (Figure 2) shows other differences as well.

Claim 2: Three-Clawed Digits on the Hand

There are modern birds, such as hoatzins, that possess claws, and one- to two-wing claws are found in nine different orders of extant (living) birds.[13] *Confuciusornis*, an extinct bird, had three claws.[14]

Claim 3: Teeth in Jaws

Though not present in known birds today, teeth are present in a number of enantiornithines (extinct birds). *Sapeornis*[15] and *Pengornis*[16] are examples of this group.

---

11. Peter Wellnhofer, *Archaeopteryx: The Icon of Evolution* (Munich: Dr. Friedrich Pfeil, 2009); and Phil Senter et al., "New Dromaeosaurids (Dinosauria: Theropoda) from the Lower Cretaceous of Utah, and the Evolution of the Dromaeosaurid tail," *PLoS One* 7, no. 5 (2012): e36790, https://doi.org/10.1371/journal.pone.0036790.

12. Jingmai O'Connor et al., "Unique Caudal Plumage of Jeholornis and Complex Tail Evolution in Early Bird," *Proceedings of the National Academy of Sciences* 110, no. 43 (2013): 17404–17408, https://doi.org/10.1073/pnas.1316979110.

13. Harvey I. Fisher, "The Occurrence of Vestigial Claws on the Wings of Bird," *American Midland Naturalist* 23 (1940): 234.

14. Luis Chiappe et al., "Anatomy and Systematics of the Confuciusornithidae (Theropoda: Aves) from the Late Mesozoic of Northeastern China," *Bulletin of the American Museum of Natural History* 242 (1999): 1–89.

15. Y. Wang et al., "A Previously Undescribed Specimen Reveals New Information on the Dentition of *Sapeornis chaoyangensis*," *Cretaceous Research* 74 (2017): 1–10.

16. J.K. O'Connor and L.M. Chiappe, "A Revision of Enantiornithine (Aves: Ornithothoraces) Skull Morphology," *Journal of Systematic Palaeontology* 9 (2011): 135–157; and Z. Zhou, J. Clarke, and F. Zhang, "Insight into Diversity, Body Size and Morphological Evolution from the Largest Early Cretaceous Enantiornithine Bird," *Journal of Anatomy* 212 (2008): 565–577.

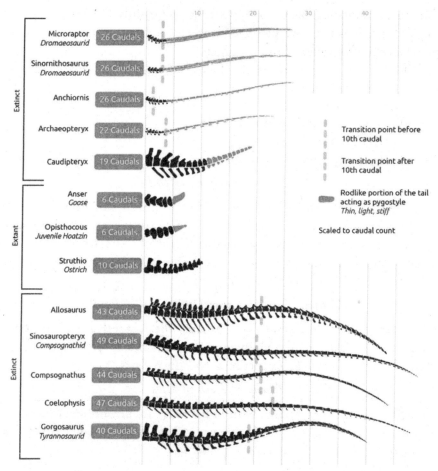

Figure 2. Tail comparison diagram (Credit: Joel Leineweber). Top two sections, supposed dinosaurs and living birds show the same tail characteristics in clear contrast to those of dinosaurs, shown in the bottom section.

Chickens, the lab rats of the bird world, have been found to grow teeth while developing when the *talpid2* gene is activated, based on research at Max Planck Institute in Tubingen, Germany. Since birds largely have this gene, they have the genetic potential to grow teeth, but only if the gene is "turned on" or activated.[17]

Therefore, none of these supposed dinosaur characteristics found in *Archaeopteryx* are restricted to dinosaurs, but are indeed common bird traits. *Archaeopteryx* was a bird and nothing more.

---

17. Admin Editors, "Chickens Still Have Genes for Growing Teeth," *Knowledge Nuts*, January 5, 2021, https://knowledgenuts.com/chickens-still-have-genes-for-growing-teeth/.

What Is *Sinosauropteryx*?

Sinosauropteryx is a theropod dinosaur. It has not been found with any feathers. But secularists (and creationists who follow suit) have advanced an argument that because it had the presence of melanosomes, then they leap to say it had feathers.

Melanosomes are a trait common in feathers, particularly involved in their pigmentation. However, the supposed presence of melanosomes preserved in fossils is also questioned by many scientists who argue that the structures could be artifacts from bacterial activity and not true melanosomes. Also devastating to the argument that these are remnants of feathers is the fact that there is no confirmation of the branching structure of a feather of *Sinosauropteryx*.[18]

What About Coloring?

Melanosomes are organelles within specialized cells (melanocytes) where melanin pigments are found. These organelles are visible and have been shown to be distinct from structures formed by bacteria by the use of TEM (transmission electron microscopy). Yet in most of the papers that mentioned the presence of melanosomes in the fossil material, the scientists did not perform any of this specialized TEM analysis that would distinguish between the bacterial structures and melanosomes.

What about the supposedly orange-and-white banded tail on *Sinosauropteryx?* There was no report on any TEM or chemical analyses being done on the specimens used in that study. The claim about the tail is instead based on reconstructions and circular reasoning:

> From reconstructions based on exceptional fossils, the color pattern is compared to predicted optimal countershading transitions based on 3D reconstructions of the animal's abdomen, imaged in different lighting environments. Reconstructed patterns match well with those predicted for animals living in open habitats.[19]

But such markings on *Sinosauropteryx* go against the forested habitat that is presumed for the Jehol habitats (in northeast China) in which *Sinosauropteryx* supposedly lived. That sort of striped camouflage would have worked best in open habitats, not in the forests that it supposedly lived in, as they acknowledge, so the tail reconstruction does not even make sense:

---

18. Alan Feduccia, *Romancing the Birds and Dinosaurs: Forays in Postmodern Paleontology* (Irvine, CA: Brown Walker Press, 2020).

19. Maria E. McNamara et al., "Experimental Maturation of Feathers: Implications for Reconstructions of Fossil Feather Colour," *Biology Letters* 9, no. 3 (2013): http://doi.org/10.1098/rsbl.2013.0184.

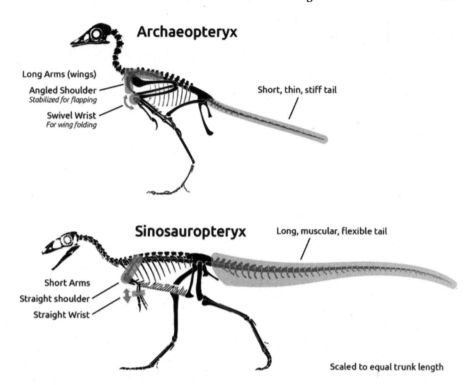

Figure 3. Skeletal drawings of *Archaeopteryx* and *Sinosauropteryx* adapted from Scott Hartman's skeletal drawings, 2013 and 2020, respectively.[20] *Archaeopteryx* presents bird characteristics, and *Sinosauropteryx* presents dinosaur characteristics.

> Most groups of terrestrial vertebrates in Jehol show a strong tendency toward forest-living adaptations. *Sinosauropteryx*, however, appears to be an exception to this rule.[21]

Experiments by Dr. McNamara and colleagues show that the evidence of color is lost and the shape of melanosomes is affected by temperature and pressure.[22] So reconstructions of colors based on the shapes of melanosomes

20. Theagarten Lingham-Soliar, Alan Feduccia, and Xiaolin Wang, "A New Chinese Specimen Indicates That 'Protofeathers' in the Early Cretaceous Theropod Dinosaur Sinosauropteryx Are Degraded Collagen Fibres," *Proceedings of The Royal Society Biological Sciences* 274 (2007): 1823–1829, https://doi.org/10.1098/rspb.2007.0352.

21. F.M. Smithwick et al., "Countershading and Stripes in the Theropod Dinosaur *Sinosauropteryx* Reveal Heterogeneous Habitats in the Early Cretaceous Jehol Biota," *Current Biology* 27, no. 21 (2017): 3337–3343.e2.

22. Maria E. McNamara et al., "Experimental Maturation of Feathers: Implications for Reconstructions of Fossil Feather Colour," *Biology Letters* 9, no. 3 (2013): http://doi.org/10.1098/rsbl.2013.0184.

need to be "treated with caution."[23] Also, the reconstructions and modeling, which are based on evolutionary assumptions about past habitats, try to force the idea there is evidence for feathers on *Sinosauropteryx*. In other words, there is no obvious evidence definitively substantiating the claim this dinosaur had feathers. Besides all that, *Sinosauropteryx* presents the skeletal anatomy of a dinosaur (Figure 3). It's obvious that *Archaeopteryx* is a bird and *Sinosauropteryx* is a dinosaur.

Other Specimens

What about other specimens that have feathers and are supposed dinosaurs? In many of these cases, they are not dinosaurs. They are birds. *Sinornithosaurus* shares similarities with *Archaeopteryx* and belongs to the family Dromaeosauridae, which has been considered by some evolutionary scientists to have many genera that could be classified as birds. Those scientists also consider that most maniraptorans (another group of theropods) are birds, not dinosaurs.[24]

Caudipteryx, Microraptor, and *Anchiornis* present many characteristics of birds. The comparison between *Sinosauropteryx*'s wrist and *Archaeopteryx*'s, *Caudipteryx*'s, *Anchiornis*'s, and *Microraptor*'s wrists is shown in Figure 4. The swivel wrist is an anatomical structure related to flight that *Sinosauropteryx* does not have because it is a dinosaur. But the others, being birds, do have it.[25]

Figure 4 is a forelimb motion and range comparison diagram. In the left column, the forelimb motion and range of supposed dinosaurs and extant birds are clearly distinctive and contrast to those of dinosaurs in the right column. The extinct genera are adapted from Hartman 2015, 2015, 2013, 2022, 2022, respectively.[26] Living birds are shown in the upper part of the

23. Ibid.
24. F.M. Smithwick et al., "On the Purported Presence of Fossilized Collagen Fibres in an Ichthyosaur and a Theropod Dinosaur," *Palaeontology* 60 (2017): 409–422.
25. Christophe Hendrickx, Scott Hartman, and Octávio Mateus, "An Overview of Non-Avian Theropod Discoveries and Classification," *PalArch's Journal of Vertebrate Palaeontology* 12 (2015): 1–73; see also Scott Hartman, "Dr. Scott Hartman's Skeletal Drawing: *Sinornithosaurus* Adult & Juvenile," last modified 2015, https://www.skeletaldrawing.com/theropods/sinosauropteryx.
26. Scott Hartman, "Dr. Scott Hartman's Skeletal Drawing: *Microraptor gui*," last modified 2015, https://www.skeletaldrawing.com/theropods/mircroraptor; Scott Hartman, "Dr. Scott Hartman's Skeletal Drawing: *Sinornithosaurus* adult and juvenile. Last modified 2015, https://www.skeletaldrawing.com/theropods/sinornithosaurus; Hendrickx, Christophe, "An overview," 1–73; Scott Hartman, "Dr. Scott Hartman's Skeletal Drawing: *Caudipteryx*," last modified 2022, https://www.skeletaldrawing.com/theropods/caudipteryx; and Scott Hartman, "Dr. Scott Hartman's Skeletal Drawing: *Anchiornis huxleyi*," last modified 2022, https://www.skeletaldrawing.com/theropods/anchiornis.

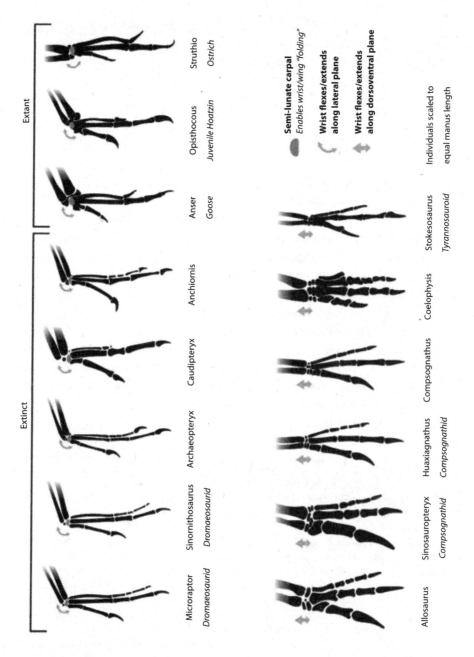

Figure 4

left column: Anser,[27] hoatzin,[28] and the ostrich were drawn from specimen photos. The extinct genera are adapted from Hartman 2012, 2020, 2018, 2022, 2019, 2013.[29]

Are *Yutyrannus* and *Beipiaosaurus* Feathered Dinosaurs?

Two more specimens that garner attention are *Yutyrannus* and *Beipiaosaurus*. These two genera present feathers or feather-like structures and thus represent "feathered dinosaurs." However, the papers first published on those genera[30] mention the presence of only filamentous structures, not complete, complex, and functional feathers. Filamentous structures could be called "feathers" or "feather-like" only if the *new evolutionary definition for feathers* (a redefinition based on evolutionary assumptions) is applied.

In this view, a filamentous structure is one of the first stages of supposed "feather evolution," and therefore such a structure can be called a feather (sadly, some creationists buy into this false idea). But if a *feather* is defined as a complete, complex, and functional structure, then, no, a filament should not be called a feather nor even a feather-like structure.

Consider another problem with defining filaments as feathers — *hair* is a filament and by this new definition, then mammals, which have filaments of hair, can be called feathered! Humans would have feathers too by this definition. That will make you think twice when you look in the mirror! This breaks down to an absurd definition.

27. "The Origin and Evolution of Bird Wings," *The Pterosaur Heresies*, June 12, 2015, https://pterosaurheresies.wordpress.com/2015/06/12/the-origin-and-evolution-of-bird-wings/.

28. G.P. Wagner and Jacques A. Gauthier, "1,2,3 = 2,3,4: A Solution to the Problem of the Homology of the Digits in the Avian Hand," *Proceedings of the National Academy of Science* 96, no. 9 (1999): 5111–5116, https://doi.org/10.1073/pnas.96.9.511.

29. Scott Hartman, "Dr. Scott Hartman's Skeletal Drawing: *Allosaurus fragilis*," last modified 2012, https://www.skeletaldrawing.com/theropods/allosaurus-fragilis; Scott Hartman, "Dr. Scott Hartman's Skeletal Drawing: *Sinosauropteryx prima*," last modified 2020, https://www.skeletaldrawing.com/theropods/sinosauropteryx; Scott Hartman, "Dr. Scott Hartman's Skeletal Drawing: *Huaxiagnathus orientalis*," last modified 2018, https://www.skeletaldrawing.com/theropods/huaxiagnathus; Scott Hartman, "Dr. Scott Hartman's Skeletal Drawing: *Compsognathus longpipes*," last modified 2022, https://www.skeletaldrawing.com/theropods/compsognathus-type; Scott Hartman, "Dr. Scott Hartman's Skeletal Drawing: *Coelophysis bauri*," last modified 2019, https://www.skeletaldrawing.com/theropods/coelophysis; and Scott Hartman, "Dr. Scott Hartman's Skeletal Drawing: *Stokesosaurus clevelandi*," last modified 2013, https://www.skeletaldrawing.com/theropods/stokesosaurus.

30. Xing Xu et al., "A Gigantic Feathered Dinosaur from the Lower Cretaceous of China," *Nature* 484 (2012): 92–95, https://www.nature.com/articles/nature10906; Xing Xu, Zhi-lu Tang, and Xiao-lin Wang, "A Therizinosauroid Dinosaur with Integumentary Structures from China," *Nature* 399 (1999): 350–354, https://doi.org/10.1038/20670.

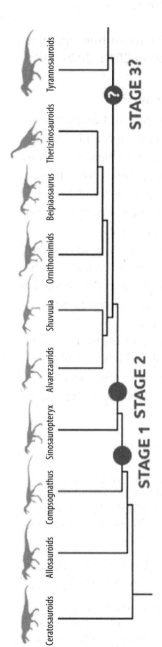

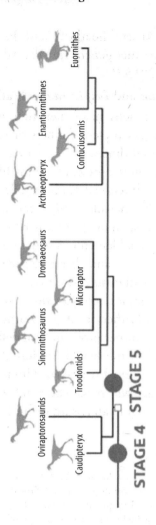

Figure 5. Stages of the supposed "feather evolution."

Stages 4 and 5 are only found in birds.

Caudipteryx, Microraptor, Sinornithosaurus, and *Archaeopteryx* are some genera mentioned as dinosaurs, but they all show stages 4 and 5 of feathers in the supposed "feather evolution." Now those stages are considered modern feathers[31] because they are like those found only on birds today (Figure 5).[32]

There is no reasonable explanation not to classify *Caudipteryx, Microraptor, Sinornithosaurus,* and *Archaeopteryx* as birds or *Sinosauropteryx, Yutyrannus,* and *Beipiaosaurus* as dinosaurs (simply without feathers).

Other Considerations

The secular data should not be ignored, **but they need to be critically analyzed rather than implicitly trusted.** Scientists, whether creationists or evolutionists, can do good observational science, but one has to carefully search out biases and assumptions in interpretations of the evidence.

Note that this perspective of uncritically using secular datasets also brings problems for some creationists and for their statistical baraminological analyses[33] (studies of created kinds) that use such secular datasets to perform their studies. When these creationists accept many of the evolutionists' assumptions regarding classification, they can end up with wrong conclusions.

This uncritical use of evolutionary datasets is dangerous within the creationist community. Sadly, many creationists are also using these datasets in models that are built on the assumption of "common design equals common ancestry" instead of models where "common design equals common designer."

Some creationists have been attempting to further support feathered dinosaur arguments by appealing to a baraminological analysis that argue confirms there were kinds of dinosaurs that had feathers and others that did not. But the baraminological analysis is based on an approach that depends on a statistical analysis of data on the features found in fossils. Without going through all the statistical details, there are large problems with these analyses.

First, the data is exclusively derived from the evolutionary literature. That in itself should warn researchers they cannot accept it without question.

---

31. Matthew P. Martyniuk, *A Field Guide to Mesozoic Birds and Other Winged Dinosaurs* (Vernon, NJ: Pan Aves Publishing, 2012).

32. Richard O. Prum and Alan H. Brush, "Which Came First, the Feather or the Bird?" *Scientific American* 288, no. 3 (2003): 84–93, http://www.jstor.org/stable/26060207.

33. Harry F. Sanders and Matthew Cserhati, "Statistics, Baraminology, and Interpretations: A Critical Evaluation of Current Morphology-Based Baraminology Methods," *Creation Research Society Quarterly* 58, no. 3 (2022): 175–192.

Further, the interpretation embedded in the data relies on the assumption that similarity is equivalent to a relationship. This is equivalent to the evolutionists using homology (similar structures) to argue for evolution: something creationists have long decried.

The other problem with statistical baraminology is that it produces results that are not reliable in groups where we know the correct answer. For example, a study of chickens and their relatives suggested four separate kinds,[34] yet hybrid data showed it was a single kind. As creationists are skeptical of radiometric dating because it fails in correctly dating rocks of known ages, they should also be cautious about statistical baraminology that fails to correctly classify known groups.

The overriding issue is not primarily paleontological. The problem is the uncritical acceptance of the consensus interpretation regarding feathered dinosaurs and trying to find ways to fit that into the Scripture. The history of why evolutionists have been so adamant about "feathered dinosaurs" (to "prove" their evolutionary ideas) should at least make us suspicious of this claim. Thus, every researcher should be diligent to ensure they are not unwittingly accepting certain aspects of evolutionary assumptions.

As shown, there are problems with the claims of feathered dinosaurs. While it is theoretically possible that God could have created dinosaurs with feathers, evidence for such a claim is currently lacking. Christians would be wise to critically review any claim made by evolutionary scientists to see if it matches both Scripture and the available evidence, even if that claim is repeated by creationists.

An Open Door?

The question of feathered dinosaurs is not merely an academic exercise with little real-world application. This is a big issue because at its core, the idea of dinosaurs displaying a coat of feathers is an evolutionary one, meant to bolster their claim that birds and dinosaurs are related and that birds are actually dinosaurs.

Because the idea is based on little observational evidence and much evolutionary speculation, storytelling, and assumptions, it opens the door for other similarly unfounded evolutionary ideas to creep into the biblical creation community. As creationists, we must be very careful not to allow compromise with evolutionary ideas to creep into our research, or biblical faithfulness could eventually be lost by either this generation or the next.

---

34. M. McConnachie and T.R. Brophy, "A Baraminological Analysis of the Landfowl (Aves: Galliformes)," *Occasional Papers of the Baraminology Study Group* 11, (2008): 9–10, https://digitalcommons.liberty.edu/cgi/viewcontent.cgi?article=1194&context=bio_chem_fac_pubs.

Image Credits

Answers in Genesis: p. 66, p. 76 (4); p. 80, p. 86, p. 99, p. 152, p. 153 (top), p. 156, p. 164, p. 171, p. 211, p. 239

Berea College Special Collections and Archives: p. 197

Bodie Hodge: p. 23, p. 37, p. 83, p. 116, p. 155 (bottom right)

Joel Leineweber: p. 237

Dan Lietha: p. 111

Public Domain: p. 10, p. 12 (left), p. 153 (bottom), p. 234

Science Photo Library: p. 90

Scientific America (March 2003): p. 234

Shutterstock: p. 8, p. 12 (right), p. 53 (2), p. 73 (3), p. 83 (4), p. 88, p. 177 (bottom)

Smithsonian: p. 213

A Library of Answers
for Families and Churches

Over 100 faith-affirming answers to some of the
most-questioned topics about faith, science, & the Bible.

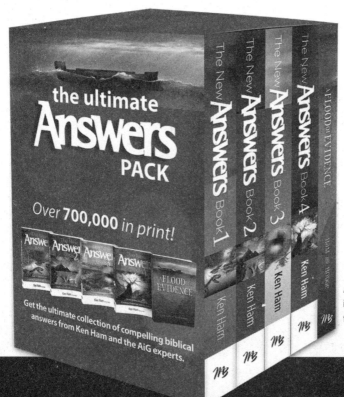

Also available
in digital
format.